C000002901

THE SPELLS THAT
CONTROL US

MESMERIZATION

WHY WE ARE LOSING OUR
MINDS TO GLOBAL CULTURE

By GEE THOMSON

Thames & Hudson

MESMER

IZATION

CONT

First published in the United Kingdom in 2008 by Thames & Hudson Ltd, 181A High Holborn, London WC1V 7QX

www.thamesandhudson.com

British Library Cataloguing-in-Publication Data A catalogue record for this book is available from the British Library

ISBN 978-0-500-97679-1

Printed and published by River Books, Bangkok

TENTS

WHO W
WHAT W
WHO W
WHAT W
AND

VE ARE

VE FEEL

VE FEAR

E BELIEVE

WHY

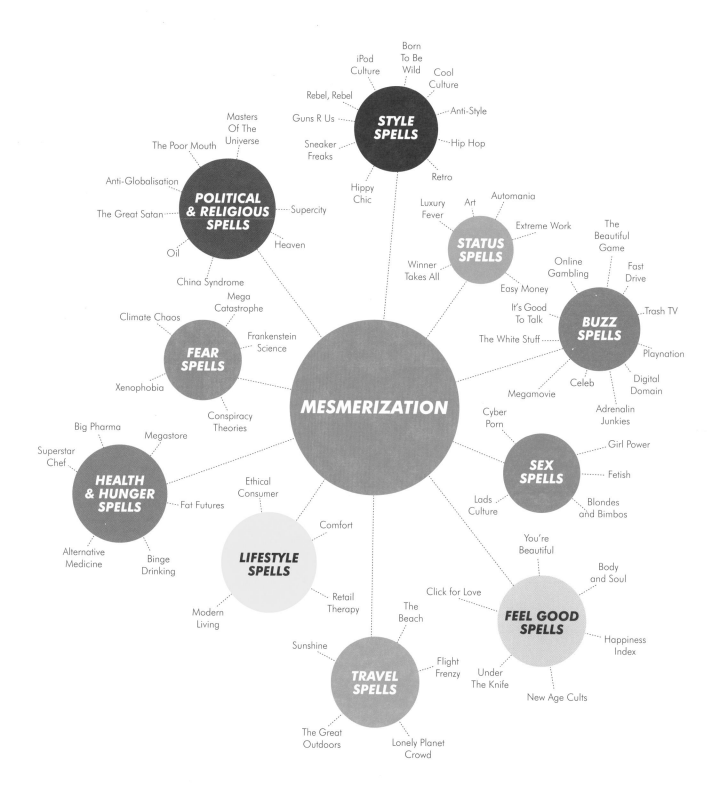

When starting this book (now some years back...), a lot of people questioned the use of the term 'spells', for describing the prescriptions that together make up the maps of culture within Mesmerization. Conjuring up images of shamans, witches and cauldrons of bubbling potions, the word was hardly an appropriate metaphor for our present, hi-tech age of ever-more-connected communication. But there's more to the term; it also reflects our innate propensity to be spellbound, the desire to be entranced, to be mesmerized; a propensity, that despite the modern, rational, scientific world we live in, we are still unable to shake off.

In a paper, 'Technology and Magic', printed in *Anthropology Today*, Alfred Gell referred to the 'technology of enchantment'. The author explained how, over the centuries, an array of psychological strategies and techniques had evolved to secure the acquiescence of the people. These involved the Arts, Music and dance – and were liberally used by those in power – the church, the monarchy and the establishment. In today's multi-media age, such techniques have become hugely complex and sophisticated; the 'magicians', the worldwide ranks of the image makers and the cultural elite. Add speed, frequency and repetition into the equation and the way is open for an extremely potent and viral image universe.

Speaking at the TED conference in California (which are incidentally available as downloadable podcasts), American philosopher, Daniel Dennett, referred to a term, 'meme', familiar to some which was first coined by Richard Dawkins in his publication, *The Selfish Gene*. Dennett described memes as 'information packets with attitude', that like viruses, can spread rapidly through populations. In the same lecture, Dennett mentioned a second book, *Guns, Germs and Steel: The Fates of Human Societies*, by Jared Diamond, to draw another impressive analogy. Diamond's publication detailed how, over the past millennium, germs, more than guns and steel, had conquered and subdued the Western hemisphere. Expansionist Europe, had wiped out millions of indigenous peoples, together with their culture, because they had no immunity to Western diseases. More soberly, in the context of memes, Dennett concluded; 'And we're doing it again. Doing it with toxic ideas – wiping out whole cultures, languages, hierarchies and practices'.

The point of this book, *Mesmerization*, is twofold. Firstly, if we have a clear understanding of how our most dominant spells work, we can lessen their effect. But secondly, and perhaps more importantly, it is to demonstrate a latent potential. Knowing how cultural memes can evolve and be made to spread, we have the ability, to not only mitigate the effect of some of the more damaging variants, but also to produce 'more benign mutations' to counter negative effects: we can influence, and to some extent, control our psychological landscape. And just in case sceptics might think this a dangerous idea, be aware – it's already going on all around us – though most of these spells might not be working in our best interests.

FROM FAITH TO FASHION, *PSYCHO-BABBLE TO CYBER-SEX – DECODING THE GREAT CULTURAL AND COMMERCIAL SPELLS OF OUR MODERN AGE.*

There's been an explosion of commentary on our age.
From empire building to downsizing, empowerment to the
'inner you', group sex to no sex, we are being preached to,
persuaded, instructed and indoctrinated.

Every second of the day a bewildering wave of new imagery and information fills our news bulletins, magazines and media channels. As we compress more and more into our lives, the ability to see more, do more, experience more, travel further and faster, defines our age. Speed rules: 'fast delivery', 'instant access', 'always-on technology' have become the mantras that propel us towards a better, brighter future. Time pressed at work and at home, our propensity for pre-packaged entertainment and clip culture sees the sound bites of celebrities and glamour models triumph over the words of those of high standing or repute. Marketing billboards across the globe promise individuality and authenticity, yet we have never been so much the same. In an era of globalisation and free trade, disparities of wealth have become both shocking and surreal. Millions in Africa work for less than a dollar a day, while on the other side of the world, in Silicon Valley, fresh-faced entrepreneurs are making a million in less than a second. Our future concerns are likewise of epic scale. Each of us, by our small actions, has collectively sown the seeds of a future environmental catastrophe, giving us the unenviable capability to alter the world's climate dramatically.

It was the 19th-century microbiologist Lóuis Pasteur, who, staring down at the growth of bacteria in his Petri dish and pondering the nature of germs, used it as an analogy for 'the mob'. He saw such undesirable influences as being like small infectious creatures that, though hidden, were always waiting to subvert and take over decent, law-abiding society. If we were borrow this analogy but reverse its perspective – reduce our complex world to the scale of Pasteur's Petri dish – which human activities, observed from a distance, would provide us with clues as to our common existence, the character of the global mind?

Those rare individuals who have been fortunate enough to stare down on the world from space have spoken of the spiritual impact of seeing the Earth looking so small within our surrounding galaxy. The experience of witnessing the undoubted beauty of the planet is mixed with a sense of its fragility and vulnerability within the context of the dark universe around it. Natural features dominate: jagged coastlines, coral atolls, river deltas, glaciers and mountain ranges. It's only at around 1,000 metres above the surface of the Earth that the first man-made effects intrude. A latticework of vapour trails from jet engines would betray the movement of aircraft. Over the skies of America alone, up to 5,000 are in the air at any one time. Lower still, the sea lanes of the world would reveal a different perspective. Day and night, a constant traffic of more than 4,000 cargo ships is shifting ten million containers across the seas. At one port on the coast of Dubai, 300 artificial islands have been formed into the shape of a map of the world. A mile from the shore in the city centre, the world's tallest building, the Burj Dubai, stretches towards the sky.

It is one of thousands of recently constructed skyscrapers, adding to a building frenzy that has seen more high-rise buildings completed globally in the last ten years than in the whole of the last century. The majority house corporations and small businesses. Neatly seated at desk terminals, one billion office workers will be staring at computer screens. Behind the Word documents, emails and complex financial spreadsheets, it is chatlines, blogs and lunchtime porn that predominate. Away from the city centres, suburbia tells a different tale. Traffic congestion is an integral part of most world capitals. Six hundred million vehicles crowd the roads of the globe. Many of these are parked up on the forecourts of large, out-of-town shopping malls. Inside, 24 million shoppers are piling up trolleys with food. Many will have purchased a magazine. On the front cover, a famous international footballer shares space with his ultra-thin wife. A million trees every hour will hit the forest floor to feed this celebrity addiction, the images they hold (currency for less than a day) destined to end their days amongst the 26 million tons of waste we throw into landfill sites across the UK (180 million tons in the US). A cursory glance through the mountains of rubbish provides other clues to our behaviour: 500 million discarded mobile phones, 50 million tons of junked electronic goods and computers, a staggering 500 billion plastic bags. Such is the scale of global consumption; almost everything we do, make or throw away, has an adverse effect on somebody, somewhere.

At this juncture, if, like Pasteur pondering the behaviour of germs in his Petri dish, we were to pause and ask, what is it that motivates and shapes the actions of this seething mass of humanity, how would we answer?

History gives a very good account of our lives and culture being guided by grand principles and virtue. Our buildings, institutions and galleries, bulging with rare heritage and artefacts, reflect these solid, traditional values. We frame our sense of nationhood in the aggrandising language of 'civilisation'; reason and rationality through science, moral integrity guided by religion, and artistic merit given eloquence by poets and playwrights. Our centres of learning instil theories and histories in the minds of our young; of geography, science, philosophy and literature. The influences contained in years of education should be considerable. Yet to what extent do virtue, wisdom or the accumulated knowledge of centuries explain our snapshot of teeming human activity? How much do they really govern the movement of crowds, or is something else more intrusive taking over our minds?

To the layman, landscape and mountain scenes betray very little of their past. But to geologists, the existence of valleys, lakes and jagged peaks are clues to a dramatic and sometimes violent history. So it is with the human mind. How we respond to our present cultural environment betrays the ghosts of our cultural past. Fear of the night, of wild animals and demons condition our terror of the dark. Magic, superstition and illusions created a propensity for grand spectacle and mass entertainment. But the deepest dent on our psyche, imprinted by centuries of indoctrination and ceremony, was, without doubt, organised religion.

Much has been written about the importance of Charles Darwin's *On the Origin of the Species*. Though it concerned itself predominantly with theories of natural and sexual selection, few at the time can have been aware of the potential disruptive social effects of this modest book (least of all the cautious publishers; only 1,250 copies were initially printed). Beyond evolution, Darwin introduced a perspective that fundamentally changed how humans viewed themselves in this world. Now, more than a hundred years later, many of us pass churches and religious sites with cold indifference. We associate such gloomy places less with peace and sanctuary than with creepy rituals and unwelcome rules. With the true significance of faith relegated to the periphery of our thoughts, it's hard to appreciate the profound importance of the seismic shift caused by Darwinism and the deep scar it left on human consciousness.

Science might have explained away the creation of the world in six days with grand theories such as the Big Bang and ridiculed the possibility of miracles with rational empirical facts, but religion was never just about Bible stories and monotonous priests reciting the litany. It was about social infrastructure. With the majority of people living and working on the land, churches and cathedrals were the only dominant architecture in an often featureless landscape. Such buildings, mesmerising in their imagery, light and sound, provided a sense of belonging, security for the community, the comfort of prayer in adversity and a place to disengage from a world of fear, suffering and poverty. They also supplied knowledge: an understanding of the natural world, our place in the cosmos, where we had come from and where we were going. The voice from the pulpit, though harsh and sometimes chastising, was also consoling, even ennobling, lifting hearts and minds. And within the parables of the Bible, interwoven between the familiar codes for moral behaviour, there was also the mundane: how to conduct yourself in society and business, and how to get along with your neighbours. Religion was a social fabric: a network of trust and reciprocity that brought cohesiveness and strength to a group (albeit strengths which could also be directed aggressively against rivals). But above all, faith was a narrative of hope: Despite all the appalling oppression of this world, paradise awaited you. Everyone had a place and a purpose. And this was the big, central, controlling idea.

For a large proportion of the Western world, the extinguishing of this 'guiding light' had a deep impact on human psychology. The loss of such mental comforts and securities, together with the failure of 'rational science' to provide a replacement (quantum physics was understandable to a few, string theory to virtually no one), left what the writer Jean-Paul Sartre described as a 'God-sized hole in our psyche'. **In place of the fixed landscape of faith, where winding roads corralled the faithful to the promised land, now there was only the desolate plain; a barren, uncertain void, in which few truths survived.**

This might look nihilistic, as indeed it was to many 20th century philosophers who struggled to create meaning within the wreckage of faith. But it also provided the ideal humus for our modern age. Conditions ripe for an explosion of new thinking – good and bad. The 'emptiness' in Western minds was like a tower block abandoned after a riot: eventually the squatters invade. The appropriation of our spiritual space came from diverse extremes. Extraordinary advances and ideas from science and technology mixed and conflicted with their obverse – unreason and irrationality, ushering in an era of DIY faiths, narcissistic cults and new age mystics. The crowd had a hunger for spectacle, illusions and magic, which knowledge and reason could not provide. Cinema, the precursor to modern-day mass television entertainment, bringing with it celebrity culture and star adoration, was quick to realise this need for sensationalism and fantasy.

But there was no more able 'forager into human souls' than advertising. Absorbing social insights from Freud's own nephew, Edmund Bernays, whom some have christened 'the father of spin', advertising became one of the great unsung success stories of the post-war economy. Its formula was succinct: concepts of happiness, tied to material gain, created a continually evolving state of desire which ensured that a finite level of contentment could never be attained. Such constructs, of lifestyle and comfort, provided the fuel for consumerism, which, in accelerating worldwide growth, also lifted millions from poverty, and lined the pockets of the global middle class. Being finely tuned to human frailties, such as desire, status fears and vanity ('vices' previously held in check by puritanical propriety), its message was especially potent to the spiritually bereft. The promises of nirvana and spiritual fulfilment were labels that could be attached to a bewildering array of products: from cars to pot noodles or even drain-cleaning solvents. Paradise could be attained through the cash tills.

All in the mind

With our actions no longer in the hands of destiny, or directed by the beneficial hand of some distant deity, human behaviour, instincts and emotions entered the realm of science. Luminaries and neurologists such as Daniel Dennett, Antonio Damasio and Joseph LeDoux have made dramatic inroads into the nature of feelings and emotions. Running in parallel with advances brought about by PET (positron emission tomography) scanners, which are capable of producing three-dimensional images of brain activity, such developments have also shed some light on the workings of consciousness. Gerald Edelman, famous for his work on the immune system and later for his theories on neuroscience, described our minds as being like an orchestra of players, their 'creation' dependent on the collective interaction of individual inputs: 'Every act of perception is to some degree an act of creation and every act of memory is to some degree an act of imagination.' His views come into conflict with the mechanistic account of the mind-body, proposed by the late Francis Crick, co-discoverer of the structure of DNA. In his book *The Astonishing Hypothesis*, Crick surmised that consciousness might be like computer software: 'You, your joys and your sorrows, your memories and your ambitions, your sense of personal identity and free will, are in fact no more than the behavior of a vast assembly of nerve cells and their associated molecules. As Lewis Carroll's Alice might have phrased it, "You are nothing but a pack of neurons." '

The Meme Machine

But a pure understanding of our physical selves as being directed by physiology and genes is not sufficient to explain human behaviour. It has long been accepted that much of our social conditioning comes from cultural influences in our environments. **Richard Dawkins, author of *The Selfish Gene*, was the first to coin the term 'meme'. He described memes as cultural genes – ideas that by becoming popular can be said to replicate and spread from person to person.** Memes can be virtually anything: fashion codes, memorable tunes, ideas for doing things, social trends, styles of architecture and design (such as the current vogue for titanium architecture or blob-shaped car design), or web-based contagious ideas. As well as spreading by word of mouth, memes are amplified by modern media: television, lifestyle magazines and now the internet. The large majority of memes which thrive today, by virtue of their repetition, volume, visibility and sheer weight in our media environment, are either commercial or conceal some commercial imperative. And it will be no surprise to discover that the most successful and potent in contemporary culture are those that, in attuning themselves to our evolutionary conditioning, press familiar buttons, such as sex, hunger, power or status. Interviewed in *The Guardian*, Daniel Dennett summarised the power of the meme industry: 'There are millions of people in this world who make their living trying to propagate memes. Everyone in advertising, everyone in public relations, everyone in religion.'

The potency of such messages today is greatly enhanced by the fact that the environment for such ideas, rather than being previously confined to local groups or national populations, has now become truly global. Memes have become viral and highly contagious. The latest fashions from Paris will, only seconds later, be in the cutting rooms of the sweatshops of Mumbai. A celebrity haircut on the front page of *OK!* will be rapidly copied by girls from Brazil to Bratislava. A graffiti motif from the hand of an edgy street artist in LA will almost spontaneously appear in the subways and streets of Moscow, Tokyo and London. A crass video, shot and edited by two unknown students in a bed-sit in South Korea, can be seen instantly by millions, their jokey antics inducing copycat behaviour worldwide.

Mobile phones with camcorder capability were designed for a future where, it was believed by the manufacturers, we would all be busy recording babies, birthdays and celebrations to forward to our families. Few anticipated 'happy slapping', where gangs used their video handsets to record scenes of violence against victims and forwarded the pictures to their mates 'for a laugh', nor did they imagine that teenage girls would use the networks to exchange scenes of themselves 'making out'.

Commercial memes and messages have multiplied in similar ways: a rush for the latest cutting-edge sneaker; a new addictive computer game; the latest hip, 'unspoiled' destination that unwittingly precipitates a rush. Political and social spells are just as virulent: a misjudged sound bite that rallies a nation to war (Tony Blair's 45-minute 'intelligence' on Iraq's missile capability); a smear campaign or sex scandal destroying trust in a previously dependable president or prime minister; or the image of a dying polar bear on an iceberg, instantly galvanising public action on climate change despite ten years of urgent testimony from some of the brightest minds in the scientific community.

Seeding themselves across all cultures, such **viral spells are like physical forces, attracting us to some things and repelling us from others. Bit by bit, behaviour is transformed. Our sense of who we are, why we do things, what we believe, becomes increasingly instigated by these control paradigms – often without our realising it.** Much of the emotional fabric of personalities – what we feel about ourselves, our ideas about happiness and contentment in the context of our sometimes frail self-esteem – are framed by these background voices and the complex interplay of their influences.

State of anxiety

And then there is fear: epic Hollywood-style anxieties – of terror attack, nuclear holocaust, flu pandemics, or asteroid attack – that merge to create a background hum that overshadows our day to day existence. Blended with our small, nagging, personal anxieties – that we don't measure up, that we 'look like shit', aren't popular or sexy or the most amusing person at the party – fear becomes the ever-present ghost state that makes us vulnerable to the commercial 'noise' that surrounds us and becomes instrumental in shaping our decision making. Competitive concerns, anxieties over our status and our positional worth compared to our neighbours, friends and family are some of the most powerful controllers of behaviour. In contemporary culture, such comparisons are that much more acute when those 'friends' and 'neighbours' are the world's most glamorous celebrities, brought into the intimacy of our homes by reality TV, the internet and lifestyle magazines.

A constantly evolving competitive climate induces the need to reassert ourselves continually; to be cooler, more heroic, sexier. **Lifestyle media have grown especially adept at providing the ammunition with which to defend our identities, feeding us with the symbols and material icons which ultimately we use to promote ourselves.** More than flesh and bones, our sense of self is wrapped up in these spells; in loft apartments with hi-tech kitchens, expensive art, powerful cars, label fashions and the latest must-have gadget. By projecting states of strength and individuality, these identities become shields to mask our frailties. When people don't like the way they feel about themselves, they reach out for something that will transform them – to temporarily shut off the anxiety state. And at school, the office or a party, increased social and sexual competition ensures that this hunger for re-invention and novelty is a constant necessity.

From the academic to the showgirl, we are all susceptible to these spells, ever anxious to shore up our self-esteem. As John Seabrook writes in his book *Nobrow: The Culture of Marketing, the Marketing of Culture,* we are all in the supermarket, just in different aisles. We take what components we want from the media environment and make them our own. Such Legoland lifestyles become constructs we can dip into then discard. Often we are blithely unaware of the blazing contradictions we deploy: raunch culture pushing empowerment, the eco-tour to Costa Rica – 4000 air miles away. Emotional rebel virtues will let us rail against the corrupting evils of multi-nationals at late-night dinner parties, but in the cold light of day rational voices whispering 'two for the price of one', 'choice and convenience' and 'easy parking' will soon see us scuttling back to the megastores.

Anger Management

Dissent and subversion have always acted as correctives to periods of decadence. But with torn jeans, body adornment and graffiti already part of high-street style, contemporary rebel sub-cultures have lost their power to shock what was once the bourgeois establishment. With their clothes, music and terminology rapidly absorbed into the mainstream, such urban sub-cultures have become yet another stylistic ingredient in the heady youth market mix. Art directed and given the Photoshop sheen, these edgy, controversial poses have been called on to shift everything from hair gel to insurance. **The angry anthems of anti-capitalism, which once marshalled the crowds at Berkeley and Woodstock, are now catchy jingles for global corporations.** Yes, suburban man still has inner rage, but now he can express this rebellion by wearing funky sneakers to the office.

Pump up the Volume

Social memes and commercial spells, potent though they are, would be nothing without a transmission medium. New technology, the internet, broadband communications, mobile media and instant messaging have added an entirely new dimension to the power of such messages. Speed and rapid exponential growth have been added to the equation. **Our contemporary commercial and media infrastructure, from lifestyle publishing, to TV and the web, has both perfected the art of triggering emotional responses using highly provocative visual metaphors, and provided a single and surprisingly coherent conduit for the worldwide dissemination and amplification of information.** Its fastest growing sector, new media, doesn't just extend the reach of viral content, it favours the meme.

The transition from old-style media – newspapers, magazines and television – to online and mobile communication and entertainment has also marked a change in how content is filtered, organised and given prominence before it is finally served up to audiences. This represents a subtle shift from editors as mediators and curators of content to the ruling (some would say tyranny) of the 'most-viewed'. The algorithms that underlie the success of two cornerstones of the internet, Google and YouTube, ranking choice by the most popular, the most linked to and the most clicked-on, create a domino effect.

Searching for virtually anything online will inevitably bring up millions of options. But the majority of users inevitably settle for the first two within a 'top ten' or 'best of results' within the page. Such selections exponentially reinforce an already dominant hold. Thus, small incremental advantages set off a stampede effect that can very quickly become a chain reaction. This explains why the most searched-for information within the web is likely to be the night-time misdemeanors of a celebrity in Paris and why the most insanely whacky, mind-bogglingly funny video clip is, ultimately, not that funny. It also explains why a relatively modest innovation such as Google (its superiority built on a few lines of software code) may become the centre of the entire media universe, with its hold on information searches likely to spread to the manner in which we absorb news, view television entertainment, and even read books.

More importantly, these techniques and technologies have come from the fringes to mould the formulas for persuasion that we see operated every day. **So effective have these delivery strategies become, that the commercial methodology has turned into a standard, a benchmark, that all communicators are forced to attain – whether they are governments, charities, news channels, environmental activists, or even terrorists;** all have to compete to be seen and heard amongst the continuous 'noise' of popular culture screaming for our attention.

The Great Distortion

The machinery of media and communication, made fluid and interconnected by new technology, has become analogous to a global mind. It's a filter that rewards and amplifies certain information and knowledge, determining what gets said, seen and made. In doing so, it lays down the blueprint for our concepts of 'lifestyle'. It's a cultural force that is profound, influencing worldwide our ideas on happiness, morality, sex, social behaviour and interaction, thus colouring our attitudes to other nations and cultures, the poor, the young and the old. In every area of our lives, be it science, health, conflict or politics, popular stories become dominant. They become paramount because they adhere to certain principles that are attuned to this global consciousness. When the primary power of a message becomes its ability to multiply fast, or become viral, it's no surprise that many, seeking audiences and fast publicity, resort to sex and shock strategies in order to be heard. Such themes have become increasingly potent because they have been forced to evolve continually (become more controversial, more explicit), in order to have the same effect in an image environment saturated with similar content.

Richard Brodie, original programmer of Microsoft Word, no less, and writer of *Virus of the Mind: The New Science of the Meme,* has suggested the reason that memes which utilise sex and power continue to have a stranglehold over us is that they touch certain emotional nerves tied to our evolutionary past. Conversely, those that fail to hit these primordial switches risk becoming invisible. Difficult or awkward stories, truths that are unpalatable or which contain nuances that are hard to reduce to simple bite-sized headlines, don't proliferate or survive. Our collective propensity to be swayed by images and messages that spread by virtue of such strategies has created a global distortion – one that, like gravity in a black hole, warps our perspective, putting an undue emphasis on short-term sensationalism (more often the simple alleviation of boredom), against more abstract (some would say dated) ideals of depth of experience and knowledge. **Every truth or tenet has a context and perspective. But sometimes a sensational headline, or a dramatic image trumps all else, irrespective of the rights and wrongs, and becomes the singular truth that is accepted. Once entrenched, such paradigms become very difficult to dislodge.** When it comes to the front-page, the opinions of a football star or a celebrity will win over those of an academic or a Nobel Prize-winner. In Iraq, the almost daily sight of billions of dollars of ordnance igniting the city failed to awaken a sense of injustice with the public; it took a handful of snaps – the shocking, surreal scenes of Abu Ghraib prison – to destroy the moral cause. Everyday horrors in Gaza fill our TV news – but not the less visible massacres of the Congo, Southern Sudan or Burma. On a smaller scale, the pros and cons of GM food, an issue deemed too complex for the public to digest, was given memorable clarity by the headline 'Frankenstein Food'. Such evocative hyperbole not only encouraged a general perception that GM crops were mad, bad and ugly, but also undermined the public's trust in the impartiality of scientists, who were now perceived to be in the pay of the big corporations. Global warming was another complicated issue needing reduction to fit the demands of the front page or TV news bulletin. Scientists standing in front of complex graphs and figures were never going to cut it with the public; they needed stars. And whilst we will readily buy into the altruism of Hollywood film stars photographed in front of their 'green' electric cars, few will see any contradiction in their jetting back to their 200ft yachts in private planes. Such blatant inconsistencies only add to the general climate of confusion.

This multiplicity of content coming at us by the hour is overloading our ability to deal effectively with information. To manage the deluge, the mind takes short cuts. Introspection and independence of thought is divorced for the sake of the global buzz. Sociologist Sherry Turkle, writing in *New Scientist,* sets out how the 'always on' wired world is transforming human psychology: 'It seems to be part of a larger trend in media culture for people not to know what they think until they get a sense of what everyone else thinks. But we learn about what everyone else thinks by reading highly polarised opinions that encourage choosing sides rather than thinking things through.'

A more serious casualty of the 'rush of stuff' is our perception of reality. *With every possible interpretation of a news event or opinion somewhere out there on the web, anything, however crazy, has a home. Those who believe in the weird and the irrational can now take comfort in the fact that millions of others also subscribe to their narrow world views.* The net result? Few believe anything anymore; conspiracy theories and extremism proliferate. We can tailor our moral cloth to suit our circumstance and our lifestyle.

Neophilia: Rush for the New

Across Europe, approximately 187,000 new products are launched every year. On the internet, a new blog site is born every half-second. The fashion industry, previously confined to seasons (spring, summer, autumn, winter), now entices consumers into stores with the promise of a constant flow of new designs and accessories. Budget travel has turned 'the great getaway' from something that we indulged in once a year, to a trifle that we can knock off in a weekend. Life becomes a checklist of must-have experiences that need to be tried and ticked off with ever more dizzying speed.

But if we can hit the brakes for even a second and pause to reflect, how much of what we experience as 'the newest', 'the coolest', 'the fastest', leaves us with any real emotional resonance? Does this mass of new products, knowledge and information flying around the airwaves equate to greater contentment, knowledge and information? Have we become so conditioned and attuned to the dictates of viral culture, that in confusing a state of happiness with the technical accumulation of such possessions and experiences, we fear its opposite – the discontent engendered by the ordinary, the slightly less wonderful, the everyday? The vast majority of commercial spells appeal to our failings: that we don't have this, that we aren't so beautiful, that we can't go so fast. But maybe that's okay; we don't have to have the coolest, the best, the quickest.

Alain de Botton, writing in *The Architecture of Happiness,* describes an aspect of medieval Japan in which attention was directed towards simplicity: 'A word emerged, *wabi,* of which no Western language, tellingly, has a direct equivalent, which identified beauty with unpretentious, simple, unfinished, transient things. There was *wabi* to be enjoyed in an evening spent alone in a cottage in the woods hearing the rain fall. There was *wabi* in old ill-matching sets of crockery, in plain buckets, in walls with blemishes and in rough, weathered stones covered in moss and lichen.' Yes, paradise does exist on an obscure beach on a remote Thai island, seven thousand miles away, but it is also just down the road.

The Wired Generation

Fondly described as 'commercial gold' by international brands, the young are the demographic most targeted by this brave new media environment. Interconnected like no generation before and brought up on a constant diet of stimulus and arousal – computer games, social networking sites, blogs, clip culture and portable media – they are not only developing a dependence on technological novelty, but are also becoming attuned to its content. *For millions of teenagers worldwide, the virtual world of online communities, avatars and multi-player gaming is the only reality that they have any deep emotional engagement with.* Traditionalists might abhor such developments. But in the context of sometimes soulless home lives, often the result of family conflict or a lack of stability, the community of cyberworlds becomes a more dependable and rewarding alternative. More crucially, if individuals chose to reject real life for the myriad pleasures of cyberspace, does that activity become their real reality? The point at which over-indulgence bleeds into obsessive behaviour, and excessive behaviour into addiction, is debatable. Ever since obsessive gamers Eric Harris and Dylan Klebold downed their computer controls for sawn-off shotguns and killed 12 students at Columbine High School in Colorado, discussions about the damaging effects of game playing have filled column inches, including alarming insights from psychologists. Scientific studies have shown that the same neurological reactions and processes that underlie the behaviour of a crack addict, also dominate the actions of a games player.

Scientist Sabine Grusser-Sinopoli, who heads a research laboratory into behavioural addictions at the Charite Medical University of Berlin, puts such findings into a wider context. She argues that all addictions are essentially the same, and that the biological impulses that govern drug addiction are similar to those in any excessive behaviour – be that shopping, binge drinking, cyber porn, or even stamp collecting. Once again, the young prove to be more susceptible to obsessive traits. Social pressures come from several extremes: concerned parents pushing for higher grades and better academic performance; 'cool stress' (peer pressure at school to be constantly hip and 'with it'); and a sense of self that is besieged by status anxieties seeded by popular culture, MTV and TV advertising. Paradoxically, kids in affluent families, who might be expected to benefit from a 'land of plenty', suffer three times the average rate of depression and mental illness, precipitated by such addictions. Obsessive behaviour has its own dynamic. It comes to dominate people's lives and, in extreme cases, destroys them. As Sabine Grusser-Sinopoli concludes: 'People aren't doing it because they like it, they're doing it because they have to.'

In a 2006 study in the US, conducted by the Pew Internet and American Life Project, it was estimated that a typical 21-year-old has already played 5000 hours of computer games and spent 3500 hours online. It's a set of disturbing statistics: 8500 hours of activity over six years amounts to approximately four hours of gaming and online activity a day. What ever happened to the great outdoors? In a second survey, again in the US, conducted by the Centre of Internet studies, one in eight people were showing signs of being addicted to the internet or online gaming. Such addictions bring their own concerns. It has been claimed by neurologists that the repeated activation of certain reward circuits of the brain, can be so strong as to cause certain neural circuits to undergo change. This is known as neural plasticity, where repeated experiences can permanently alter the organisation of the brain, increasing our hunger for sensory inputs of a similar nature.

Where pleasure and excitement are bonded to particular emotions within neural maps inside the mind, re-imprinting of the same input reinforces a sense of euphoria. Just as a painter finds the sublime in a rocky landscape, or a priest is moved by an evocative passage in the Old Testament, young minds are becoming more turned on by interacting with digital worlds and virtual partners than with interaction with real people in normal life.

Peter Whybrow, Director of the Semel Institute of Neuroscience at the University of California in Los Angeles and author of *American Mania,* blames our inflationary commercial environment for the massive increase of addictions of all kinds. Worldwide affluence and the sudden availability of everything is putting our reward systems into overload. Whybrow believes that desire for material possessions and our thirst for novelty have come from the fringes to occupy centre stage: 'Technology and the marketplace are no longer invaders that can be shut out from the everyday world – they *are* the everyday world.'

The Global Rush

Obsessive and addictive behaviour at the individual level has its own concerns – anxieties that range from petty fears over status, to stress-related disorders, depression and, in some extreme cases, even suicide. But at the international level the dominance of viral culture takes on an altogether more harrowing perspective. Western civilisation's most potent meme is the spell of modern lifestyle, embodied in its technology, products, homes, entertainment, music and architecture. And it is this single universal dream, propelled by notions of 'faster', 'more comfort' and 'newer', that drives the global mind. Such spells have become the role models that the majority of the world are following – or aspire to emulate. These are the cultural bulldozers of our collective consciousness, shaping the psychological landscape of our mind. It's a 'one size fits all' prescription that comes with a barb in its tail. Nearly 70 years of the post-war economy have created both extraordinary success stories and catastrophic failures. Commercialism and globalisation are two stories told back to back. Empowerment/repression, freedom/enslavement, wealth creation/impoverishment; your version will be largely dependent on where you were born. The future heralds an even greater dichotomy: How do we balance the need for future progress, where global affluence will lift millions in developing nations (such as India and the Far East) out of poverty, against a juggernaut culture that, in using more of the world's energy resources, will have a deeper impact on environmental degradation, resource conflict and global warming?

World economies are precarious at best. The well-being of billions of us, rich and poor, is dependent (either directly or indirectly) on the health of international trade. Our jobs, hopes of promotion, ability to pay off our debts and mortgages and fund our children's education is dependent on economic harmony. **Does wonderland and its dreams of the good life become a necessary illusion, an 'optimum state' that we need to quietly accept, even protect, in order to maintain fragile economic stability and keep the dreaded spectre of world recession at bay?** Fundamental change is clearly necessary. But inspired political vision and resolve is conspicuously missing. Enzio Manzini, professor at the University of Milan, likens the process of moving from a high consumer world, to a low waste society, to changing the engines of an aircraft in mid-flight. Perhaps the still painful memory of the failure of two of the most disastrous social experiments of the last century have undermined our courage for innovation and sweeping social change?

Megacorp: The Evil Empire

When the UK supermarket brand Tesco opened its first stores in Thailand in 1998, reaction was mixed. Angry competitors hit the business with a wall of lawsuits, some even claiming that the extreme cold within the shopping aisles (due to the air-conditioning) was hazardous to health. One disgruntled local took more extreme measures, targeting the food store with an anti-tank rocket. The story had all the ingredients of an age-old David and Goliath saga: the defenseless poor driven out by the greed of an all-powerful international conglomerate.

Ever since mythical anti-tech zealot Ned Ludd (inspiration behind the Luddite movement), set about destroying two stocking frames in a factory in Nottingham in 1811, the image of big business as being evil, corrupting and selfish has been a familiar tale, emphasised by centuries of literature, poetry and philosophical musings. Charles Fourier, a French 16th century utopian philosopher, was one of the first to write about the predatory nature of competition: that one man's success could only be brought about by the failure of another. William Blake's memorable poem *And did those feet in ancient time* vividly described the dehumanising effects of industrialisation and its 'dark satanic mills'. Joseph Conrad, writing in *An Outcast of the Islands,* decried the loss of sailing vessels and condemned the steamships of merchants, which 'tore down the veil of terrible beauty in order that greedy and faithless landlubbers might pocket dividends'. Marx and Engels railed against the enslavement brought about by modern capitalism, mocking the shallow ways of the bourgeoisie, who were transfixed by trivial possessions. In the 1960s, some Western academics and students found solace in the spiritual, anti-materialistic values of Eastern spiritualism, its message of community and simplicity a welcome antidote to the sudden acquisitiveness of their parents seduced by the new consumer age.

Today, the abuse of corporate power has become the focus of books such as Naomi Klein's *No Logo* and Kalle Lasn's *Adbusters* and has inspired social action events such as Buy Nothing Day and TV Turnoff Week. Contemporary artists ridicule international conglomerates with towering installations and canvases, whilst the concept of the 'ogre in the office' has provided an endless stream of content for stand-up comics and satirical commentators. **Many on the hard left, see the grim forebodings of climate change as a godsend: global warming heralds a new puritanical ideology of lean, communal living, that will finally bring the great capitalist machine to a painful, juddering halt.** Driven by notions of corporate greed, waste, exploitation and the 'pathological pursuit of profit', Megacorp exists in our minds as Public Enemy Number One.

Few have questioned the veracity of this deeply engrained paradigm. Most of our fears of the future (the foremost being environmental, such as climate change, pollution and the scarcity of resources), have been built on the supposition that businesses, and their consumers, won't change. But perhaps this pessimism is unfounded. Under pressure from both government legislation and environmental pressure groups, there is evidence that some sectors of industry are taking the message of change on board. The vast majority of big businesses, like everything else in this world, have been forced to evolve. Over the last century, the development of international trade and globalisation has run in parallel with a history of reform. From improvements in labour hours, working conditions, workers' rights, fair pay and moves to prevent sex and age discrimination, businesses have (mostly reluctantly) evolved for the better. And just as labour practices have revolutionised corporations, is it unrealistic to envisage that future restrictions, such as curbs on energy use, lean production, longevity of design and the need to make products both sustainable and recyclable, can be implemented in the same manner as our historic reforms, residing not as an adjunct to a company's operation, but at its core?

Indeed, recent examples have shown that in some cases, businesses have often had to move faster than governments in setting future goals, not resisting change, but embracing it. In the US, where the Bush administration has been dragging its feet over initiatives such as the 1997 Kyoto Protocol, companies like Dupont, Caterpillar and Alcoa have made their own approaches to Congress, calling for the implementation of cap-and-trade schemes for greenhouse gases. General Electric has set into motion a proactive strategy, Ecoimagination, that will double its investment in cleaner, alternative energy to $1.5 billion by 2010. Google has urged the computer industry to adopt a single 12-volt standard for all PCs that will save billions of kilowatt hours worldwide. The UK retail giant Marks & Spencer announced a five-year plan to re-engineer itself as a carbon-neutral, zero-waste, ethical trading business, at a cost of £200 million.

Sceptics have derided the idea that big business can change its ways. They see such attempts as superficial gloss or public relations exercises – a 'greenwash' to cover a multitude of sins. In their view, corporate altruism always comes with strings attached, and these efforts are, at best, only a very pale shade of green. Matt Ridley, writing in *The Origin of Virtue,* questions whether any altruism can exist as a selfless act. As individuals we are often altruistic, knowing that our good deeds build up social capital, thereby contributing to our future interests. Though some have argued that benevolence motivated by vanity or self-interest is not *real* benevolence, surely all that matters is that such initiatives bring about worthwhile change. Instigating corporate strategies should not only represent an opportunity for good public relations; legislation should also ensure that such moves make sound economic sense.

Jeff Immelt, Chairman of GE, in initiating a substantial investment in cleaner technologies, clearly wanted to distance himself from starry-eyed idealists by declaring that his aim was 'not a hobby to make people feel good', but a strategy to find value in energy efficiency. Richard Branson, who is a skilled self-publicist as well as an entrepreneur, was one of the first to realize that alternative industries could be made compatible with profit; he first invested $60 million in ethanol fuels, then promised a $25 million reward to the best inventor of a process to remove CO_2 from the atmosphere. Even the global investment bankers Goldman Sachs have redirected their focus. Internal policy forbids the bankrolling of projects that 'significantly convert or degrade a critical natural habitat'. In 2007 they brokered a deal with Texas Pacific Group and the energy utility, TXU Corp, that was dependent on making a $400 million investment in energy-saving initiatives. In a statement published in *Newsweek*, Goldman Sachs stated that its environmental efforts were aimed at creating 'long-term value for our shareholders'.

Revolution downloading...

By contrast, the creative industry – from architecture to product design, media and advertising – have come surprisingly late to the party, considering their professed thirst for innovation and the need to always be seen to be at the 'cutting edge'. Yet these are disciplines that will also be vital in solving our future problems. Yes, we can implement rush measures today, but their effect will be limited in relationship to a problem whose timescale is measured in hundreds of years. **The real future, in the shape of highly efficient cars, low energy homes, new energy technologies and the restructuring of how we produce and source our food and consumer products, has yet to be invented.** The focus will be on manufacturing. Unregulated production will need to be replaced by a 'dust to dust' design philosophy: a new discipline and aesthetic that governs a product's entire life cycle – from the sourcing of sustainable materials and local industries, to low-energy manufacturing techniques and the production of designs that are durable and easily recyclable. On the marketing front, our image makers will need to engineer the transition from a norm in which we are persuaded to make lots of cheap purchases (that we soon replace and discard), to one in which we buy fewer products (though they are of better quality and cost more) that are designed to last. The short emotional kick of novelty must be replaced by the longer-lasting satisfaction of finding pleasure in products that age. But above all, a low-carbon lifestyle will need a dynamic that makes it viral, visible and saleable to all of the world's consumers. Desire made compatible with virtue. **A 'green' horizon shouldn't fill us with dread, or be viewed as a monk-like sentence devoid of fun or colour. Why can't such an alternative be seen as a future that makes our lives more fulfilling and rewarding?** It's a question of perception. Just as technology forms a cornerstone of our contemporary lifestyle, issues of the environment, sustainability and low emissions must become the lead dynamic in our future economy. Fifty years ago, creative professionals effectively transformed the global economy in the post-war era; it's certainly within their powers to achieve such a change again.

Critics will argue that such exacting measures will be both open to abuse and impossible to police globally. Equally, it would be naïve to suppose that such moves alone can suddenly make companies everywhere paragons of virtue and moral probity. Examples of brands cynically appropriating environmental and charitable measures merely to conceal malpractice are common. But in doing so, they have failed to appreciate that a fundamental shift has occurred in contemporary culture.

Gone are the days when business managers could cosy up to a handful of media proprietors and use the threat of removing advertising from their publications as a means to ensure protection for their brands. With the gradual erosion in the power of newspapers and broadcasters, control of information, content and entertainment, is shifting from editors and programme directors to online communities and networks. Mobile media, blogs and community networks such as YouTube (now owned by Google) and MySpace, are becoming the favored environments for mass communication. Interconnected and socially aware, with a sharp nose for misdemeanours, the web lights up with the slightest whiff of wrong-doing. Like a people's central intelligence agency, this connected community is vigilant – it has all-seeing eyes and finely tuned ears. And they're everywhere: in London and New York but also, more importantly, in Hong Kong and Mumbai.

Nike witnesed such an effect in 2001, after putting online their very ingenious personalisation concept, Nike ID, which allowed customers to customise their sneakers with a word or slogan. MIT graduate student Jonah Peretti was one such user. Taking at face value Nike's declaration of 'freedom', Peretti cheekily decided to design his sneakers with the word 'sweatshop' running down the sides. Nike refused to deliver. The managers who made such a decision can have had little idea of the damage it would cause. Peretti's online correspondence with the international brand, first shared amongst mates, went on to gain coverage in more than 300 newspapers and spread like wildfire across the web. The resulting carnage at the hands of bloggers worldwide was millions of dollars of adverse publicity for the brand.

Such examples have demonstrated the power of the wired world. It has the ability to create sudden popularity for things that consumers approve of, but also the obverse effect: the unnerving capability to destroy brands within the same alarming timescale, if the target market chooses to turn again them.

This introduction started with the analogy of micro-organisms in a Petri dish. And like Pasteur, governments and businesses have shared the microbiologists' fear of the actions and opinions of the mob. But Pasteur was not just guilty of pessimism in his assumption that the actions of the masses (like bacteria) would be wholly negative, he was being paranoid. Interconnected protest groups like *Avaaz.org* (meaning voice in several languages) and advocacy movements like Australia's *GetUp.org.au* have already proved the benefits of e-protest. The structure of the wired world has the potential to change the entire nature of democracy, giving voters the ability to actively participate in debate and get involved with forming legislation. As software and hardware become more sophisticated, it is not unreasonable to suppose that one day, we might all have a genuine voice. Coordinated effectively, such a movement would provide an effective counter-balance to the shortcomings and inaction of both global government and corporate power.

In his book *The Tipping Point: How Little Things Can Make a Big Difference*, Malcolm Gladwell concludes that: 'What must underlie successful epidemics, in the end, is a bedrock belief that change is possible, that people can radically transform their behaviour or beliefs in the face of the right kind of impetus.' **Just as there is no greater contributor to inertia than the debilitating idea that we can't do anything about our circumstances, there is nothing more inspiring than the notion that all of us, irrespective of wealth, creed, or colour, can influence beneficial change.**

THE VIRAL FACTORY, HOW THE MODERN WORLD TARGETS THE CENTRAL NERVOUS SYSTEM

This book aims to decode the most potent cultural and commercial spells of our age – the ideas that shape our lives, excite our desires and fuel our addictions. It will demonstrate the power of our lifestyle paradigms: how they work, spread, influence change and shape global behaviour.

The difficulties of establishing objectivity and truth have long been the subject of academic debate. Felipe Fernandez Armesto, writing in his book *Truth*, challenged our preconceptions about fixed viewpoints. History was compared to 'a nymph glimpsed bathing between leaves; the more you shift perspective, the more is revealed. If you want to see her whole you have to dodge and slip between many different standpoints.'

In the same way, popular culture can appear indecipherable. To provide clarity, this publication has tried to peel away the outer layer of a subject, rather like an orange, to reveal the different segments inside, each component comprising a different facet of the whole: emotions, fears and aspirations, mixed with visual stimuli and reward. From the exercise of power over the people through religion and mega-catastrophe to the stylistic – cool, anti-style and hip-hop – viral memes might give the impression of being bewilderingly complex but more often there is simplicity. From the entrepeneur to the politician, the academic to the pole dancer, the same psychology is in operation. Driven by the same hungers and desires – individuality, recognition, affection or material wealth – we shelter behind identities to shield our frailties and sense of self.

The second challenge was to make these ideas approachable to a wider audience. The spells of *Mesmerization* are not a theory of thinking. Unlike fixed schematics, such as maps or plans, they aim to provide a framework in which ideas and concepts can be better explained. In decoding such constructs, the spells are there as a catalyst; to fire up a sense of enquiry, make us question, be sceptical, be curious.

Armed with a greater awareness of how such control strategies work and manipulate our consciousness, we will be better able to 'read' the media: to put together the different, sometimes contradictory fragments of a reality to form our own viewpoints – to make a distinction between the real and the vague, the seminal and the same, the innovators and the imitators, the prophets and the plagiarisers, the genuine voices of change and the mere echoes. In the words of James Gleick in *Faster*, 'Try to distinguish between the little nattering demons that can fill every moment and the greater, quieter spirits that can enrich the passing hours.'

AN EXPLANATION OF THE SPELLS IN MESMERIZATION

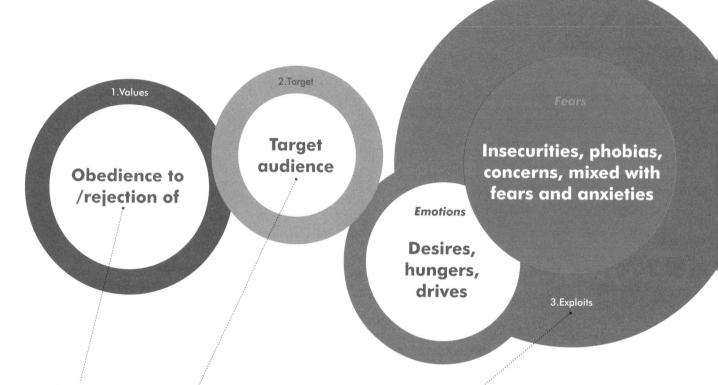

1. Subject Values
Effective viral spells and memes (contagious cultural and commercial ideas) are defined by their values: obediences to certain beliefs, concepts and traits of behaviour, are framed by their obverse – rejection, opposition, even hatred of opposing views and principles.

2. Target Audience
Global connectivity and mobile communications has given viral ideas and messages added potency. Not only has the audience for such memes and spells become truly international – a simple message, image, or video, has the ability to be seen by millions within the space of seconds – its message is in turn replicated to further induce copycat behaviour.

3. Triggering desire in the context of fears
Cultural and commercial spells attract our attention because they are designed to target our unconscious emotions. It's an appeal that stimulates past memories, associations, desires, hungers and drives. These combine with our 'memories of the future' – our hopes, aspirations and ambitions.

Such emotions are given additional impetus in the context of our fears. Our harbored insecurities and inadequacies at both a personal level – hair loss, being overweight, being a loser – are combined with our collective 'background' fears – global warming, international terrorism, bird-flu epidemics. Into this cauldron of anxieties bleed our irrational fears – conspiracy theories, asteroid attack or abduction by aliens.

This composite of emotions (explained in both a personal and social perspective), becomes the humus on which the majority of our popular cultural spells feed.

Promise

Either: wish fulfillment or alleviation of suffering

Visual spell

Imagery, style, iconography

4.Seduces with

5.Reward

Cultural spells and memes will only spread and evolve if they successfully effect a reaction that leads to an outcome, reward or exchange.

4. Seducing with visual spells

Spells that are effective and contagious, do so by delivering a promise or proposition, fused with a highly emotional visual metaphor, wrapped in an aesthetic style (such as 'cool', 'girl-power' or 'rebel chic'), that because of its unquestioned acceptance within the lexicon of popular culture, is able to override our normally astute and often rational resistance to the noise of cultural and commercial clutter.

The analogy with viruses is further endorsed by the fact that, in order for contemporary spells to spread rapidly through the transmission medium (global media, TV and the internet), memes are forced to become that much more virulent than their previous strain – sexier than, cooler than, better than – in order to achieve cut-through in an already saturated, competitive environment. Modern lifestyle, to remain relevant, must continually evolve and inflate.

5. Reward (*Reality check*)

Such is the weight of our most popular cultural and commercial spells in media across the world, that certain of our most potent prescriptions have the power to engrain modes of behaviour, that in being constantly repeated and replicated, become difficult to dislodge. Often such paradigms grow to be so established that they reshape, even distort many of our accepted notions of social conduct and culture. Extreme states can lead to compulsive behaviours: obsessions, even damaging addictions are often the result. The summary section of each spell, in the form of a 'reality check', is an attempt to address this imbalance.

MESMER

COOL CULTURE
RUSH FOR IDENTITY

BORN TO BE WILD
SELL OUT FOR $TARDOM
IPOD CULTURE
DESIGN ICON OF OUR TIMES

ANTI-STYLE
AGAINST THE MAINSTREAM
RETRO
YEARNING FOR THE PAST

YLE
LLS

HIP HOP
GET RICH OR DIE

REBEL, REBEL
COUNTER CULTURE
GUNS R US
INSTANT RESPECT

SNEAKER FREAKS
DEFINES WHO YOU ARE
HIPPY CHIC
DROP OUT, OPT OUT, CHILL OUT

COOL
CULTURE

In a world where we are daily besieged by images of the impossibly rich, beautiful and powerful, 'Cool' has become a strategy to maintain self-esteem by promoting oneself as having opted out of conventional society and the homogeneity of a middle-class lifestyle to create one's own set of values. Originally an attitude of dissent, used by underdogs, slaves, or political prisoners, to cope with intolerance and repression, Cool has evolved since the fifties to become the central theme of today's youth sub-culture. Co-opted by the consumer marketplace, a veneer of 'cool' has become an essential ingredient in the promotional/advertising mix, for brands, products, even borrowed as the watchword for the UK's labour goverment, ever-anxious to maintain an edge of credibility with the fickle youth market, that now ironically, embraces everyone, from six year-olds demanding their first mobile phone to Grandpa picking up his pension in his latest, edgy sneakers.

Cool is a powerful director of social behaviour, dividing what is acceptable in life from what is perceived to be dull and boring. But by creating such harsh divisions it also impoverishes our human experience. Much of what is truly remarkable in life is housed in institutions, churches and galleries, which to the style aficionadas are perceived as being 'uncool' and thus off limits. Obedience to the dictates of what is acceptable lifestyle, the 'hip', 'the latest', 'the newest', has made us culturally undemanding, narrowing and limiting our experiences and choices. As we roll ever onwards with the 'cool crowd', such spells merely anchor us to convention, leaving us blithely unaware that we have hitched what remains of our individuality to the bandwagon that is now corporate culture.

COOL CULTURE

Rush for Identity

Emotional Context:
- Cool used to be the exclusive domain of the young. Part of its power was the generational thing; a declaration of 'non-cooperation' on one's own terms – do not assess me by your outdated standards, wealth, status etc.
- For teenagers and adolescents, the great anxiety was not to be square, not to be old, to conceal one's identity and insecurities behind a mask of defiance and ironic impassivity. Such concerns make the youth easy prey for the marketers and brands, each peddling their own variations of the cool aesthetic and lifestyle.

Social context:
- In a society in which the majority can be defined as being 'bourgeois', Cool has become the ultimate 'Anti-Bourgeois' strategy, the ideal antidote for the middle classes to distance themselves from accusations of being 'square', 'grey suited', or 'mondeo man' – even Grandpa wears Freedom Nikes. And it is a strategy that is global, as relevant in the markets of Mumbai as much as in London's Notting Hill.

1. Values

WHAT'S HOT
WHAT'S HIP
WHAT'S NEW

2. Target

GLOBAL YOUTH
(IN FACT EVERYONE)

Emotions

BE SOMEONE
DIFFERENT

3. Exploits

Fears

I'M SQUARE
I'M BLAND
I'M A LOSER

Obedience to:
- Cutting-edge style
- First with the fashion
- Neophilia; an obsession with novelty
- Attitude of rebellious nonconformity
- Counter culture
- Oddball, off-the-wall behaviour
- Cult of individuality
- Inner defence strategy
- Desire for recognition
- Ironic detachment
- Slavish obedience to what's 'in', what's 'out', i.e. the latest tech gadgets and accessories (iPod etc)

Rejection of:
- Bourgeois conformity
- Traditional social mores
- Conventional status symbols
- Uptight guy in grey suit
- Showing over-eagerness, overt ambition
- Bland bureaucracy
- Conservative, parental values
- Living at home
- Old school club, privileged background
- Bankers and financial over-achievers

Personal Fears:
- The horror of being like one's parents
- Fear of aging (and for the old – fear of not being young)
- Fear of exclusion, of not being accepted, not in the 'in' gang
- Social inadequacy
- Fear of ridicule or embarrassment
- Fear of being thought of as being bland, lacking credibility. (In confusing individuality with the possession of certain products and labels, the fear remains, that unless we own certain brands and commodities, we have no 'visible' personality)

World Fears:
- Surrendering to the system
- A life of work and drugery with no end
- Mortgage, 2.5 kids, a life of debt

4.Seduces with

Promise

ACCEPTANCE,
AUTHENTICITY,
INDIVIDUALITY

5.Reward

Visual spell

URBAN CUTTING-EDGE,
STREET STYLE,
THE NEW COOL

STAND OUT
FROM THE CROWD

Reality check:

Cool ends up as a straight formula – to succeed one has to be ground breaking, non conformist and cutting edge. But if everyone is being ground breaking and non-conformist, it becomes the norm.

Cool gives the impression of being the voice of the street and the individual. Extravagant displays of deconstructed graphics are an attempt to create distance from the dull monotony of corporate culture and competitive marketing. In reality an obsession with the hottest, the latest, the newest, builds in style and fashion obsolescence with ever greater efficiency. So vital and effective have such style strategies become in accelerating consumerism, that cool has ironically become a powerful driver of global capitalism, an ideology it originally set out to subvert – how cool is that?

Iconography:
• Rock stars and rock chicks
• Rebels, outcasts and underdogs
• Cult movies and music
• Sex, drugs and rock and roll
• Urban street culture, graffiti, guerrilla style
• Sunglasses, jeans, t-shirt
• Zen-style mysticism

Style/Aesthetic:
• Effortless, of-the-moment creativity
• Edgy, deconstructed, cutting-edge graphics
• The unorthodox, unexpected
• Quirky, surreal imagery
• Ironic imagery
• Oddball cartoons and animation
• Provocative sexual imagery
• Porn, sleaze chic

Promise:
• Find meaning, authenticity in life
• Enhance individuality and self identity
• Difference, exclusivity, mark of distinction
• Cool by association (with brand X)
• Part of the 'in crowd', join the zeitgeist
• Cutting-edge, hip credentials
• The new elite

Future Vision:
• As products become homogenous worldwide, the pressure is on to be different. Cool supplies this 'edge'. But in becoming the dominant international currency, 'Cool' has debased its value and become as bland an adjective as saying that something is nice. We might think we're being angry, radical and subversive, but in reality we're just promoting our own subservience to the great global machine.

Dick Pountain & David Robins
Cool Rules

In the days of slavery, cool was part of a survival mentality a defence mechanism invented to cope with continuous exploitation, discrimination and disadvantage: it deployed ironic detachment and emotional impassivity to enable its bearer to withstand the domineering orders, abuse and insults of the overseer without succumbing to depression or to a rage that might incur flogging or even execution.

David Brooks
Bobos in Paradise

Marx told us that classes inevitably conflict, but sometimes they just blur. The values of the bourgeois mainstream culture have merged. That culture war has ended, at least within the educated class. In its place that class has created a third culture, which is a reconciliation between the previous two. The educated elites didn't set out to create this reconciliation. It is the product of millions of individual efforts to have things both ways. But it is now the dominant tone of our age. In the resolution between the culture and the counterculture, it is impossible to tell who co-opted whom, because in reality the bohemians and the bourgeois co-opted each other. They emerge from this process as bourgeois bohemians, or Bobos.

Joseph Heath & Andrew Potter
The Rebel Sell, how Counterculture became Consumer Culture

The turnover in cool is fantastic, and it exposes one of the deepest ironies of countercultural movements. – countercultural rebellion has given us even faster cycles of obsolescence in fashion, all in the name of individuality.

Derek Draper
The Independent

There is something about our culture that pushes us towards activities that are hypnotically shallow, rather than committing to something more profoundly.

Jessica Brinton
Sunday Times

We never used to have this problem. From the moment in the 1950's when 'cool' was first used to mean 'hot', it was obvious who had it and who didn't. Steve McQueen was cool. Wild at Heart Debbie Harry was cool. Tortured Kurt Cobain was cool. Cool people were different and, by definition, out of reach. And there was no difficulty when it came to 'uncool' either. Grandpa was uncool, simply by virtue of his age and his tragic taste in knitwear. So was the Birdie song and that ultimate Essex boy status symbol, the Ford Escort.

Then, sometime in the early 1990's, the marketing industry decided that, in the name of democracy, everyone had the right to be cool. And so it was that the tiniest details of our daily lives were transformed into lifestyle accessories.

Rick Poyner
Obey the Giant – Life in the Image World

It's time to accept that cool, as a signifier of meaningful rebellion, is belly-up in the water. It is profoundly manipulative and makes no sense at all as a mass frame of mind. If you still want to be a rebel, go right ahead and kick out the jams, but it will have to be a rebellion out of cool. There is no other way. Kalle Lasn of Adbusters calls for nothing less at this point, than the uncooling of America' – its icons, signs, fashions and spectacles. 'The only battle still worth fighting and winning,' he writes in *Culture Jam*, 'the only one that can set us free, is The People versus The Corporate Cool Machine.'

John de Graaf, David Wann, Thomas H. Naylor
Affluenza: The All-Consuming Epidemic

Felicia Edwards, an African American mother of two, who lives in a small apartment in a Hartford, Connecticut, housing project, worries about the pressures her children feel to wear the designer-label clothes they see on other children in their school. 'These schools tend to be like fashion shows', she says with a shake of her head. 'There's a lot of peer pressure that can lead to crime. Kids in school have killed other kids over a pair of sneakers'.

Born to be Wild

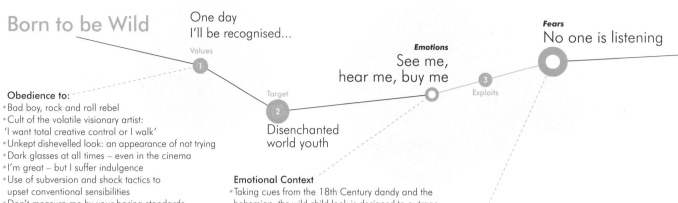

Values — One day I'll be recognised...

Target — Disenchanted world youth

Emotions — See me, hear me, buy me

Exploits

Fears — No one is listening

Obedience to:
- Bad boy, rock and roll rebel
- Cult of the volatile visionary artist: 'I want total creative control or I walk'
- Unkept dishevelled look: an appearance of not trying
- Dark glasses at all times – even in the cinema
- I'm great – but I suffer indulgence
- Use of subversion and shock tactics to upset conventional sensibilities
- Don't measure me by your boring standards
- Swiping at rivals (like, they're so shit)
- Being misunderstood, reputation for erratic, unhinged behaviour
- Hitting the road to self destruction – live fast, die young

Rejection of:
- Manufactured pop, mainstream music/MTV
- Commercialism and big business
- Conventional, conservative values and manners
- Responsibilities: marriage, mortgage, kids, schools
- The hated bourgeois (though they might be buying the records)
- Greatest Hits CD compilations
- Bankers, accountants, blood-sucking lawyers

Emotional Context
- Taking cues from the 18th Century dandy and the bohemian, the wild child look is designed to outrage – 'don't measure me by your sick, sad, bourgeois standards, I'm different'. Like any uniform it is clear in its intentions: look at me, recognize me, listen to me. Yes, it still has anger. But a lot of that anger is engendered by the realization that Rock was the invention of their grandads.

Social context
- Music has a resonance and meaning that is hard wired into our psyche. Steven Pinker, author of *How the Mind Works*, speculates that music might have come before language as a means to project emotions. It was also extremely successful at promoting one's appeal to the opposite sex. So not much has changed...

Personal Fears:
- No one is listening
- Selling out to the system (i.e. getting a normal job)
- Sex, drugs, rock and roll; not getting enough of it
- Failing to make the big break
- Going gets tough, book into rehab
- The same insecurities that propel rock stars to seek success in the limelight are the same vulnerabilities that drag them down in disillusionment.

World Fears:
- Rock music fears, since the 50's, have remained essentially the same: anti-imperialism (Vietnam/Iraq), third world poverty (Bangladesh/Africa), the environment and anti-capitalism (Exxon/Nike)

iPod Culture

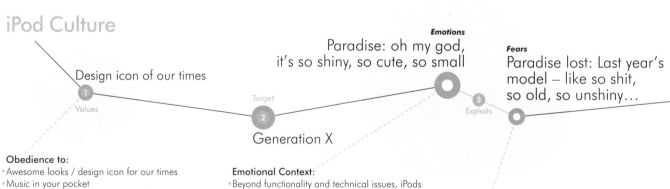

Values — Design icon of our times

Target — Generation X

Emotions — Paradise: oh my god, it's so shiny, so cute, so small

Exploits

Fears — Paradise lost: Last year's model – like so shit, so old, so unshiny...

Obedience to:
- Awesome looks / design icon for our times
- Music in your pocket
- Freedom & individuality: be yourself, it's who you are
- Bite-sized lifestyle
- Small is beautiful
- Perfect blend of style, simplicity and technology
- Cult status following, total devotion to the brand
- Celeb endorsement
- Podcasting and vodcasting
- Never ending model: always a new iPod, iPhone, iTouch on the horizon

Rejection of:
- Any other brand
- Mobile phones offering music
- Tapes and vinyl
- Big old-style stereos

Emotional Context:
- Beyond functionality and technical issues, iPods are about desire and style. People who wouldn't buy an MP3 player buy an iPod. Beyond cool there is something of the fetish in its appeal. Apple stores have become cathedrals of style. Fiercely loyal, obsessive Apple devotees have been likened to a cult, anxiously waiting for new product announcements.

Social context:
- The iPod success was not predictable. Unlike Sony and the Walkman, Apple had no previous music experience. Other competitors were faster to market. So why the runaway success? The iPod phenomenon reflects a growing trend in the consumer market. Small, incremental advantages, equate to massive, runaway success. It is this methodology which will have the greatest impact on future design and business.

Personal Fears:
- Theft: nightmare scenario
- Scratches on the facia: total nervous breakdown
- Battery life: slow disillusionment
- Dropping it onto a hard floor (lifetime of music gone in a nano second)

World Fears:
- Like a shark in water, the iPod needs constant momentum and innovation. The success of Apple hinges on a product barely bigger than a matchbox. Fashion is fickle. The iPod could rapidly become yesterday's brand.
- In 2007, a fake e-mail about a delay in the iPhone was enough to knock $4 billion off the company stock.

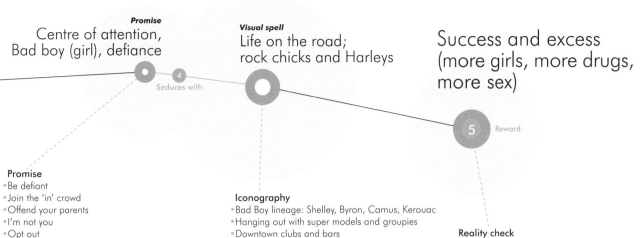

Centre of attention,
Bad boy (girl), defiance

Life on the road;
rock chicks and Harleys

Success and excess
(more girls, more drugs, more sex)

Seduces with 4

5 Reward

Promise
- Be defiant
- Join the 'in' crowd
- Offend your parents
- I'm not you
- Opt out
- Attitude of angry youth rebellion

Future Vision
- Since its inception more than 50 years ago, rock and roll has remained remarkably enduring. As young musicians 'discover' the real visionaries of the 50's and 60's, Dylan, Neil Young, Jim Morrison, it's a formula that has been endlessly reinvented. Rock music was the angry voice of youth feared by the establishment. Now tamed by commercialism, band branding and the download revolution it merely serves up neatly packaged dissent. Rock stars are selling rebellion within a system that is anything but rebellious.

Iconography
- Bad Boy lineage: Shelley, Byron, Camus, Kerouac
- Hanging out with super models and groupies
- Downtown clubs and bars
- Trashing hotels and expensive sports cars
- Spinal Tap style rock histrionics
- Rebel clothes, ripped t-shirts, jeans, jackets, long unkept hair: Jagger, Morrison, Doherty
- Wall of Fender guitars

Style/Aesthetic
- Life on the road/Easy Rider
- Backstage at the gig
- Lines of cocaine on the recording studio floor
- In the spotlight: a sea of faces to the horizon
- Poster legends: Santana, Led Zeppelin, Hendrix
- MTV controversy: Smack my Bitch Up
- Rock star hideaway: chicks by the pool in the South of France

Reality check
- There's nothing new about the bad boy look. It has remained virtually untouched since the time of Byron and Shelley more than 200 years ago. The look might promote rebel credentials and angry defiance, but having become a staple ingredient of high street style, even haute couture for decades, its a style that's as predictable as a suit from Saville Row.

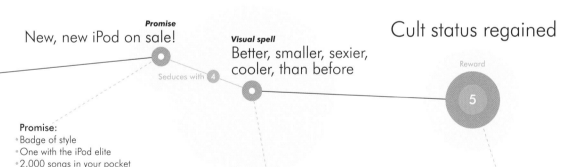

New, new iPod on sale!

Better, smaller, sexier,
cooler, than before

Cult status regained

Seduces with 4

Reward

5

Promise:
- Badge of style
- One with the iPod elite
- 2,000 songs in your pocket
- Music on the move
- Youth and vitality
- Freedom to roam
- Definition of cool
- Escape: shut off the world outside

Future Vision:
- To survive future competition iPods and iPhones will need to be more than just music. Future iPods and iPhones will embrace every aspect of your life, photographs, home videos, television, movies, future appointments and mobile communication. Such products will be an extension of the self – and you could lose it.
- Having sold more than 100 million units, the iPod is the fastest selling music player in history.

Iconography:
- Dark silhouettes, white headphones
- Cool dudes in loft apartments
- Music on the move: skateboarding, jogging, skating, running

Style/Aesthetic:
- Understated simplicity
- The wheel
- Clear functionality
- Slow evolution and perfection of design
- Freedom, vitality, youth

Reality check:
- The cult of iPod has gone beyond the straight music player. It's an attitude, a culture. These emotional values, combined with an aesthetic that reflects simplicity, individuality, and freedom, have impacted on several aspects of lifestyle: fashion, automotive design, even architecture (micro houses).

Anti-Style

① Go against the mainstream
Values

② Indie crowd
Target

Emotions
Fierce defense
of individuality
③
Exploits

Fears
Bland ubiquity of
mainstream cool

Obedience to:
- It's all about individuality, attitude, originality; don't go with the crowd, dare to be different
- Indie culture, youth and rebellion
- Break the rules, go against the mainstream
- Self-deprecating humour, ironic detachment
- Underground music and culture
- Don't buy 'fashion', don't buy 'style'
- So uncool it must be cool
- 'We are not branded'

Rejection of:
- Conservative, middle class, parental values
- Mainstream commercial cool
- Anything to do with authority or the establishment
- Shallow bourgeois consumerism
- Global brands, multi-nationals, big spend advertising
- Smug high-flying, over-achievers
- Grey suit employment

Emotional Context
- Anti-style is ruled by a hunger for recognition within a world regarded as being made conservative and ubiquitous by notions of popular mainstream cool. It is a defence of self-esteem, by finding strength and self-worth in new found individuality and difference.

Social context
- Anti-style is style thinking for a new generation anxious to distance themselves from the dire middle-class values of their parents. Over exposed to commercialism, it is a struggle for a new identity that turns against overt materialism and needless consumption. It is a fear that you are somehow diminished if you let yourself be influenced by marketing and that brands and labels only serve as badges to promote your own gullibility.

Personal Fears
- Being like everyone else
- Dread of aging, conforming, losing one's youthful identity
- Working just for money
- Fear of embarrassment, ridicule, lacking credibility, or rejection by peer group
- Being perceived as having middle-class values and tastes

World Fears
- A world of dull conformity
- Globalisation, pollution, industrialisation
- Over exploitation of resources
- World conflict
- Souless materialism

Retro

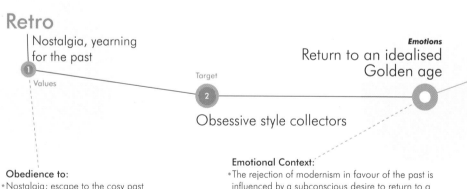

① Nostalgia, yearning for the past
Values

Target
②
Obsessive style collectors

Emotions
Return to an idealised
Golden age
③
Exploits

Fears
Loss of identity in
the modern world

Obedience to:
- Nostalgia; escape to the cosy past
- Golden age of the 50's
- A return to authenticity; an aesthetic purity that is lost in mass-produced, modern design
- An uncritical celebration of an idealised age
- Retro clothes; vintage-style pumps, polka-dot dresses
- Retro cars and motorbikes; VW Camper vans, Morris Oxfords, Harleys and Triumphs
- Retro games; Pacman and Tetrus on Atari computers
- The music of early Rock & Roll, Soul and R&B

Rejection of:
- Soulless, modern highstreet produce
- Cold hi-tech design
- Cutting edge (but soon redundant) design
- Fussy fashion dictators and style gurus
- The relentless drive for the 'new new'

Emotional Context:
- The rejection of modernism in favour of the past is influenced by a subconscious desire to return to a better era. It is to rewind to a period in which family harmony was the cornerstone of social values, as yet untarnished by modern-day stress and crime. Somewhat idealised in childhood eyes, the everyday products of that past, household electronics and cars, become symbols for what is essentially, a complete fantasy.

Social context:
- The 50's in the eyes of the collectors, was an idyllic, progressive age, the dawn of mass consumerism and full of optimism. The advertising of the time, spared of contemporary cynicism and irony, reflected this complete faith in the future; cars were liberation, a high-school romance in the back seat. Domestic appliances freed one from a life of drudgery. Sleek airliners introduced a new world of excitement and 'boy's own' adventure.

Personal Fears:
- Being the same, running with the crowd
- Loss of identity in the boring modern world
- Contemporary life, by its ubiquity and conformity, is dull and uninspiring

World Fears:
- Our obsession with TV makeovers and modern architecture will see the past erased and forgotten at the bottom of a skip

Beyond fashion & style

Promise
New edgy attitude & authenticity

Visual spell
No style, snap shot, girl-next-door aesthetic

Seduces with · 4

Reward · 5

Promise
- The new 'cutting edge'
- Be part of a new attitude
- Authenticity, 'the real you' over corporate banality
- Dignity through individuality
- Distance yourself from the mainstream and the style dictators
- You're not a number
- Identity for the knowing few

Future Vision
- Anti-style, like other counter-culture terms such as anti-capitalism and anti-globalisation, gives the impression of being subversive, beyond fashion and style. But like other over-used adjectives, 'cutting edge' and 'avant garde', the look and feel of anti-style apes any other new trend or culture – just as contrived and artificial and as likely to conceal a commercial imperative.

Iconography
- Imagery of daily life, street locations
- Naff old cars
- Retro technology, 50's furniture and interiors
- Graffiti, street art, camouflage look, edgy graphics
- Tart/sleaze/porn style
- Butlins style (i.e. naff style)
- Ironic juxtaposition of overtly popular mainstream culture with the 'new' cool
- Fringe magazines: *Dazed & Confused*, *Sleazenation*

Style/Aesthetic
- No style, snap shot aesthetic
- 'Girl next door' beauty – not professional models
- Ethnic diversity
- Offbeat quirky humour, often voyeuristic
- Spontaneity – honesty of the moment
- Drug, club culture

Reality check
- With even Grandpa wearing supposedly rebel brands such as Nike and Oakley, style needed a new haven for 'cool', an adjective, that now debased by commercialism, is as bland as saying something is 'nice'.
- Though originally intending to turn its back against marketing, style and fashion, Anti-style has merely created a new language of advertising and brand promotion in a different guise. Anti-style might be perceived by some as being at the forefront of cutting-edge style, basking in rare moments of anti-conformist credibility, but once such style constructs become absorbed into the ever-hungry mainstream, such iconography becomes yet another visual language waiting in line to be debunked.

Oddball individuality

Promise
Happy days are here again

Visual spell
Retro cars, clothes, scooters

Seduces with · 4

Reward · 5

Promise:
- Golden age; the good old days
- Happy days are here again
- Return to a time of simple, honest values; the postman was always on time, you could walk safely in the streets, and you could kiss a girl without getting a seriously infectious disease

Future Vision:
- The future holds no interest save to further frame one's nostalgia for the better past

Iconography:
- Leafy suburbia
- Highschool graduation parties
- Chrome-clad burger bars
- Italian scooters: Vespa, Paiggio
- 50's cars and motorcycles
- The romance of flight: TWA, BOAC
- Nostalgia TV (*Happy Days*)
- The space age; anything with fins on; lights, trains, toasters

Style/Aesthetic:
- Soft golden glow, sepia tint
- Retro styling; A design language used by luxury brands, US and Japanese manufacturers. Designs from car companies such as Jaguar, Ford and Chrysler, combined classic forms with contemporary, modern aesthetics

Reality check:
- Retro is a distillation of an entire period of history into a handful of bakelite objects. It is the fun and the groovy without the pain and the complexity (i.e. no Vietnam, Reds under the bed or threat of nuclear inferno). Retro paid no heed to the reality, buying instead into the 'advertised', dreamy ideal.

Hip Hop

From its early US roots in emceeing (a person who raps to inspire the people), DJing and blockparties in the mid 1970's, the controversial Hip Hop music revolution has risen to become one of the dominant rebel music movements, even to the extent of being endorsed by 'family' brands such as Coke and Reebok. In style, attitude and behaviour, everything about Hip Hop, Rap and its derivatives, is a wanton, even confrontational display of power, clothes, dance, body movement and language. The appropriation of symbols of affluence, such as Rolexes and gold rings, are there both to impress and provoke: 'I'm so tough no one can take it off me'.

Critics have accused the movement and its stars of advocating violence. Rap bands have argued that they are just describing reality – 'talking about what was happening'. But 'Keeping it real' is part of the problem. Rap is so locked into its macho image, that aggression, getting locked up and shootings are all there to promote authenticity and to distance themselves from being perceived as 'studio gangsters'.

This glamorisation of the 'warzone' makes it all the more difficult for young blacks to escape it. More positive role models are needed to encourage the young away from gang culture to aspire to future careers in professional employment, either as doctors, lawyers, entrepreneurs, even Presidents of America.

Hip Hop
GET RICH OR DIE

1.Values

I AM WHAT I AM

3.Exploits

Fears

BEING A NOBODY

Emotions

DON'T FU*K WITH ME

2.Target

WORLD URBAN YOUTH

Obedience to...
- Authenticity: Keeping it real
- 'Visibility', street presence and credibility
- Hyper macho, tough guy defiance
- 'Look at me', 'in yer face', narcissism
- Big on opulence, luxury, excess: Bling-bling jewellery, cool mobile phones
- Gangsta chic street style and attitude: limited edition sneakers, shades, guns as fashion accessories
- Concealment of emotions (showing weakness)
- Bangin bitches and 'hoes'
- 'Steaming' – gang rushing a bank
- Urban culture: graffiti, underground art
- Risen-up-from-the-ghetto narrative

Rejection of...
- Education (uncool)
- White, conservative values
- Parental, middle-class sensibilities
- Being a TV gangsta, tamed by pop culture
- Authority: the law, bureaucrats and politicians
- Freeloaders, faggots, phoneys, and bitch feminists
- Wiggers – 'white niggers':Singers who mimic hip-hop culture
- Snitches and low-life
- Stuffy intellectual snobs and academics
- Machine car washes

Emotions
- Much of the anger behind Rap and Hip Hop is engendered by disadvantage (49% of black families in the USA are single parent), and exclusion from what they perceive to be a white-dominated world that starts from being denied the best education and ends in an inability to secure professional employment. Oppressed young blacks see a belligerent adversarial stance as the only 'authentic' response to social discrimination. In the ghetto 'career options' are limited. There are few ways to escape poverty. For those in search of easy riches, guns, prostitution and inevitably drugs, are the only fast way out.

Social context
- Hip Hop has been a central component of youth subculture since the mid 70's. Fostering an attitude of defiance, it follows in the footsteps of previous 'angry' music movements, in mixing lyrics that glamorise violence and guns, macho tough-guy posturing and chauvinistic attitudes to 'hoes and bitches'. Its purpose remains the same – to threaten 'the fabric of society', panic the stuffy middle classes, upset conservative sensibilities – and this explains its success worldwide. Practically every nation has its own version of ghetto culture: Asian Hip Hop, African Rap, even Danish Hip Hop. And it is these variants that will ensure that this music style remains prominent.

Personal Fears
- Having no presence, status, respect
- Showing weakness
- Being uncool, unreal
- Being white
- Running scared
- Being excluded from the gang

World Fears
- White man's world – and they've ****ed it up

Promise
- Power share: become part of a bigger movement
- Strength and security in solidarity
- Group status, power, money
- Respect, recognition, fear
- The high life: drugs, fast cars, hot bitches
- Shock the stuffy establishment

Future View
- Hip Hop follows an age-old formula: angry music that is more controversial to the establishment than the last incarnation. Its outward style – clothes, shoes, haircut, music and language – will change. Not its product.

5.Reward

HAVE WHAT YOU WANT: SKY'S THE LIMIT

Reality Check

In breaking into mainstream music, Hip Hop uses familiar 'shock' tactics to court controversy, upset conservative 'white' values and get air time with an ever-complicit media ready to absorb its provocative imagery of sex, guns and violence. Bands and now brands will argue, 'keep it real', 'tell it like it is', and sell soft drinks and sneakers off the movement. Unsurprisingly Hip Hop has evolved to become like any other rebel music movement: Big Business, replete with corporate offices, pretty PA's and bullish lawyers. In its wake it leaves an untold social story – an increase in rape and domestic violence, rising crime and more deaths from gangland shootings. The spread of turf wars between Hispanic and Black gangs, has added an altogether more harrowing dimension to gang culture.

4.Seduces with

Promise

FOR THE TAKING

Visual spell

FROM BROOKLYN TO THE BOARDROOM, RAGS TO ROLEXES

Iconography:
- Hoods, lose cut jeans, sneaker culture
- Bling: visible jewellery, gold, Rolexes, diamonds
- High status cars: Chevys, Humvies, Bentleys.
- Pimp-my-ride: chrome hubs, massive speakers, air-brush paint job
- Big mansions, pools, underlit bars
- Pimp, drug culture
- Gun glamour: bodyguards, knives, AK 47s
- Music-video porn
- Hot bitches, sluts and hookers in bikinis
- The 'street' as urban battleground
- Anger management: cashing in with CDs, hip hop porn DVDs, fashion and sneaker lines, commercials

Ian McEwan,
Enduring Love

It's a big deal when you point a gun at someone.
Basically you're giving them permission to kill you.

Dick Pountain & David Robins,
Cool Rules

Many modern egos are held together by the
powerful spiritual adhesive that is cool. A carefully
cultivated cool pose can keep the lid on the most
intense feelings and violent emotions. In the street
culture of America's inner-cities, as glorified in
gangster rap, cool is considered such an important
source of respect that people will commit homicide
in order to maintain it.

Jacques Barzun,
From Dawn to Decadence

This antagonism between faith and moral conduct
has been repeatedly manifested in western culture.
A latter-day form of it appears in the scorn of 'the
bourgeois and his values.' Respectability seems
dull and cowardly to sin and crime.

Joseph Heath & Andrew Potter,
The Rebel Sell, How Counterculture became Consumer Culture

Some myths die hard. One can see the same cycle repeating itself in hip hop. The counterculture idea here takes the form of a romantic view of ghetto life and gang culture. Successful rappers must fight hard to retain their street cred, to 'keep it real'. They'll pack guns, do time, even get shot up, just to prove that they're not just 'studio gangstas'.

Sarah Harris,
Hip Hop, Radical in its Roots

In the 1980's, feminists had a saying: 'pornography is the theory, and rape is the practice.' It may seem a little extreme, and I know it's over simplified, but I believe that today the music videos, the images and the lyrics are the theory, and the disrespect and abuse of women are the practice.

Saul Austerlitz
Money for Nothing

It was not until the early 1990's, the era of 'O.P.P.' and 'Baby Got Back', that women as lust objects, intended to be ogled, made their first steady inroads into the music video. Taking a page out of heavy metal's playbook, hip-hop would increasingly depend on the bodaciousness of the female bodies on display to sell their videos, with male performers routinely paired with stunningly beautiful women as proof of their virility.

Rebel, rebel

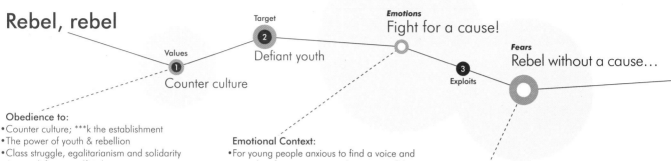

Values ①
Counter culture

Target ②
Defiant youth

Emotions
Fight for a cause!

Fears
Rebel without a cause…

③ **Exploits**

Obedience to:
- Counter culture; ***k the establishment
- The power of youth & rebellion
- Class struggle, egalitarianism and solidarity
- Anger, defiance, self-righteousness
- Breaking the rules
- Fight for what you believe in
- Outlaw mentality; the romantic notion of fighting for the underdog

Rejection of:
- Authority (teachers, parents, the law)
- Mainstream concepts of cool
- Being bourgeois and middle class
- Obsessions with mindless materialism, wealth & status
- The establishment, corporations & commercialism
- Mass media & Hollywood culture
- Squares and 'suits', anyone in a uniform

Emotional Context:
- For young people anxious to find a voice and struggling for recognition in the context of their own insecurities, the rebel is a call to individuality, 'to be someone', to distance oneself from an increasingly conformist society. From mythology to the present day, Robin Hood to Che Guervera, the outcast, the loan romantic hero battling for a moral cause, has held strong appeal. Sadly, today, this is more likely to be a rush to the fashion boutique rather than a call to the barricades.

Social context:
- Modern life – work, mortgage, home, wife & kids is life without 'edge'. The imagery of the rebel awakens that residue of anger that is in us all; 'fight for a cause', 'dare to be different', 'counter corporate conformity' – buy the sneakers. Whereas genuine rebellions furthered the cause of the masses, 'rebellion' in our age is a flight from the masses, serving only to enhance our vanity.

Personal Fears:
- Fear of conforming
- Fear of being uncool
- Lack of recognition
- Growing old, being like one's parents

World Fears:
- Power of global capitalism ransacking the planet
- Autocratic government and authority
- Corruption and injustice
- Neo-fascists
- Concerns over the environment
- Loss of community and spiritual values

Guns R Us

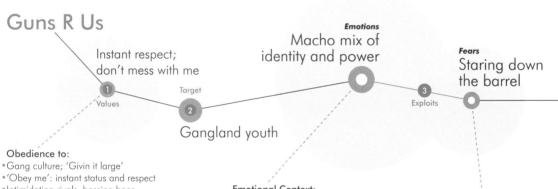

Values ①
Instant respect; don't mess with me

Target ②
Gangland youth

Emotions
Macho mix of identity and power

Fears
Staring down the barrel

③ **Exploits**

Obedience to:
- Gang culture; 'Givin it large'
- 'Obey me': instant status and respect
- Intimidating rivals, bossing hoes
- In the ghetto, just how it is; a means to get drugs and money
- Guns equalise: regardless of age or sex, nothing stops a bullet
- Machismo: shooting skills are a mark of a man
- Part of US culture, the right to protect; the Wild West, Al Capone, *Miami Vice*, National Rifle Association
- Symbol of defiance against timid liberal norms

Rejection of:
- Showing disrespect (which can amount to knocking someone's drink over)
- Gun control lobby
- Gungrabbers, Police and law enforcement, Government legislation
- Bleating liberals; Michael Moore (Director of *Bowling for Columbine*) – 'guns are a cancer killing society'

Emotional Context:
- For the young, guns hold a deep emotional fascination, a macho mix of identity and power that is hard to resist. Glamorised on video games such as Hitman and by rap artists on MTV, handguns and AK 47s are perceived as being cool, an icon of style, like a fashion accessory.

Social context:
- In the US, the 240 million guns in circulation, cause about 14,000 fatalities and 60,000 injuries per annum. The powerful lobby group, the National Rifle Association, considers gun ownership a civil right protected by the Bill of Rights (the threat of gun control is seen as an infringement of liberty and personal freedom).
- Every year, worldwide, small arms cause more fatalities than the two bombs dropped on Hiroshima and Nagasaki.

Personal Fears:
- In ghetto life, everyone else is armed
- Without a gun you have no respect
- Getting caught in the crossfire (i.e. an innocent)

World Fears:
- Gun control
- Us and them
- Future Armageddon (better be armed for the coming conflict)

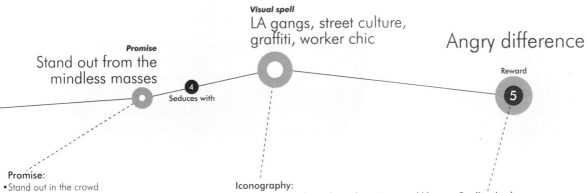

Angry difference

Stand out from the mindless masses
Promise

4 Seduces with

LA gangs, street culture, graffiti, worker chic
Visual spell

5 Reward

Promise:
- Stand out in the crowd
- 'Don't mess with me' difference
- Uncompromising individuality
- Youth, energy, vibrancy
- You're not a wanker
- Chic street-fighter ethic
- Promote your non-conformity and rebelliousness

Future Vision:
- Corporations, ever anxious to distance themselves from the image of being uncaring global monoliths, and to maintain that essential youthful appeal (their most profitable demographic), employ 'cool hunters' to sniff out the latest cutting-edge culture. The angry, anti-corporate look becomes a style that can be affixed to any product to enhance its 'street' credentials; from multi-national banking groups to global software companies.

Iconography:
- Gritty reality; real people, real situations, real life
- Graffiti, deconstructed edgy graphics and tattoos
- Worker chic
- Rock music
- Soviet graphic style, revolutionary slogans, AK 47s, black berets, camouflage look
- Che Guevara (the Marxist Revolutionary of the 1960's and the Osama Bin Laden of his time who believed that the US was the source of all evil, a style icon that has, ironically, sold more fashion merchandise than Mickey Mouse)

Style/Aesthetic:
- Subversive, cutting-edge style and fashion
- Anarchic, aggressive imagery
- Shock tactics, breaking sexual taboos
- Underdog v fatcats, honest workers v corrupt capitalists
- Anti-gloss aesthetic

Reality check:
- Rebel brands, promoted with the imagery of counter culture, skateboarding, street and graffiti art, give a remarkably good impression of being youthful, small-scale enterprises, despite their rising prominence in the pages of Fortune 500. Middle-aged, middle-class men and women, buying such brands as badges of youthful vibrancy and protest, are in reality only promoting their own gullibility; i.e. anger without cause, commitment or courage.

Do you feel lucky punk?

Don't walk in fear
Promise

4 Seduces with

Bikini babes with machine guns
Visual spell

5 Reward

Promise:
- Don't mess with me cool
- Provocative machismo; try to take it off me
- Be one with the gang; sense of belonging
- Instant street cred; don't walk in fear, walk with respect

Future Vision:
- With no active will in the US to curb gun ownership, technology and new materials will ensure a steady flow of even smaller more lethal weapons finding their way onto the street.
- The increased violence and realism of computer games will provide the aspirational stimulus further desensitising young people to violence until it proves too late.

Iconography:
- Judgement day; retribution is coming
- Hip Hop, Rapper, tough guy cool: 50 Cent, So Solid Crew
- Violent computer games: Hitman, Grand Theft Auto, Vice City
- Mainstream TV and movies; *Scarface*, *Grindhouse*
- Large black SUV's
- Drugs, Hip Hop Honeys, money
- Ghetto guns; Uzi, AK 47, Scorpion
- Oiled bikini clad babes with machine guns
- Russian, East European mafia

Style/Aesthetic:
- Night time, city lights, neon
- The ghetto, sin city, vice dens, strip joints
- Back alleys and clubs
- Volatile mix of fashion cool, guns and girls

Reality check:
- A television programme or a computer game is not going to turn a well-adjusted young boy into a raving homicidal maniac. But the human mind is malleable; a relentless daily diet of glamorised violence certainly has the potential to tip an already unstable mind into that of an unstable killer. The escalation of violence on TV and in games rises in parallel with gun-related deaths. Content incites crime. It's a clear enough correlation. The only people to dispute this are those with commercial interests either trading directly on violence or the depiction of violence.

Sneaker Freaks

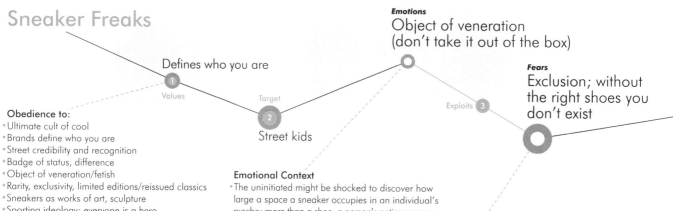

Emotions
Object of veneration
(don't take it out of the box)

Defines who you are

① Values

② Target

Street kids

Fears
Exclusion; without the right shoes you don't exist

Exploits **③**

Obedience to:
- Ultimate cult of cool
- Brands define who you are
- Street credibility and recognition
- Badge of status, difference
- Object of veneration/fetish
- Rarity, exclusivity, limited editions/reissued classics
- Sneakers as works of art, sculpture
- Sporting ideology: everyone is a hero, a future Ronaldinho, a new Tiger Woods
- All in the detail (belief that an edgy graphic will enhance your performance)
- Just do it: cut through the lethargy
- 'What the Dunk?' – (Dunks are considered the most significant shoe of the decade by sneaker aficionados)

Rejection of:
- Counterfeits
- Cheap Asian imports
- Last month's model
- Off the shelf products

Emotional Context
- The uninitiated might be shocked to discover how large a space a sneaker occupies in an individual's pysche; more than a shoe, a person's entire persona, beliefs, credibility, status, is vested in his/her choice of footwear. When you walk into a room people look at your feet. You become invisible without the right brand.

Social context
- Sneaker culture originated in the underprivileged ghettos of New York in the 70's. Shoes were venerated both as status symbols and something that (like a car) needed constant care. Hyped by style magazines, blogs and internet sites, sneakers have become a $30 billion industry. Its products embody individualism, youth and rebellion. Values that have appeal to every teenager (and unfortunately their dads).

Personal Fears
- Diminished status, low self-esteem, lack of recognition
- Exclusion from the 'in group', the tribe, the crowd
- Scratches on brand new sneakers

World Fears
- No world beyond the sneaker

Hippy Chic

Emotions
Free love, one with the universe

Values **①**

Target **②**

③ Exploits

Drop out, opt out, chill out

New hip generation

Fears
Being subsumed by evil capitalism

Obedience to:
- Drop out, opt out, chill out
- Alternative everything
- Flower power
- Self-discovery, freedom of expression, wander the world
- Anything counter culture: psychedelic art, underground music
- Eastern mysticism, Buddhism, Zen
- Bohemian, community living
- Recreational drugs: cannabis, hallucinogenic mushrooms

Rejection of:
- Stuffy conservative parental sensibilities
- Obsessive materialism and status seeking
- Grey suited, middle management, mindless bureaucracy
- Global corporations
- Advertising and mass consumerism

Emotional Context:
- To behave like a hippy – free love, long hair, drugs and hippy clothes – was to antagonise conservative mores, promote one's disaffection with society and signal a rejection of conventional measures of status. Now that Hippy style has become a middle class, even luxury class, affectation, there is something of the Marie Antoinette about the style – chic to look poor for a day.

Social context:
- Once the domain of tie dye and ripped jeans, Hippy Chic is now high couture style; John Galliano has released designs for Christian Dior under the slogan, 'Dior for Peace'.
- The merchant bankers of globalisation now charter helicopters to the Glastonbury festival. Luxury hippy chic is a $1,000 a night ethnic villa on the beach in Bali.

Personal Fears:
- Self identity being destroyed by the system
- Loss of individualism and self-esteem
- Modern life smothering self-expression, creativity
- Pressure to conform
- Getting older (and with it, the encumbrances that force you to compromise – mortgages, job for life, marriage, kids at school)

World Fears:
- Global corporations ransacking the earth's resources
- Pollution from industry and commerce
- Globalisation swamping indigenous cultures
- Heavy-handed US imperialism
- Climate change
- Corrupting oil politics

Promise
Exclusivity, buying you superiority, credibility in the street

Seduces with 4

Visual spell
New edgy graphic

Reward 5

Promise
- High altar of cool
- Exclusivity, credibility, superiority
- Freedom: the open road
- The equaliser: be like the stars
- Instant credibility, fitness, vitality
- Recognition: be someone
- Run with the cool crowd

Future Vision
- Advances in 3D printing will further enhance the ability to personalise your own sneakers. New technology promises more capability. Micro processers in the sole can control both the shock absorption in the heel, and your iTunes music library.

Iconography
- Brand frenzy: latest Vans, Converse All Stars, Nikes
- Streetsports: skateboarding, break dancing, parkour, basketball, football
- Rappers and Hip Hop stars, 50 Cent, Jay Z,
- Hot chicks and cars
- Pop culture: MTV, music videos, graffiti artists, deconstructed graphics and zany animation

Style/Aesthetic
- Sneaker culture is a global billion dollar industry dominated by a handful of powerful US brands. It's an international business that takes its style and fashion cues from the look and 'attitude' of the street: the ghettos of Harlem and the Bronx. Angry rebellion, anti-establishment and anti-authority stances are all part of the big brand aesthetic.

Reality check
- The frenzy created by sneaker culture and its 'sneaker pimps' has reinvigorated an industry knocked by accusations of child labour and slave wages. The viral nature of blogs – Hyperbeat, Sneaker Freaker and Sole Collector – ensure buzz and cult status, inspiring shoe collectors worldwide to hoard shoes, not to wear, but to add to towering, obsessive collections.

Visual spell
Gaia, Mother earth

Promise
Return to simplicity, harmony, community

4 *Seduces with*

Get back to the garden

5 *Reward*

Promise:
- Alternative lifestyle
- Freedom, peace, love on earth
- Back to nature
- The commune: one happy family
- The Tao (harmony with all things)
- Zen simplicity – finding beauty in the ordinary

Future Vision:
- Back to the future? The ideals of the 60's Revolution, of a return to simplicity, low energy use, self-sufficiency, local economies, and a rejection of materialism were the original blueprint for Green Living.

Iconography:
- Barefoot living
- Sandals, kaftans, sarongs, tie dye
- Peasant, gypsy chic, Indian saris, sequins, embroidery
- Magic bus: India, Asia, Morocco
- Yoga, meditation, Tai Chi
- Long windswept hair
- Sleeping on the beach
- Festivals: Woodstock, Glastonbury
- Veggie food, organic produce
- Summer of Love: Grateful Dead, Janis Joplin, Jefferson Airplane

Style/Aesthetic:
- Gaia, Mother earth
- Psychedelic graphics and colours
- Ethereal, natural beauty
- Chill-out outlook on life
- All the time in the world
- Slow down

Reality check:
- Despite its rebellious, anti-corporate, anti-consumer origins in the 60's, Hippy Style has ended up as yet another facet of the great consumer fashion machine it professed to distance itself from. It poses a central dilemma for protest groups. How can authentic movements be heard if their styles, their music and their voice become instantly absorbed and made banal by commercial culture?

STA

SPE

LUXURY FEVER
LIFE IN THE RICH LANE

WINNER TAKES ALL
CASH IS KING

EXTREME WORK
FAST TRACK TO THE TOP

TUS
LLS

EASY MONEY
LIVE FOR THE MOMENT

ART!
STATUS ON THE WALL

AUTOMANIA
THE NEED FOR SPEED

LUXURY

FEVER

Life in the Rich Lane

Radha Chadha & Paul Husband
The Cult of the Luxury Brand

From presidents to office ladies, from captains of industry to university students, from well-heeled socialites to housewives buying fish in the local wet markets – in Japan, even the fish mongers tuck away their cash receipts in Louis Vuitton bags – every section of society, every country in Asia, is falling under the spell of Western luxury brands.

Robert Frank
Richistan, A Journey through the 21st Century Wealth Boom and the Lives of the New Rich

The rich will become less and less attached to their own countries and more like global citizens of Richistan. They will invest around the world, rather than putting all their money back into their own communities or countries. They will think, live and buy as Richistanis, not as Americans, Indians or Russians.

Globally, ideas of luxury have become ubiquitous. Spirited to a luxury shopping mall anywhere in the world, we would be hard pressed to tell if we were in Moscow or Milan. The glitzy architecture, brands, names, styles and surly shop assistants are virtually the same.

The necessary acquisition of the right brands has become a check list of stock experiences; modernist Manhattan apartment, designer Italian furniture, Yacht in the South of France, bespoke Range Rover, Cartier watches and wardrobes filled with Dior dresses. This has become base level luxury. To really make a dent with the elite, difference comes with a large price tag. Trophy assets – modern art, vintage wines, exotic cars – become the rare commodities that buy personality and caché. There is nothing like a room filled with Rothko paintings to raise your status from dull hedge fund investor, to shrewd, sophisticated, international culture collector. As billionaires emerge from the new economies of Russia, China and India, this finite supply of such prestige assets will ensure that prices will continually inflate.

LUXURY
FEVER
LIFE IN THE RICH LANE

1.Values

2.Target

3.Exploits

IT'S ABOUT
BEING SEEN

ASPIRING
MILLIONAIRES

Fears

HE'S GOT A BIGGER...

Emotions

SHOW IT
SPEND IT
LOVE IT
REVEL IN IT

Obedience to
- Conspicuous luxury, 'It's about being seen'
- Seeking out the best, the most comfortable, the most expensive (money no object)
- Rare, trophy assets; exclusive cars, jewellery, wine
- Personal art consultant
- Jet-set lifestyle; European mansions, beautiful people, luxury toys
- Invitations to 'A' list events and openings
- Concierge, bespoke services
- Children at private schools, tutors at weekends
- Loft apartments in world capitals
- Luxury seaside villa and personal yacht
- Do anything, anytime, anywhere
- Fast track service
- Gated communities – keep 'them' out

Rejection of...
- Down sizing and economising
- Crowds, queuing, waiting
- Mixing with the underclass
- Reserve, self-restraint, modesty
- Slow life, quiet life (i.e. dull life)
- Communal living; sharing bathrooms, kitchens
- Household chores and supermarket shopping
- Whinging intellectuals and lefty liberals, moaning on about equality and wealth disparity
- Global 'boring' – scientists blah,blah,blah

Emotional Context
- As symbols of status escalate in value and price, the cost of exclusivity is a ground that is continually shifting upwards. The super-rich are driven by positional status anxiety. Recent hi-tech success stories have seen ideas of self-worth sky rocket. Such incalculable amounts of wealth only further diminish one's own standing and the need to amass more, spend more and show more.

Social context
- Twenty years ago, it was considered improper, verging on vulgar to boast about wealth. With a new generation of celeb, super-model and internet billionaires joining the ranks of the elite, it is now acceptable to aspire openly to flying first class. TV shows such as *Martha Stewart* and *The Apprentice*, with Donald Trump, have even afforded the business man with pop idol status. Why be made to feel guilty about making loads of money?

Personal Fears
- 'Other' people: their noise, their company, their germs
- Travelling economy, using public transport
- Crash and burn; could all be gone tomorrow
- Siege mentality; everyone's after my money
- Stalkers and kidnappers
- Visit from the tax authorities
- Getting old; money still can't buy youth
- I'm ridiculously rich – but I'm bland and boring… People only laugh at my jokes because I'm paying for the champagne
- Despite my millions – god, I feel miserable

World Fears
- We're under attack
- Global recession – party over, financial bubble bursting
- I feel miserable

4.Seduces with

Visual spell

GOLD, GLTIZ, GLAMOUR:
HARBOUR AT ST TROPEZ,
SUPERMODELS
&
CHAMPAGNE

Promise

HIGH-ROLLING
STATUS GAME

Reality check

For the mega rich, less interested in cerebral ideas and culture, an individual's worth is measured in material possessions and wealth. High status brands and acquisitions, a rare Jackson Pollock, an ostentatious Bugatti, the finesse of a Fendi handbag, become the powerful visual language that articulates their importance, gives meaning to their existence and keeps unpalatable truths at bay (aging, kids on drugs, partner an alcoholic). By finding beauty and contentment only in prestige assets, the rich are as much enslaved by their emotional incontinence and the considerable resources and manpower needed to sustain these illusions, than for the rare moments of pleasure and escape that such luxuries provide.

MONEY BUYS YOU
EVERYTHING

Promise
- Exclusive, members-only lifestyle
- Live life to the fullest
- • Be loved and admired
- Never a dull moment
- Pride of place in the harbour in Monaco
- Supermodels, footballers and rockstars at your table
- Champagne on tap

Future Vision
- The return of luxury fever reflects a boom in new money from a wave of new millionaires emerging from India, China and Russia. This new affluence will crowd an already saturated luxury market, pushing up the prices of anything of any rarity: paintings, sculpture, jewellery, vintage wines. Houses in destination capitals, with 'beneficial' tax regimes, such as London, and New York, will also come under pressure, as more of the international set rush to snap up a diminishing stock.

Iconography
- Tuxedo, cigars, Crystal Champagne, casinos
- Girls, fast cars, mansions and pools
- Uber premium brands: Cartier, Chanel, Bulgari, Riva, Ferrari
- Private jets and yachts
- Personal trainers and laser surgeons
- Offshore accounts
- Bejewelled pets
- Star studded charity auctions (nothing like outbidding your rivals to enhance your financial standing)
- Manhatten pizza (with caviar and lobster for $1000)

Style/Aesthetic
- Status, glamour, sex
- World of the beautiful people
- Diamonds are forever
- Effortless consumption
- High style sophistication

Winner takes all

Cash is King

Article in *Fast Company* on the launch of Jefferson Han's revolutionary screen technology, Perceptive Pixel.

In this Googly age, it only takes a random genius to conceive a technology so powerful that it plows under the landscape and remakes it in its own image.

The numbers say it all: Google founders, Sergey Brin and Larry Page, personal wealth, $18 billion. Internet call company, Skype, created by Niklas Zennstrom and Janus Friis, sold to Ebay for $4 billion. YouTube, a site for user generated content, barely a year in operation, taken over by Google (again) for $1.6 billion. Private equity king, Stephen Schwarzman, who engineered one of the largest leveraged buyouts, the $39 billion purchase of Equity Office Property, earns roughly $1 million a day.

Such success stories preach a powerful message to the young; irrespective of your colour, age, social connections, or financial power, if you had vision, ideas, and ambition, success was yours for the taking. But this was no ordinary success. Such was the structure of the new global economy, that for an idea with legs, with scalability, there was virtually no ceiling on financial reward. The winner takes all.

New levels of success have an impact that is global. The accentuated divide between average earners and the mega rich, throws into sharp relief our own modest endeavours. Relative to those in the stratosphere of wealth, everyone's status becomes further diminished, as we all aspire to the next rung on the ladder.

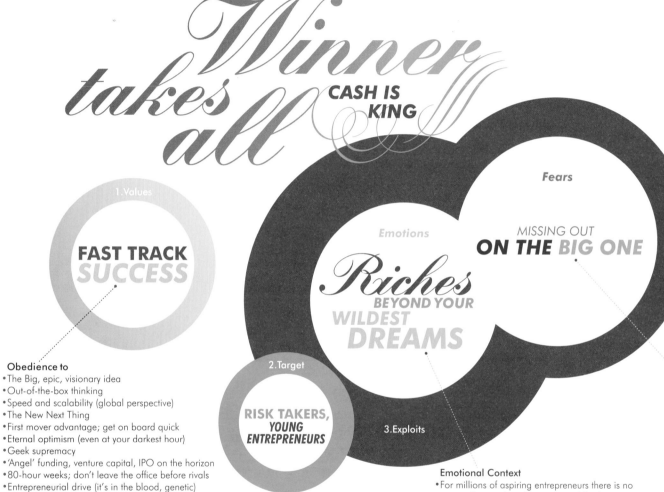

Winner takes all

CASH IS KING

1.Values

FAST TRACK SUCCESS

Emotions

Riches
BEYOND YOUR
WILDEST
DREAMS

Fears

MISSING OUT
ON THE BIG ONE

2.Target

RISK TAKERS, *YOUNG ENTREPRENEURS*

3.Exploits

Obedience to
- The Big, epic, visionary idea
- Out-of-the-box thinking
- Speed and scalability (global perspective)
- The New Next Thing
- First mover advantage; get on board quick
- Eternal optimism (even at your darkest hour)
- Geek supremacy
- 'Angel' funding, venture capital, IPO on the horizon
- 80-hour weeks; don't leave the office before rivals
- Entrepreneurial drive (it's in the blood, genetic)
- Raw ambition in the driving seat (why be ashamed of success? Wealth and its creation benefit everyone)
- Mega bonus packages
- Hostile takeovers, leveraged buyouts, hedge funds, partnership in elite private equity funds
- 'Liquidity Event' – when an entrepreneur cashes in their shares

Rejection of
- Risk adverse, small-time caution, playing it safe
- Lack of drive, courage, conviction
- Local scale and vision
- Self-doubt and pessimism
- 9 to 5 work ethic
- Old school stodgy corporate strategy; playing it by the book
- Resistance to change
- Passive attitude to work and life
- 'Airhead' lifestyles, new-age thinking, travelling the world

Emotional Context
- For millions of aspiring entrepreneurs there is no greater fantasy than the promise of the American dream – ordinary, young people can make billions; and you don't need a massive inheritance, fat sugar daddy, or stuffy Harvard Degree, you need a single, simple, ingenious idea.

Social context
- The seemingly instant success of entrepreneurs, such as the eBay, Google, YouTube and MySpace founders has created a frenzy of hype in the ability of technology to transform simple ideas (sometimes a small advantage embodied by a line of software code), into extraordinary reward (i.e. a monetisation machine).
- Likewise, in the financial markets, the rise of private equity funds have seen small advantages, often percentage points, produce inordinate returns for the privileged insiders – elite clubs few of us will ever get entry to.
- In the US, one percent of the top earners, pocketed more than 40 percent of the country's earnings.
- People have never been richer – there are now more than 1,000 billionaires worldwide.

Promise
- Be part of the new mega rich elite
- Hollywood glamour lifestyle
- The world as your playground; yachts the size of houses, private jets the size of yachts
- Fast toys, girls, toy-boys, champagne and jewellery
- Mansions filled with every conceivable electronic labour-saving device and gadget
- Invest in pet projects: personal sports car company, bankroll Hollywood movies as a hobbie

Future Vision
- The ability of the internet to spread contagious ideas, 'the next, new thing', has massively enhanced the effect of 'winner takes all'. It's a phenomenon that will only become more pronounced, as more power and money becomes concentrated in fewer, larger companies, resulting in steeper gains for those individuals with interests in them, massively inflating ideas of individual wealth.
- Will this widening inequality contribute to greater resentment and a less caring society in which admiration sours to animosity?

4.Seduces with

Promise

MANSIONS, CARS GIRLS, YACHTS
YOURS FOR THE TAKING

5.Reward

Wealth
STRATOSPHERE

Reality check
The concept of 'winner takes all' lifts ideas of success to new levels. Because of the global nature of products and the speed of the internet to spread viral ideas, the marketplace favours the first, the best, the coolest. From MP3 players such as the iPod, to search engines like Google and community websites such as MySpace and YouTube, audiences tend to congregate behind a single dominant player. Speed and global reach vastly accellerates take up. And for those in possession of these unique winning formulas it meant there was no ceiling on reward or success.

Visual spell

TWENTY SOMETHING CEO
COVER OF
FORBES MAGAZINE

Personal Fears
- Status anxiety
- Social inadequacy
- Under achieving
- Peer competition
- Lack of recognition
- Missing the big opportunity
- Wasting one's life
- Failure
- Everyone's getting rich but me
- Without money you're no one
- Losing one's BlackBerry

World Fears
- World recession
- Global stock market meltdown

Iconography
- College boy geek at the helm of billion-dollar enterprise
- Basement startups – birth of the next big idea
- Success hasn't changed me; CEO in modest T-shirt, faded jeans and sneakers
- Billionaire on a skateboard with a BlackBerry
- Ferraris and Porsches in Silicon Valley forecourts
- Wall Street elite: private equity gurus
- Quirky, loud, comfy sofas in groovy reception
- Yachts in the Med with boys' toys lashed to the deck
- Home – more miniature (100 room plus) city

Style/Aesthetic
- The underdog – loan geek v large stodgy, incumbent corporation

Extreme Work

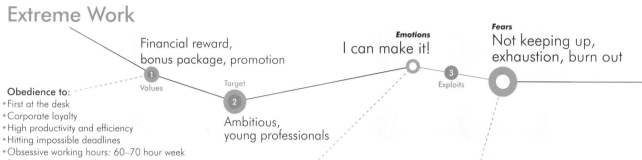

Values ①

Financial reward,
bonus package, promotion

Target ②

Ambitious,
young professionals

Emotions
I can make it!

Exploits ③

Fears
Not keeping up,
exhaustion, burn out

Obedience to:
- First at the desk
- Corporate loyalty
- High productivity and efficiency
- Hitting impossible deadlines
- Obsessive working hours: 60–70 hour week
- Dog-eat-dog competition
- Office lingo: 'Think outside the box', 'Value added', 'The bottom line'
- 'Always on' comms: BlackBerry, PDA, mobile
- Snappy Powerpoint presentations
- Six figure end-of-year bonus-packages
- Exhilaration of success/promotion

Rejection of:
- Expectations of job security for life
- Extended sick leave
- Sloppy time keeping
- Dozing on the job
- Out to lunch
- Taking time off to be with the kids
- Long vacations
- Opting out of the rat race; travelling the world
- Bad behaviour on the photocopying machine

Emotional Context:
- The American dream; no matter where you come from, colour or creed, if you work hard, have ambition and discipline, you can achieve anything – world-class airlines, media empires, global coffee brands. Success has no limits.

Social context:
- Whereas in Europe work is viewed as a necessary chore, in the Far East, Confucian thinking sees work as a rewarding and ennobling pursuit. Such principles together with fiercely competitive labour markets have created a work crisis in Europe and the US. In order to compete effectively, hard-won social advances, unemployment benefits, and pensions are now under threat. The European model, and the 35 hour week, is no longer viable.

Personal Fears:
- 'You're fired'
- Early redundancy, gardening leave
- Burn out, exhaustion
- No time to socialise, too tired for sex
- Erosion of time off
- Being passed over for promotion
- Tech stress ('Always on' technology – mobile calls, e-mail, voice-mail, conference calls, multi-tasking – has speeded up communication, but added to stress and the fear that you can't turn off
- Is there life after work? Probably not

World Fears:
- Global recession
- Company bankruptcy
- Relocation abroad
- Stock market crash

Easy Money

Values ①

Instant 'get it now' gratification

Target ②

Retail junkies

Emotions
Fast ticket to
the goodlife

Exploits ③

Fears
The Great
Credit Crash...

Obedience to:
- Credit cards and debt are a way of life
- Spending is fun, sexy, recreational
- Instant gratification
- Spoil yourself, you deserve it
- Live for the moment, throw caution to the winds
- Neverland strategy; put off the day of reckoning
- (Economic success story; the credit card boom has raised standards of living worldwide. Its rise has been instrumental in powering the global economy.)

Rejection of:
- Financial caution
- Making 'rainy day' savings
- Boring sensibility 'living within your means'
- Delayed gratification
- Nagging Victorian frugality
- Paying attention to the small print

Emotional Context
- We used to be anxious about borrowing. Now it's become hip and cool. For the young, tempted by the good life, iPods, the latest fashions, going out on the piss – credit cards are like fashion accessories, fun and easy. Promoted with catchy tunes and colourful cartoon characters, young people fail to make the connection between borrowing and spending.

Social context
- Previously limited to low-wage earners, the prospect of spiralling debt is affecting every demographic of society; from students struggling with educational loans, women (three quarters are in debt), high-wage earners (bigger mortgages, school loans), to senior citizens (the pensions shortfall leading to a rise in credit card use). Life's choices become compromised by the need to service a lifetime of repayments. Such problems have a high emotional impact; constant stress, ill health and depression and the inability to work to pay off debt.

Personal Fears
- Not being able to afford the next shiny new thing
- Becoming addicted to shopping
- Getting out of control, up to your neck in debt
- Prospect of personal bankruptcy
- Rising cost of borrowing
- Knock on the door from the loan sharks/debt collectors

World Fears
- World financial credit crisis
- Interest rate rise

Work the dream

Promise
Recognition, opportunity, power

Visual spell
New laptop, Blackberry, PDA

Seduces with

Reward
⑤

Promise:
- Fast track promotion
- Corporate parking place
- Executive share options
- Company car
- Personal assistant
- Corporate entertainment; tickets for the big game
- Corner office
- Business-class travel
- Seat on the board; Directorship

Future Vision:
- For those in the Western world, the unpalatable truth is that to maintain high living standards, everyone will have to work longer, more efficiently, for most of their lives. The concept of a golden retirement has become a pipe dream. For some retirement has been replaced by a return to the workplace. Fair return for a lifetime of toil? It remains to be seen if future generations will buy it.

Iconography:
- 'Always on' tech; BlackBerry, mobile phone
- Portable laptop
- Name on the door
- Business-class lounge
- Employee of the month
- Rising sales forecast
- Handshake sealing the deal
- Sharp shirt and suit
- German executive car
- Personal assistant

Style/Aesthetic:
- Hyper efficiency
- Global cooperation and expertise
- Do anything mentality
- High-tech sophistication
- Backbone of civilisation

Reality check:
- Our inability to switch off, combined with longer working hours and an erosion of free time, has contributed to work exhaustion, feelings of constant tiredness and levels of stress. Yes, we earn more and our standards of living have never been higher, but alcoholism is increasing and depression has risen to become the single most commmon illness in the western world.
- At executive levels, exhaustion is leading to a dependence on drugs (cocaine and ecstasy), as a necessary prescription.

Live for the moment!

Visual spell
Credit with a cuddly cartoon face

Promise
Dream life, dream car, dream house today

Seduces with

Reward
⑤

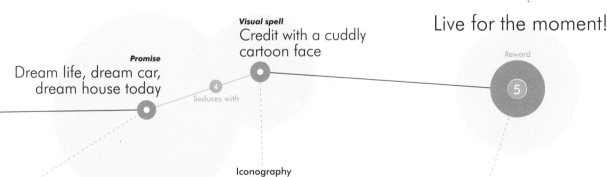

Promise
- Buy it now
- Money is easy
- Low stress, carefree loans
- Dreams come true today
- Who says you can't afford it? Whatever you want, we have a solution; cheap home loans, car loans, TV for the World Cup loans

Future Vision
- A failure to confront the debt crisis will make future solutions all the more painful. Eventually there will be a day of reckoning. But with consumer spending accounting for up to two thirds of GDP in developed countries, an integral factor in the wealth of nations, it is understandable why governments are in no hurry to curtail borrowing.

Iconography
- Debt has a friendly face, often a short skirt and sings a catchy tune.
- Advertising likes to anthropomorphosize credit cards, with soft, touchy-feely, cartoon characters, always ready, always willing to come to one's assistance.
- A trip to the highstreet bank maintains this aura of easy affability, with hip, comfy armchairs and beaming managers with garish ties.

Style/Aesthetic
- The future's bright; leave your financial woes behind. (in actuality they are just beginning and here to stay for the rest of your life).

Reality check:
- Experiments in neurology have led some economists and psychologists to suspect that the ease of modern-day shopping, where credit cards provide instant gratification, has meant that impulse purchase buys are divorced from the reality of handing over actual money and the hardship that this involves, (the feeling of pain is processed in a different region of the brain). Without such restraining instincts we become immune to the accumulation of debt. As a result, from Asia to Europe and the US, we have never borrowed so much. There is real concern that we are heading for a debt crisis (personal debt in the UK is increasing by £1 million every five minutes).

ART!

Status on the wall

George Walden
The New Elites

The only thing at issue is the quality of the art. We all have our views. What is conventionally called avant-garde art seems to me to have enjoyed a brief but brilliant period in the early decades of the 20th century. Once it was innovative, witty, intelligent and genuinely troubling, not least by its associations with the Universal Scientific utopias of communism or the violence and rationalism of fascism. Today the question mark over allegedly avant-garde work no longer concerns its legitimacy as art: it is its authenticity on any level.

As with all prestige asset markets, the Art world has grown into a billion dollar industry. A flood of new money has besieged the galleries of London and New York. In the frenzy to acquire star artists, such as Rothko, de Kooning, Jasper Johns, or Cy Twombly, prices have rocketed. Its effect has been to inflate the values of all but the most meagre works. Driven by power, ego, hype and money, absurd prices are being paid for contemporary art. And everyone is in on the market: hedge fund managers from Wall Street, tech-billionaires from LA, oligarchs from Moscow, and new industrialists from Shanghai.

But with individual pieces crossing the $100 million mark, do prices still have a relationship with aesthetic values and our own appreciation of them as objects of unrivalled beauty? Should we be 100 times more over awed? Does a Rothko, mass produced in every exacting detail, and stacked two to a penny in Walmart conjure up the same excitement? Obviously not.

Prices do not reflect beauty perse – but beauty combined with rarity. Star artists prominently placed at the centre of Manhattan apartments are less about intrinsic creative values, than an embodiment of pure currency; a more powerful statement in oil and canvas of an individual's idea of self worth, than grand houses, yachts or jets could ever hope to achieve.

ART!

Status on the wall

1.Values

2.Target

Uber-rich banker collectors, pop stars, speculative investors

Rush for new undiscovered talent

Fears

Being out-bid

Emotions

Ego, power, money

3.Exploits

Obedience to:
- The new 'hot' discovery; finding and buying into the latest hip undiscovered talent
- Cult of the artist; young, tortured, debauched, but gifted
- Buying it by the metre; wallpaper for new loft apartment in New York
- Personal art consultant – latest extravagance for the mega-rich
- Shock statement – i.e. for bankers with zero charisma to promote 'edgy' credentials
- The cutting edge; street art, protest art, guerrilla art, activist art, kids-just-outta-art school art
- The big gallery opening; 'A' list celebs, the beautiful and the bohemian, exotic cocktails, Japanese finger food, Swiss banker as sponsor

Rejection of:
- Trad, classical, figurative art
- Cheap or mass-produced art
- Popular media and culture
- Established galleries and museums
- Democrisation of art; anyone can paint
- Big popular shows that pull in the crowds (although success stories like Tate Modern in London are becoming increasingly adept at encouraging the public to engage with art and culture)

Emotional Context:
- Great art has powerful appeal because it has a strong emotional signature that resonates with its audience. In today's highly volatile market, where too much money is chasing a dwindling commodity, that 'signature' is more often than not, the $. Prices are of no concern. They act only to reflect ideas of an individual's net worth. And in the rush for status, new buyers, who know nothing about art, are snapping up everything that comes to market.

Social context:
- It has always been a large part of the blueprint for modern art to shock and violate conservative, bourgeois norms. But when shock is the antics of middle-class suburbia, controversy a salacious video on the internet and weird is the pictures from Abu Ghraib on mainstream TV, the task becomes harder everytime. Who is there left to shock?

Promise:
- Be part of the new 'ultra chic' elite
- Elevate your status above the philistine mob
- Buy distinction; a mark of sophistication
- 'A' list invitations to private views
- Wealth statement, big, brash and beautiful dominating the New York loft apartment
- Intimidate and impress friends and enemies

Future Vision:
- The future is the past. Everyday a new wave of artists loot the past, pillaging what they can from the likes of Duchamp, Cocteau and Picasso, and injecting cheap twists to make it their own. But with the currency of shock so over used, art is suffering from inspiration fatigue. As the French poet, Paul Valéry remarked, 'Everything changes but the Avant Garde'.

4.Seduces with

5.Reward

Promise

Buy personality, status, prominence

Power game in canvas

Reality check

Art is a differentiator, distancing the moneyed elite from the mob. Even an appreciation of art is an acquired, singular taste. Verbose terminology is used both to bewilder and intimidate the uninitiated; if you don't get it, you're thick, if you're shocked you're a prude, what is cliché is irony, what is dull, social commentary, what is pornographic, obscene only to those that 'see' pornography in it. And if you object to the price you certainly can't afford it.

Visual spell

SENSATIONALISM;
Shock, sex, the
ordinary and the
mundane, made
monumental

Personal Fears:
- Being out-bid by rivals
- Missing out on the 'new' new talent
- Buying the wrong new talent
- Buying a fraud

World Fears:
- Bottom falling out of the international art market; plummeting prices, stock becoming worthless

Imagery/Style
- Sensationalism; art as Victorian freak show: Damien Hirst's cow in formaldehyde
- Shock show: Chapman Brother's 'Sex'
- The mundane: Tracy Emin's 'My Bed'
- Disgust: perfomance artist Hermann Nitsch – who slaughters live animals in his 'art'
- New kid on the block: Banksy, graffiti artist

AUTOMANIA

The Need for Speed

Jeremy Clarkson
Born to be Riled

The safety lobby with their meat free fridges and their green tinted specs had their 15 minutes of fame in 1991, but they must now realize that Gordon Gecko is back in the driving seat, with his foot flat down in a tire squealing slide back to 1986.

The automobile is the centre-piece of the great jigsaw puzzle that makes up western lifestyle. Its gleaming, pristine, sculptural form, occupies pride of place on the forecourt of the idyll which is the suburban home, lovingly polished by its owner.

Film culture reinforced the potency of this symbol in modern life. James Dean, 'chickie' racing for the cliff face in 'Rebel Without a Cause' endowed the car with instant, rebellious, cool. Steve McQueen, the laconic cop, chasing underworld lowlife in *Bullitt,* across the roller-coaster roads of San Francisco, emphasized the quiet talking, gear-shifting, macho man at the wheel.

The ever unruffled, and very British secret agent, James Bond, traditionally at the hand of an Aston Martin (that would inevitably end up destroyed) made them desirable and sexy. The adrenaline rush of *The Fast and the Furious*, street racing in comic-book style through LA and Tokyo, blurred the line between reality and computer games. More recently, the Pixar-animated *Cars*, anthropomorphised trucks and cars, giving them feelings, making them cute. And televised worldwide, Jeremy Clarkson's petrolhead show, *Top Gear*, made the car the voice of manliness, liberated from the growing interference of grey bureaucracy, conformity and political correctness. Counter to this wave of auto culture, a lone voice, Al Gore's *An Inconvenient Truth,* preached the irresponsibility of car ownership, singling out the automobile as being global warming culprit number one.

Around 25% of CO_2 emissions come from cars and light trucks. Luxury 4x4's are an obvious target. But a more pressing issue is the mass-market — the ordinary, unremarkable saloons that account for 95% of world sales. And as such concerns rush to the top of the news agenda, the hunt is on for quick-fix solutions. There are none. Global warming is an issue with a timescale measured in hundreds of years. It will take 10 years for the automotive industry to develop a credible solution and at least another ten years before such innovations are adopted worldwide. Only then will meaningful emissions cuts be achievable.

Personal Fears
- Status anxiety, keeping up with the Patels
- New, latest, faster, better, cooler model
- Stubborn stain on the leather upholstery
- Dent in the rear wing
- Convoy of caravans
- 'Green' anti-car legislation and road usage tax
- Speeding cameras and fines
- Price at the pump
- Death on the road (1.4 million people die on the world's roads)

World Fears
- A world without cars
- The oil really might run out
- A world populated with silly electric cars

AUTOMANIA
›THE NEED FOR SPEED

1.Values

RAW EXCITEMENT, ADRENALIN RUSH

2.Target

WORLD CAR DRIVING POPULATION

Fears

NEW MODEL ANXIETY...

Emotions

SEX, SPEED, STATUS

3.Exploits

Speedometer markings: 20 40 60 80 *mph* 100 120 140 160

Obedience to:
- The car as an unashamed reflection of masculine virtues; of sexual prowess and status
- In a life of dull conformity, the car is a metaphor for a better life – freedom and individuality
- Raw excitement – a rush of blood to the head
- The car as technical achievement; symbol of human progress, art, even sculpture
- Sensory high; smell of leather, roar of exhaust, thrill of acceleration, speed, G forces in the bend
- Call of the wild; the promise of SUV's – go anywhere, get back to nature
- For the young – liberation from parental control

Rejection of:
- Environmentalists and the anti-car lobby (Bolsheviks reborn; their real agenda to destroy capitalism)
- Carbon tax, pay-per-mile tax, congestion tax, petrol tax, purchase tax – in fact any tax
- EU emissions target of 130g CO_2 per car
- Car sharing, community car schemes
- Little pathetic green cars
- Doomsters; oil running out, global warming
- Cars kill people (so does falling fruit)
- Cars are killing the planet (so are cows)
- Politically-correct wankers hogging the fast lane
- Boring bureaucrats and health and safety officials

Emotional Context
- Cars promise a dream; a seductive mix of sex, speed, status and leather luxury. And that's the big problem. In a world filled with often bland compromise, more human ingenuity, technical innovation and design, than in any other sector of commerce, has gone into fulfilling this fantasy. And cars deliver on this promise.

Social context
- More than any other technological advance, the car has had a huge impact on the way we live our lives. The needs of car users have dictated the look of our cities, how we get to work, where we live (the spread of suburbia), were we shop (the shopping mall), and how we link to other cities (the motorway networks). Rapid mobility has also impacted on our rural communities, encroached on our wildernesses and brought remote commmunities abruptly into the modern age.

Promise

- The open road; liberation, excitement, raw fun
- Comfort, luxury, sophistication
- Technical superiority; roadholding, acceleration
- Sex on wheels
- It's who you are; successful, cool, wealthy
- An appeal to the 'hero inside'
- The embodiment of the human spirit in sheet metal

Future Vision

The car sits at the centre of our future concerns. Surrounded by huge business interests (the petroleum, chemical, spare parts and insurance industries), millions of workers are reliant on the car for their livelihood. Cutting back on the car will have a profound impact on these economies.

Despite this, car populations are rapidly rising. This will mean more pollution, more congestion, more CO_2 emissions and more road deaths. Hydrogen cars are planned for the future. But the real savings are still with petrol. Cars can weigh half as much, be made twice as efficient and be driven half the distance.

Promise

THE HERO
INSIDE

5.Reward

FREEDOM
OF THE OPEN ROAD

Reality check

Of all the most persuasive spells perpetuated by advertising since the 1950's, the freedom, individuality and status of the car is the most potent. Is this imagery now so powerfully locked in people's minds that we have become psychologically blind to our predicament?

Visual spell

SCULPTURAL,
FEMININE
BEAUTY POLISHED STEEL,
CHROME EXHAUSTS

4.Seduces with

Iconography

- Empty, mountain roads
- Blonde in the passenger seat, Dire Straits on the stereo
- Route 66
- Desert locations, blue skies, puffy clouds
- Twisting corners; Italian, French Riviera
- Over-taking in the fast lane
- Spinning wheels, chrome, reflective bodywork
- Rev counter touching the red line
- Hot new concept car at an auto-show; pretty model drapped over the coachwork

Style/Aesthetic

- Speed, beauty, seductive feminine curves
- Go anywhere freedom, escape, liberty
- Hi-tech cool and sophistication
- Dream imagery

FAST DRIVE
INSTANT EVERYTHING

**IT'S GOOD
TO TALK**
MOBILE PHONE MANIA

TRASH TV
FAME GAME
MEGAMOVIE
SENSORY BOMBARDMENT

CELEB
CURRENCY OF OUR AGE

ZZ
LLS

ADRENALIN JUNKIES
LIVE LIFE TO THE MAX

THE BEAUTIFUL GAME
THE GREAT EQUALISER

PLAYNATION
SEEK AND DESTROY

DIGITAL DOMINATION
EMPIRE THAT NEVER SLEEPS

THE WHITE STUFF
LEAVE DULL REALITY BEHIND

ONLINE GAMBLING
EVERYONE IS A WINNER

Obedience to:
- The future is technology
- Transmission speed
- Processing power (GB's, GHz, MP's)
- The 'new new' tech gizmo
- Constant stimulation, excitement
- Always-on connection, instant messaging and data
- Fast-track service
- I want it now; 24-hour news, clip culture & music, online shopping & delivery
- Squeeze in more, do more, experience more, into the alotted time
- Mobile office, 24/7 availability, multi tasking

Rejection of:
- Downloading, please wait…
- Bad connection
- The slow lane
- Switching off
- Tech luddites
- Low-tech lifestyle

Personal Fears
- Systems crash
- Computer viruses
- Power failure
- Loss of data
- I'm not with it (to be one second behind the competition is failure)

World Fears
- Tech meltdown

Emotional Context
- New technology, the latest styles, new information and the speed of its delivery, exploit our deepest insecurity; being out of the loop, being out of fashion, being out of touch.
- In the highly competitive financial world, small advantages combined with speed create massive returns for the few who are first. Lack of knowledge is failure. You can't turn off.

Social context
- We have been made half crazed by the pace of technology. From computer software, instant messaging and e-mail, to labour-saving technology, entertainment and travel – speed – the ability to do more, see more, experience more, becomes the defining quality of our lives. Paradoxically, giving us more to do, to enjoy, hasn't slowed down our existence, merely created the impression that life moves too fast.

1.Values

first adopter advantage

2.Target

global tech heads & young entrepreneurs

3.Exploits

Emotions

rush of stuff to the head

Fears

in the competitive 'always on' info age, you can't turn off

fastdrive
instant everything

Promise
- Fast is first
- Speed is success
- Faster processing, transmission, commication
- First adopter superiority
- New gizmo cool; badge of status, tech-credibility
- Never be out of touch; always on connection
- Centre of the universe in the palm of your hand

Future Vision
- Electronic assistants, knowledge databases, even brain implants, promise to speed up our ability to deal more effectively and better with the deluge of information we receive. But better is subjective. Will such advances improve our lives? Or will we, by an over reliance on information in the digital world, conversely absorb less and become as individuals, less able independently to control our lives?

Iconography
- Speeding planes, trains and automobiles
- Space-age technology and satellites
- Optical fibres and electronic flashes
- Sexy cyber assistants
- Clip culture – media on the move
- Sound effects
- Rapid heartbeat

Style/Aesthetic
- Go faster graphics
- Blurred images
- Speedy computer animation

5.Reward

see more,
do more,
experience more

Reality check

We have an illusion of speed. Our latest futuristic cars have benefited from huge improvements in efficiency and power, but don't get us to our destinations any faster. Air travel, despite sophisticated advances in lightweight materials and technology, has failed to cut down on travel time.

At work, inboxes inundated with e-mails slow down the very productivity they're designed to speed up. News, data, tv and video media come at us at an ever frenetic pace. What has meaning now is meaningless ten minutes later. As a result, the human mind, besieged by content, filters out. Little registers long enough to make an impression. Are we heading towards a Teflon society in which nothing sticks or creates any resonance? We see more, but 'see' less? Speed becomes the only defining value?

Promise

speed is success,
fast is first

Visual spell

news, data, comms,
music, tv;
anything, anytime,
anywhere

4.Seduces with

IT'S GOOD TO TALK
Mobile phone mania

1.Values

NEW SHINY THING

2.Target

EVERY MAN, WOMAN AND CHILD *ON THE PLANET*

Emotions

NEOPHILIA *LUST FOR THE NEW*

3.Exploits

Fears

LAST YEARS' SAD, *OUTDATED* *MODEL*

Obedience to:
- The shiny fun, new thing
- Cool ring tones
- It's good to talk; constant chit-chat and gossip
- All-in-one gizmo: phone, PDA, e-mail, camera and music player
- Social networking (sms messaging, and instant activism)
- The new cool, latest tech 'must haves', hippest fashion accessory
- User-interface (iPhone touch screen shows the future)

Rejection of:
- Tech luddites; I can live without a mobile (only if you've a sad loser)
- No connection
- Mobile-free zone
- Making a call from a callbox
- Non-Stop interference technology...

Emotional Context:
- A major part of the success of the mobile was its appeal to both sexes; tech appeal for men, fashion and style appeal for women. The profitability of the sector is driven by rapid turnover. Neophilia, the obsessive pursuit of the new, the very best, the latest, is a powerful psychological driver. It turns out to have a biological basis. A gene for the enzyme monoamine oxidase creates a predisposition to compulsive consumer behaviour – i.e. the lust for the shiny new thing.

Social context:
- From the mid 80's 'brick' mobiles to the present day 'pay-as-you-go' flip-tops, mobile phones and their operators have become one of the most profitable sectors on the planet. 'It's good to talk'; A projected 3 billion customers in 2008 will inflate the already massive profits of the major brands. Downloadable music, video and porn, will also contribute to increased profit margins. With the convergence of phone, PDA, e-mail, internet, camera and media player, the humble mobile looks set to become the central interface into our lives.

Personal Fears:
- I can never be out of touch (disasters are waiting to happen)
- 'Always on' anxiety; you will miss the next 'big' business call
- Silence – nobody loves you (young people, reliant on constant stimulation, can't go five minutes without a call)
- Status fears; being stuck with last year's model, or a cheap ring tone
- Call addiction, especially with young people (one of the biggest non-drug addictions of our time, adding to irritability, stress and increases in personal debt)

World Fears:
- Rising crime epidemic (in the UK 10,000 mobiles are stolen every month)
- Anti-social behaviour; happy slapping, cyber stalking, kids filming and exchanging scenes of each other having sex
- Mobile phone link to brain tumours and health risks to children

Promise:
- Badge of cool, prestige, status, envy of your mates
- Never alone; friends, boy and girlfriends, mummy
- Brand credibility: Nokia, Sony Ericsson, Motorola, Apple iPhone
- The mobile executive, efficient and never out of the office (in reality 'never being out of touch' has increased working hours and contributed to job stress)
- Share your life: the ability to upload photos and video to sites such as Flickr and YouTube

Future Vision:
- The mobile phone already forms the electronics centre-piece of most peoples' lives. Artificial intelligence promises more; personal assistants, financial intelligence, cyber relationships. As such advances take over, more of ourselves, our data, memories and images, will be held in electronic form, making our emotional attachment and dependence on such devices that much stronger.

5.Reward

Promise

GLOBAL
CONNECTIVITY

Visual spell

WORLD
IN YOUR POCKET

Reality check
The technology of the mobile phone has fundamentally changed how we work, interact and socialize. As a purely functional addition to our lives it would have remained a bulky, rare extravagance. It took chit-chat and gossip to turn the mobile phone into the palm-sized, fun, fashion accessory that we all own today, making it both ubiquitous, international and for those who own the networks, a licence to print money; the single most successful product on the planet.

TECH GIZMO
FASHION ICON
STYLE ACCESSORY

4.Seduces with

Iconography:
- Instant communication
- Fun on the move: calls, text, photos, music, games
- Businessmen, women, soul-searching in international capitals
- Hi-tech environments: airports, galleries, cool offices
- Caring mother, cute loving child, waiting for the call
- Club culture: mobile as fashion accessory
- The roaming professional: island hopping, climbing mountains, never out of touch
- Enter a new universe where everyone is your friend

Style/Aesthetic:
- The future today
- The next cool thing
- Fashion and style icon
- Technology liberates
- Friends, family, business, in your pocket

Trash TV

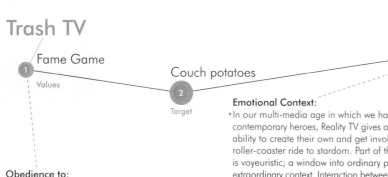

Emotions
Shameless voyeurism

Fame Game
Values

Couch potatoes
Target

Exploits **3**

Fears
Favourite voted off show

Obedience to:
- Ordinary people made extraordinary
- The new irony: if it's bad it's brilliant, if you don't like it, you don't get it
- Call up the usual suspects: dizzy peroxide blondes, oddballs and freaks
- Make it personal; close-up on the inevitable emotional break down and unguarded outburst
- Gratuitous nudity and/or steamy hot tub sex scene
- Inclusion of highly opinionated and merciless celebrity judges who are bound to come to blows
- Marvel at the banality and gullibility of the working class

Rejection of:
- Staid, traditional broadcast TV values; that television entertainment shouldn't pander to the lowest common denominator, but should also educate, enlighten and broaden the mind

Emotional Context:
- In our multi-media age in which we have few contemporary heroes, Reality TV gives audiences the ability to create their own and get involved in their roller-coaster ride to stardom. Part of the attraction is voyeuristic; a window into ordinary people in an extraordinary context. Interaction between contestants provides a potent chemistry that is designed to engineer conflict and controversy; addictive viewing, as well as being currency for celeb mags. But there is also schadenfreude, the guilty pleasure of delighting in the misfortune of others.

Social context:
- To like Reality TV is to promote your pop credibility. Those who go against the majority view and criticize such shows for being mindlessly vulgar, are not only missing the point, but are exposing themselves as being elitist, out of touch with mass culture.
- Wanabee stars, unlike their PR-controlled 'A' list, tell all and do anything for money. Reality TV thus enjoys a symbiotic relationship with celeb magazines such as *Heat* and *Hello*. It also endorses new values; show no inhibitions, let yourself go. Sentiments that gel perfectly with the message of the adman.

Personal Fears:
- I'll miss out on the 'must see' moment

World Fears:
- Favourite voted off the show

Megamovie

Blockbuster, 'must see' movie of the moment (coming to a cinema, DVD, iPod, Mobile...)
1
Values

World cinema audience
2
Target

Emotions
On the edge of your seat

3
Exploits

Fears
Stilted art-house movies

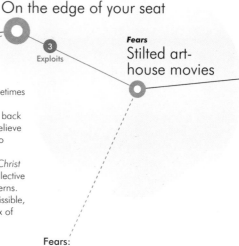

Obedience to:
- Bigger, better, sexier
- Mega summer release
- Best ever box-office opening weekend
- Big stars, mega budget, awesome special effects.
- Miss the film, buy the DVD, download from the web
- Not just a film, an event; buzz & gossip from sexy stars, magazine spreads, guest appearances on TV shows, fashion and perfume range
- Narrative that can fit on a postage stamp
- Engine room of the Hollywood money machine

Rejection of:
- Worthy, over-long, art-house movies
- Boring, 'yawn', foreign subtitles
- 'Edgy' but unknown cast
- Wordy scripts and confused narratives
- Low budget 'Indie' production values (16mm/shot on video)

Emotional Context:
- Blockbuster movies might be frivolous and sometimes stupid; but their impact on the global psyche runs deep. *Jaws* made everyone afraid to go back in the water. *Close Encounters* made us all believe in aliens and the *Blair Witch* left us petrified to leave the campfire.
- From *The Exorcist*, to *Twister*, *The Passion of Christ* and *Basic Instinct*, such movies encode our collective fears, sexual behaviour, prejudices and concerns.
- Always pushing the boundaries of what is permissible, 'Torture Porn' is Hollywood's latest potent mix of ultra-violence and sex.

Social context:
- To understand a blockbuster as being just a movie is missing the point. The scale of such ventures, from the bankers and financiers to the cast and crew, creative team, the marketing and publicity, the DVD manufacturing, to international sales, the merchandise, tourism and the sequels to follow, is like mastering the economy of a small city state. The blockbuster movie, is less about creativity, and more about the art of money generation.

Fears:
- Beware the 'A' list star peddling a political 'message movie' – kiss of death at the box office.

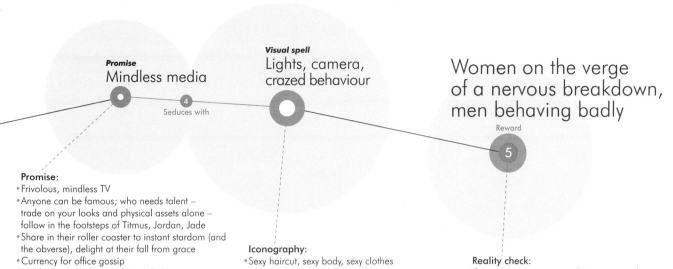

Mindless media

Visual spell
Lights, camera, crazed behaviour

Women on the verge of a nervous breakdown, men behaving badly

④ Seduces with

Reward
⑤

Promise:
- Frivolous, mindless TV
- Anyone can be famous; who needs talent – trade on your looks and physical assets alone – follow in the footsteps of Titmus, Jordan, Jade
- Share in their roller coaster to instant stardom (and the obverse), delight at their fall from grace
- Currency for office gossip
- Fodder for celeb mags – *Heat, OK!*
- Shameless self-promotion; tabloid sex story, fitness video, sex video, fashion line, tacky perfume

Future Vision:
- The rise of community networks and mobile media will cajole TV down the route of clip culture; 30-second bursts of snack TV, where selections will be judged by the tyranny of 'the most viewed'. Having to compete against the crass and the sensational, it's hard to see how long-form drama, let alone hard news or analysis, will survive within such a bite-sized environment.

Iconography:
- Sexy haircut, sexy body, sexy clothes
- 'I'm just so emotional' moment
- Tearful Mum and Dad back home
- Wanabee look-alikes, disco dancers
- High-anxiety moment – voting off contestants

Style/Aesthetic:
- Loud, brash, sensational
- New voyeurism

Reality check:
- Google's announcement that more people are now online than watch TV induced panic. Rallying under the banner that is populism, shows such as *Pop Idol*, *Big Brother*, and *Celebrity Love Island* reflect a crisis of confidence; the media of the masses is collapsing, audiences are deserting 'old school' entertainment for online clip culture. Faced with desertion, TV is going for the emotional jugular, cranking up its quota of shock, sex and sensationalism. A desperation that suggests a last rear-guard action before the rout.

Sensory bombardment

Roller-coaster of emotions, never a dull moment

Visual spell
Awesome action, FX's, shocks and sex

Reward
⑤

④ Seduces with

Promise:
- Whhaooh factor
- The experience of a lifetime for the price of a cheap indie film
- Sensory overload, never a dull moment
- Special effects, the likes of which you have never experienced (well not since the last one)
- And (rest assured), last minute, upbeat ending (despite all evidence to the contrary he gets the girl)

Future Vision:
- The latest figures from the industry show that returns from blockbuster movies have fallen whilst costs have risen. Are people losing interest? No. Cinema audiences might be low, but profits on the DVD side are racking up. And with broadband and portable media crying out for content, there will always be high demand for the next big blockbuster. And if you run out of inspiration go for the remake and extend the franchise

Iconography:
- The big epic release
- Cover of *Time* magazine
- Glamour, red carpet opening
- Ordinary man/girl on the street pitted against forces of vast, unstoppable, evil empire
- Charismatic rogue
- Twee, innocent girl, gets tough, ends up 'kicking ass' and saving the day
- Merchandise: the look, the record, the book, the make-up, the t-shirt, the fashion, the toys

Style/Aesthetic:
- Big, brash, mega, epic; a rush of imagery that dwarfs all else
- Constant twists, unexpected reverses, perpetual danger, but, against the most improbable odds, always the upbeat ending
- Cliff hanging dilemma; if A goes after B he loses C (the girl)

Reality check:
- Critics and academics criticise Hollywood for historical inaccuracy and for writing content that is formulaic and crass. But who's wining the war? Hollywood instils our memories of the future, is the lead trendsetter for all other media (TV, publications, even fashion), and blatantly rewrites and remixes our past – history, literature, religion – to suit the demographic (middle America). And just in case our kids might go unscathed, Disney rewraps our fairy tales.

CELEB

Currency of our Age

Several factors contribute to our growing obsession with fame and celebrity: the historic – our genetic propensity to worshipping anything from rocks to stars, even pepsi cans, and the proliferation of internet sites, new TV channels, brands and publications, trading on stardom. With so many hungry media outlets to feed, every permutation has been exploited: stars in their cars, celebs at home, celebs in their underwear, celebs with their boyfriends, celebs on the piss. With their identity duplicated, printed and distributed in hundreds of magazine spreads, online sites and television programmes worldwide, they are everywhere. Remarkably, considering their prominence, the vast majority have absolutely nothing to say.

For the celebs, new advances in mobile technology bring added pressures. With a camera in every pocket, everything a star does, from the extraordinary to the mundane, becomes currency. Embarrasing mishaps and minute flaws in their appearance can be displayed instantly online (such as on the notorious Perez Hilton gossip blog) for the world to gloat over spots, cold sores and embarrasing stains. The pressure is on to always look perfect. Fame has become a simple contract: celebs might gain the paradise of yachts and private villas but they lose the paradise of normal life – the right to walk the streets, the freedom to roam, to wander the world and sometimes be aimless.

Celeb

CURRENCY OF OUR AGE

1.Values

WHAT I REALLY, REALLY WANT...

2.Target

WANNABEES
(do anything for fame)

Emotions

LIGHTS, CAMERA, MAKE-UP
INSTANT RECOGNITION

3.Exploits

Fears

I'M NOT
BEAUTIFUL ENOUGH
SEXY ENOUGH
COOL ENOUGH

Obedience to:
- Instant global recognition; plucked from total obscurity to the pages of *OK! Magazine*
- 3 'A's: affluence, attractiveness, achievement
- You're beautiful, you're wonderful – don't be ashamed of your talents
- Lights, glamour, adulation
- Travelling entourage: stylists, drivers, PA, stropy PR
- Diva dressing room demands
- Million-dollar product deals
- Do anything for fame: boob job, nose job, 'who do you sleep with?'
- Stardom won't affect me – I'll still live with mum
- Who needs an education; trade on looks and physical assets alone – talent is not a prerequisite
- Check out my MySpace page

Rejection of:
- Getting through college
- Doing it the hard way; 9 to 5 job
- Turning up on time
- Taking the bus
- Queuing like the rest of us
- Family responsibilities

Emotional Context:
- The more we are exposed to celebrities (they're on our TV's, in our magazines, and on our mobile phones), the more real that relationship appears to become, increasing feelings of intimacy and loyalty as if they were genuinely close friends. But appearances can be deceptive: If stars are stunningly beautiful we have a natural tendency to believe they are also wonderfully intelligent, social, loving and have something meaningful to say.

Social context:
- Fame, previously focused on European Royalty and Hollywood, has now expanded to embrace every sector; from politicians and supermodels to TV chefs, footballers, and even their wives. In becoming the dominant currency of our media age, the desire for fame has created a filter that impacts on everything that gets said and seen. World events, news, even science, are judged to be of low media value unless they come with a celeb attached.

Personal Fears:
- Fame will pass me by
- Insecurities; I'm not beautiful enough, sexy enough, talented enough
- I want to be seen by millions, but I just want to be alone (The lens of the Paparazzi; success is a deal with the devil – you cash in your right to privacy)
- Control freak on the verge of a nervous breakdown – rehab on the horizon

World Fears:
- My 3 minutes of fame is over

Promise

ANYONE
CAN BE FAMOUS
(even **you**…)

TICKET TO
WONDERLAND

Reality check:

Sudden, incredible wealth and instant worldwide fame, just because you're wonderful and drop-dead beautiful, is a potent spell that resonates with millions of new young hopefuls dreaming of a place in Neverland. And one in a million might just make it. For the rest of us we can only live out this fantasy in the plethora of celebrity products and brands piling up in the highstreet, ever hopeful that some of that magic might just rub off on us.

But this is fantasy land with a downside – the vulnerable (often the underprivileged and poor), laid low by unrealistic ideas of their own self-esteem, succumb to depression – loneliness, drug-dependance, even suicide, – the sad reality.

Visual spell

On the tele,
Cover of OK! magazine
Sexy music video,
lingerie range

Promise:
- Leave your sad little life (and friends) behind
- Anyone can be famous; buy the lipstick, the peroxide, the fashion accessories, share the dream
- 'A list' access to exclusive clubs, openings and VIP zones
- Instant wealth: designer clothes, jewellery, expensive Swiss watches
- Playboy glamour: stretched limos, private jets, yachts, Ferraris

Future Vision:
- Our growing global infatuation with celebs, combined with instant connectivity and the increasing reach of western entertainment and brands, will ensure that those lucky few who make the grade, will rise higher and faster to fame and riches. But with rapid turnover also a driving factor, the fall from grace will be steeper and harder.
- In virtual worlds, where everyone has the ability to be a star, look glamorous, sing on their own stage, will real celebs lose their appeal?

Iconography:
- Red carpet film and restaurant openings
- Centre stage on TV chatshows
- Cover of *Vanity Fair, OK! Magazine*
- Lifestyle photoshoot: country mansion, six car garage, exotic pool, designer kitchen
- Big product endorsements, commercials
- Shocking, controversial, explicit video shoot (thus the front page of every tabloid in the country)
- Fast cars, yachts, beautiful people
- Kitsch mansions, tacky plaster statues
- Celebsafari.com: the sport of 'bagging stars', posing with a photo with them, much as you would collect 'trophies' on a safari

Style/Aesthetic:
- In the past we were used to seeing stars through the sympathetic lenses of the big star photographers such as Mario Testino and Nick Knight. Given the high gloss, art directed, photoshoped polish, our celebs had the appearance of godlike icons. But with the advent of the internet and 'a phone in every pocket', the chic and composed aesthetic has given way to a warts-an-all, caught unaware, snap-shot reality.

Boy George

If fame came with a switch-off button, it would be great, because you could just walk down the street and click it off and be like everyone else.

Joan Smith
Moralities: Sex, Money, and Power in the 21st Century:

Women, particularly women who are famous, are encouraged into a state of neurotic self obsession. Any of us can get up in the morning and look in the mirror and think: my hair needs washing. But to have that constant feeling of checking yourself, of being under scrutiny must direct energy away from more important things. It keeps women in an almost infantile state where all their self-esteem is bound up in how they look and what dress they're wearing.

Dr Raj Persaud
Sunday Times Review,
'All hail new gods of our age'

New psychological research suggests that worship of celebrities by the public has begun to take the place of religions in many people's lives. The main findings were that the lower a person's religious conviction the more likely they were to worship celebrities. Stars such as David Beckham have not only become sporting role models for millions of young boys around the world but they now influence their values and lifestyle in the way religions have traditionally provided guidance.

Alexis Petridis
The Guardian, G2 section:

The cover of *Heat* magazine features Victoria Beckham's sister exclusively revealing that her sibling likes pasta. Celebrity's currency has become as devalued as the Venezuelan bolivar, and accordingly it has become de rigueur for any musician with a fully functioning sense of dignity to mock the processes of stardom.

Sean O'Hagan
The Observer Review, 'The World's most photographed', on the photographer Tom Parker:

We live in a time when the snapshot rather than the posed portrait is the defining image of celebrity. The process of absolute control instigated by Parker in the Fifties, and insisted upon today by the phalanx of agents, PR consultants and managers that surround every celebrity, has, paradoxically created a guerrilla industry specialising in the taking and dissemination of snatched images, often captured on the run or from several hundred yards away – And while the likes of *Vanity Fair* still collude in the illusion that contemporary Holllywood stardom is an elect calling akin to old-style royalty, a rash of newer, less reverential magazines such as *Heat* revels in presenting evidence to the contrary, that celebrities are just as scrawny/over weight/badly dressed as you or me, and just as prone to tantrums, tears and hangovers. All seem redolent of an already distant era, not actually that long ago, when photography not only reflected, but informed history, when a single image could confer power and status and enshrine a public figure's reputation for posterity.

Ellis Cashmore
Celebrity Culture

Celebrity culture has offered us a distinctive vision, a beguiling one too: one in which there are few limits, an expanding range of opportunities, and inexhaustible hope. Ideas like restraint, prudence, and modesty have either been discredited or just forgotten. Celebrity culture has replaced them with impetuosity, frivolity, prodigality. Human impulses like these were once seen as vices; now they are almost virtuous.

Adrenalin Junkies

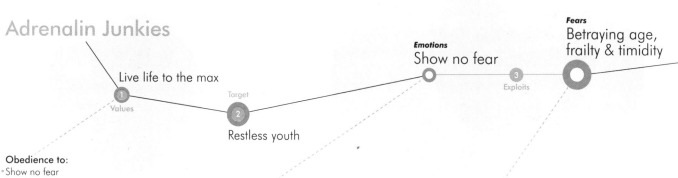

Live life to the max
① Values

Target
② Restless youth

Emotions
Show no fear

③ Exploits

Fears
Betraying age, frailty & timidity

Obedience to:
- Show no fear
- Live for the moment
- Push yourself to the limits
- Novelty seeking, risk taking
- The world as one big playground
- Natural highs; adrenaline rush to the head
- A life outdoors; man against the environment
- Untamed youthful spirit; freedom to roam
- Deep play: intense experiences

Rejection of:
- Nanny society: don't do this, don't say that, don't go there'
- Be sensible – safe rather than sorry
- Health and safety inspectors
- Traditional, conventional, 'safe' sports
- Mundane desk-bound work
- Age, and with it, risk adverse
- Chickening out – pulling back from the brink

Emotional Context:
- Extreme sports is founded on the bravado mentality; an attitude of one upmanship over rivals – 'top this'.
- It also cocks a snook at the 'tame masses', who weighed down with the anxieties of life – mortage, school fees and kids – shy from risk and play it safe.

Social context:
- Adrenalin junkie is synonymous with extreme sports and before that action sports. The intrepid wing walkers at the beginning of the 20th century were the ultimate risk takers of their day. Today, take a conventional sport, put extreme in front of it, wear cool kit (sunglasses, edgy t-shirt, sneakers), make it absurdly dangerous and (the difficult bit), show no fear.

Personal Fears:
- Conforming
- Desk-bound work life
- Tied down by family responsibilities
- Being restrained and chained by mortage, home, job
- Getting old and boring; losing one's sense of adventure and courage to go it alone

World Fears:
- The world, made tame by health & safety prerogatives, is losing its sense of danger

The Beautiful Game

The great equaliser
① Values

Nations of the World
② Target

Emotions
90 minutes of heart thumping emotion

③ Exploits

Fears
Penalty shoot out

Obedience to:
- From Argentina to Zimbabwe, the greatest game of all
- The game of the people, irrespective of wealth, economic power, or colour
- Through thick and thin, national unity, solidarity and hopefully celebration
- The acceptable face of world conflict
- Let yourself go; opportunity to scream, roar, party
- The crucial goal; victory, the cup, relief
- Star adulation: local hero becomes world hero, the most worshipped person on the planet

Rejection of:
- Sky-high salaries of football team managers
- Over-weight, over-paid, underachieving stars
- Inept, biased, or corrupt referees
- Sport of billionaires (Obscene amounts of money, snapping up the best players, creates a dominance that is killing competition)

Emotional Context:
- Football is a roller coaster of emotions. No sport is more highly charged. In 90 minutes of heart thumping, adrenalin-pumping action, the difference between total ecstasy and total misery hinges on a second. One's total identity and sense of national and local pride, is wrapped up in the destiny of 11 men and a football.
- Victory can change the spirit of a country long after the cheers have faded. Conversely, national gloom will be the prevalent mood if the reverse is true.

Social context:
- Football, more than any other sport, can justifiably be called the sport of nations. Played on dirt tracks, ghetto streets, back lots, and school playgrounds world-wide, it's the great egalitarian game, with the power to lift the poor and disadvantaged to instant stardom. All from a game that started on the green and pleasant fields of England's elite public schools.

Personal Fears:
- Team slaughtered
- Penalty shootout
- Red card
- Offside
- Serious injury
- TV going on the blink

World Fears:
- The other side

Promise
Live life on the edge

Visual spell
'You have to be shitting me..'

f***ing go for it!

4
Seduces with

Reward
5

Promise:
- Show you don't conform
- Badge of fearlessness
- Join the adrenaline elite
- Live life on the edge
- Better than sex

Future Vision:
- The adrenaline junkie has become a successful component of new media, made mainstream by such programmes as *Extreme TV* and *Jackass*, where stunts have become popular through acts of sometimes mindless stupidity and recklessness, broadcast to large international audiences; a long way from the activities of the original adrenaline junkies whose experiences were often solitary.

Iconography:
- Extreme landscapes: canyons, waves and snow bound mountains
- One man/girl against the elements
- Bright, eye-catching, lycra skin-tight gear, t-shirts, trainers
- Anything extreme: base jumping, powder skiing, kite surfing, biking, white-water kayaking, climbing, sky-diving, skateboarding, free running, parkour

Style/Aesthetic:
- Fast, slick, edgy graphics, music and flicker book-style video

Reality check:
- Extreme sports has become like any other lifestyle culture. Big business has moved in, branding everything from drinks, sports gear, hotels, TV and video games, even credit cards.
- An increasingly popular facet of the rebel demographic, millions aspire to this dare-devil world of action, but once they've read the indemnity forms, been terrified by the heights, will settle for the t-shirt, the beer and a retreat to the safe life of the couch potato.

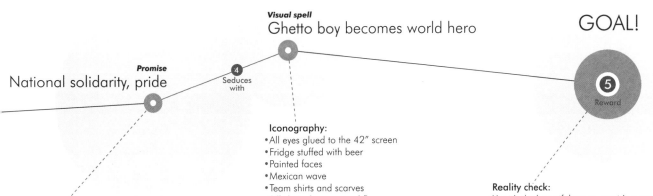

Visual spell
Ghetto boy becomes world hero

GOAL!

Promise
National solidarity, pride

4
Seduces with

5
Reward

Promise:
- Goal!
- Feelgood factor; emotional high
- You're on the winning team
- Share in the celebration and success
- Identify with the stars, the local team, the nation
- Outside of dull work and family, the chance to run wild, to muck in with the lads, to scream, to howl, to drink, to party and promote your egalitarian values

Future Vision:
- Bigger teams, bigger players, bigger egos, bigger crowds, bigger TV, mega profits

Iconography:
- All eyes glued to the 42" screen
- Fridge stuffed with beer
- Painted faces
- Mexican wave
- Team shirts and scarves
- Silly hats, banners and flags
- Designer stadium
- The latest new sports shoes
- Mid-match commentary
- High-spending footballers' wives
- Megawealth; fast cars and vulgar mansions
- Kiss-and-tell tabloid scandals; three-in-a-bed sex

Style/Aesthetic:
- Man from the street takes on Beckham
- The underdog against multi-million dollar players
- Nations as tribes
- Big, brash and beautiful

Reality check:
- Yes it's the beautiful game, yes it's a great equalizer – unknown boy from the favelas lifted onto the world stage – but its larger reality is big business; Club revenue, transfer fees, TV rights, sponsorship and mega advertising deals; sports shoes, soft drinks, merchandise, mobile media, even online sites for footballers' wives.

PLAYNATION

Seek and destroy

Steven Johnson
Everything Bad is Good for You

To non-players, games bear a superficial resemblance to music videos: flashy graphics; the layered mix of image, music, and text, the occasional burst of speed, particularly during the pre-rendered opening sequences. But what you actually do in playing a game – the way your mind works – is radically different. It's not about tolerating or aestheticizing chaos; it's about finding order and meaning in the world, and making decisions that help create that order.

No one can deny that computer games have an addictive quality that is greater than any other form of media, such as passive television viewing or an evening at the movies. Some of the youngest and brightest minds on the planet are currently employed to develop both the highly sophisticated hardware for these machines and the software to produce these elaborately crafted fantasy worlds. With the new generation of consoles on the market, such as Sony's PlayStation 3, such capabilities and complexity will only increase. Greater processing power and heightened emotional intelligence controlling characters within games, together with scenes that are able to match their Hollywood movie counterparts for big visual impact, will bring added realism to interactivity, increasing the excitement and potential of gameplay. Greater technical virtuosity will accentuate the psychological effects, the results of which are still mixed – some research shows higher IQ's and improved spatial awareness, whilst other data claims rising verbal aggression, increased violence, low attention spans and obesity.

Although the complexity of cyberspace might be indecipherable to adults, young minds take instantly to its visual grammar and constructs. Computer games have have been rightly criticized by educationalists. But might there be positive lessons from the games industry that can be co-opted by education? Could such techniques be the key to how learning in schools might be delivered to children in the future? And in potential careers, such as banking, what if the financial markets looked like a landscape out of Halo?

PLAYNATION
SEEK AND DESTROY

2.Target

HOME ALONE
KIDS
(AND YOUNG ADULTS)

3.Exploits

Fears

1.Values

REAL LIFE,
SITTING ROUND A DINNER TABLE,
TALKING ABOUT SCHOOL,
GOING SHOPPING

FAST FORWARD
GAMEPLAY

Emotions

ACTION,
ADVENTURE,
EXCITEMENT,
RUSH OF STUFF

Obedience to:
- Buzz, excitement, adrenalin rush
- Mindless fun
- Having a laugh
- Making it to the next level
- Seek and destroy
- Total escapism, instant transportation
  to fantasy worlds
- Immersive gameplay; obsessive and engaging
- Need for speed; fast cars and sexy women
- Multi game playing across the globe
- Cheat codes

Rejection of:
- School work
- Anxious parents – 'is sweet Johnny becoming
  a mindless moron?'
- Computer games desensitizes kids to violence
- Outdoors pursuits, taking a stroll
- Organised sports
- Sharing in the housework

Emotional Context:
- Yes game playing is harmless – taken in moderation.
  But MIT scans taken of the minds of hard-core
  gamers reveals a different picture. As with drugs like
  cocaine, intense game playing activates the same
  seek and reward circuitry, thus leading to addiction.
  Habitual playing of excessively violent games
  reinforces the neural networks associated with
  aggression, making it more likely to lead to violent
  behaviour in real-life situations, be that road-rage
  or taking 'vengeance' on students at High School.

Social context:
- Beyond all the hype of violence and shooting,
  gaming is becoming more about communities,
  social interaction and building relationships, whether
  with someone with similar interests in Kazakhstan
  or with on-screen avatars. In online communities
  such as Halo, Warcraft and Second Life, gamers
  are creating their own worlds with their own systems
  and activities. And as every day these virtual
  worlds become that much more alluring, and
  engaging it's understandable why we are losing
  our kids to cyberspace.

Personal Fears:
• No mates; unloved in the real world
• Family stress
• Real life is dull and monotonous
• Becoming a gaming addict (recent surveys in the US have revealed that an average 21-year old has played 5,000 hours of computer games, used the mobile 10,000 times and spent 3,500 hours online – not much time left for the real world…)

World Fears:
• Civilisation being destroyed by the evil green goblin

4.Seduces with

Promise

BE ANYONE, DO ANYTHING, SEE EVERYTHING

Visual spell

FANTASY WORLDS, SEXY AVATARS AND TRIGGER HAPPY PSYCHOS

5.Reward

REALITY SUCKS GO VIRTUAL

Reality check

Gamers see criticism of the industry as a witch hunt claiming that films and video are just as violent. Few would deny this was true; such media have the same effect. An angry kid playing violent computer games is also going to revel in violence in films and TV, increasing his chances of developing into a real life aggressive, anti social adult. And for those who are already mentally imbalanced, close to the divide, a violent computer game is going to seem like training day for the real thing.

Promise:
• Do anything anytime; a world that is denied you in real life is available in gameplay: fast cars, sex kitten girls, big guns, the ability to take out your aggression in acts of mindless violence and destruction
• Find community in cyberspace; a warm, colourful, exciting, engaging alternative world, populated by sexy fantasy characters, (in contrast to the real-world; dysfunctional, oppressive, lonely, unengaging, governed by a 'don't do that', 'don't say that' mentality.)
• There's real money in cyberspace – virtual land, virtual products, even virtual bodies are sold in games like World of Warcraft and Second Life

Future Vision:
• Game playing is still in its infancy. Greater processing power will increase the range of possibilities of game playing machines. Emotional intelligence and 3D effects will provide added realism. WiFi and faster broadband will bring like-minded communities even closer. So compelling, immersive and rewarding will these virtual worlds become, that real life, with its conflicts and petty concerns, will start to lose its appeal for younger generations.

Iconography:
• Fantasy worlds: castles, dungeons, jungles, somewhere in space
• Vice Cities: streets of LA, Soho, Miami
• The war zone: Western Front, Samurai, Ninjas
• The world as racetrack: mountains, deserts, snowfields
• Sexy avatars: chameleon, pole-dancing call girls
• The surreal: killer tomatoes, scary monsters

Style/Aesthetic:
• Stylised, computerised worlds; from Omaha Beach to gangland clubs and the bars of LA

Obedience to:
- Tech frenzy, the next big thing; get on board quick!
- Web 2.0 (and to come, 3.0)
- New 'killer' application; transforming the world as we know it
- Fluid integration of video, text and music mobile media, user-generated content, mashups, immersive sites
- Big Bang; from squalid basement to MegaEmpire in 12 months
- IPO's, angel investors, VC funds
- Thirty-something entrepreneurs
- Scalable ideas: small, often incremental advances that bring massive returns
- Blogs and the democrisation of creativity; anyone is a news reporter, everyone has an opinion, a photo or video to show – and you don't need money, help or permission to speak to the world
- Social networking site – MySpace, Facebook page
- Viral media (shock and sensationalism wins)

Rejection of:
- Slow technology
- Low technology
- No technology

Personal Fears:
- Late to market – it's already been done
- Systems crash – data loss
- Computer viruses
- Computer fraud
- Missing the big one (investing at the crest of the wave and losing a fortune)
- Symptoms of becoming a net junkie: fatigue, low achievement, social isolation, feelings of sudden rage
- How many 'friends' you don't have on your MySpace page

World Fears:
- Total tech meltdown
- Dark net (Tim Berners-Lee, inventor of the World Wide Web, warned in a BBC interview, of the rise of misinformation and the effect of 'undemocratic forces')

1.Values

NEXT NEW NEW THING

2.Target

GEEKS
SCREEN SLAVES
ANYONE
WITH A LAPTOP

3.Exploits

Emotions

TECH
FRENZY
GET ON BOARD QUICK

Fears

LATE
TO
MARKET

Emotional Context:
- The digital age plays on age-old themes: the lone spotty upstart taking on the evil empire. Start-ups, often from some dingy basement, always play it small, knowing that one day, the big diggers will move in (as with News Corp buying into MySpace, Google snapping up YouTube, Microsoft taking a chunk of Facebook and AOL buying Bebo).

Social context:
- Digital technology, from mobile media to the internet, has provided us with far greater capabilities than our low-tech counterparts. We can view video, check on stocks, go online, make conference calls, organise pictures and find obscure restaurants on GPS.
- But as we delegate more of our mundane tasks to the digital world, our mobile phones, our in-car traffic systems and online assistants, will we lose the ability to process such information ourselves? Will intelligence in fact make us more stupid? Does it matter? If we can find information so readily, why know anything anymore?

Promise:
- Be part of the new 'tech' theocracy – forge the future
- First adopter – the new next thing
- Super investment opportunity
- The 'long-tail' effect – infinite choice and the ability to sell
- Create, contribute, participate
- Reinvent yourself, be someone else: sexier, cooler, younger

Future Vision:
- Few can have foreseen the impact of the digital domain, the web and mobile media, on information, news and data, and now music, tv and films. Even fewer would have predicted the social impact of user-generated content and cyberworlds such as Second Life, where truly alternative communities have created real dollar economies.
- The virtual is becoming a genuine replacement for real life rather than an adjunct. You can get it all – sex, a laugh, gaming, go shopping, see the world, make money – without venturing further than your bedroom. And that's the sad truth – people are migrating to sites like Second Life, because their first-life (real life), isn't that rewarding.

Iconography:
- Geek with a laptop taking on the world from his mum's basement
- Silicon Valley start-ups
- Pizza-eating gawky eggheads
- Skateboarding down the corridors of power
- 20-something workforce in jeans, t-shirt and sneakers
- Working on the move; laptops, WiFi, mobile phones, PDA's
- Future tech: sexy digital assistants, cybersex, digital beauties
- Blogging on the move
- Uploading your latest crazed antics onto YouTube
- Google with everything – search, maps, ads, mobile

Style/Aesthetic:
- Fast forward to the future, bigger, faster and better than it is today
- Photoshop graphics and cool computer FXs
- Make believe, virtual worlds

5.Reward

EMPIRE
THAT NEVER SLEEPS

Reality check

Not long back, news, information and content was mediated by editors. Now the algorithm rules. Small advantages become a stampede; the domino effect. When a message's primary value becomes its ability to multiply fast and become viral, it's not surprising that anything in our age, from politics to entertainment, must adhere to certain values (such as shock, sensationalism or sex), to be heard.

Yes we have more information, but we also have more misinformation. The net result: conspiracy theories abound, we distrust government, politics, and big business. With the erosion of trust, no one believes anything anymore. Any prejudice, or narrow world view, is endorsed, not by the few, but by the millions. Can truths survive? Are they even relevant?

Promise

4.Seduces with

Visual spell

SUPER
INVESTMENT OPPORTUNITY

FROM DINGY BASEMENT TO MEDIA EMPIRE
CEO IN JEANS AND T-SHIRT

DIGITAL DOMINATION

BLOGS TO CYBERSPACE AND BEYOND: THE LIBERATION OF ME - MEDIA

The White Stuff

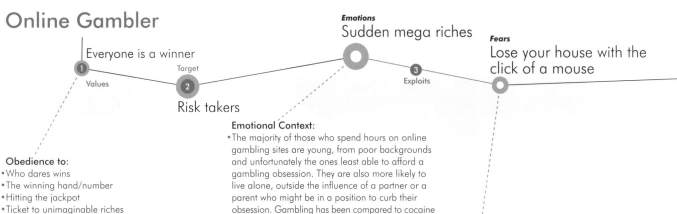

Values — 1 — Leave dull reality behind

Youth — 2 — Target

Fears — Socially and creatively inadequate without a fix

Exploits — 3

Emotions — Euphoria

Obedience to:
- 'Out of body' experiences, sense of euphoria, cool hallucinations; leave dull reality behind
- Relaxing, chilling out, getting stoned
- Rush of fun to the head
- Behaving badly; being off your trolley
- Cocaine chic; wiped-out looks of super-models and wild-boy rock stars
- Rebelliousness against and defiance of social norms

Rejection of:
- Natural highs (sports, painting a picture…)
- Drugs kill (so does paracetamol)
- Sensible, conventional, conservative values
- It will wreak your life (so will nagging parents)
- Government legislation (alcohol is just as dangerous, yet few moves are made against the global drinks industry – wonder why?)
- Reality (who needs to be reminded of it…)

Emotional Context:
- With its ability to increase awareness and confidence, cocaine is the drug of choice for City brokers, music and advertising executives and creatives. Under constant pressure to make money and be 'creative' it's easy to see how such drugs have become part of the culture. Even the ability to 'party' has become part of the job. Cocaine is as likely to come from your boss. The drug gives you a highly inflated view of who you are and your ability. In other words it makes you pig headed and obnoxious.

Social context:
- Films like *Scarface* and *Miami Vice*, TV and fashion, have made drugs cool, sexy and part of contemporary pop-culture. Kids see superstars and models doing it and think it's hip. But it's the people of the third world, in countries like Columbia and Afghanistan who are paying the price. The real impact of drugs and conflict on a world scale is poverty and prostitution, slums and ghettos, killings and kidnaps, with economies and environments devastated by corruption and lawlessness. Not a view you get from the club scene.

Personal Fears:
- Social inadequacy without a stimulant
- Creatively dull without a stimulant
- Inability to cope with pressures of work
- Exclusion from the group
- Having no direction in life – total utter boredom (not just a problem with underprivileged kids – hyper rich kids, stressed by pushy, high-profile alpha parents, and with little purpose in life, often turn to drugs to alleviate their sense of complete despair)
- Overdose, anxiety attacks, bad trips, addiction, 'meth mouth' (tooth decay)
- HIV infection

World Fears:
- Rise of the holier-than-thou majority

Online Gambler

Values — 1 — Everyone is a winner

Target — 2 — Risk takers

Emotions — Sudden mega riches

Exploits — 3

Fears — Lose your house with the click of a mouse

Obedience to:
- Who dares wins
- The winning hand/number
- Hitting the jackpot
- Ticket to unimaginable riches
- Trust in fate; this could be your lucky day
- It's good, harmless fun ($10 for a swagger never hurt anybody)
- Your lucky number
- One more throw to win it all back

Rejection of:
- Boring rationality (the odds on winning the lottery are the equivalent of one ping-pong ball in a football stadium with your name on it)
- Mealy-mouthed sceptics (the lottery is a tax on stupidity)
- Smug quips: 'who pays for the lights in Las Vegas?'

Emotional Context:
- The majority of those who spend hours on online gambling sites are young, from poor backgrounds and unfortunately the ones least able to afford a gambling obsession. They are also more likely to live alone, outside the influence of a partner or a parent who might be in a position to curb their obsession. Gambling has been compared to cocaine addition, a habit that can quickly spiral out of control. Neurologists have confirmed this. The brain activity in gamblers is similar to that observed with drug addicts.

Social context:
- Fuelled by images of James Bond in Monte Carlo casinos, gambling has a glamorous, sexy, jet-set image. The internet has introduced gambling to a much wider audience. The promise remains the same: you can make a killing. Such fantasies have ruined not just individuals, but families and communities. Day trading on movements in the money markets is rapidly becoming the addiction of the millennium. The risks are huge – you can lose your house with a click of the mouse.

Personal Fears:
- Misplaced lottery ticket
- Lady luck will pass me by
- Last minute doubt
- Losing by a single digit
- One card short
- Being dealt a bad hand
- Mounting debts/gambling addiction

World Fears:
- Best mate winning

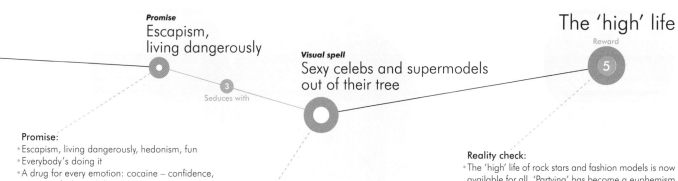

Promise
Escapism, living dangerously

Visual spell
Sexy celebs and supermodels out of their tree

3
Seduces with

Reward
5

Promise:
- Escapism, living dangerously, hedonism, fun
- Everybody's doing it
- A drug for every emotion: cocaine – confidence, ecstasy – feel good, heroin – contentment, LSD – altered states, crystal meth – sex all night, magic mushrooms – silliness, amphetamines – work all night

Future Vision:
- With all eyes focused on drugs and crime the real revolution will come from another source. The large pharmaceutical companies are looking at the bigger 'legal' picture. Advances in neurology have enabled chemists to enhance behaviour related to specific 'disorders' (though the definition of what is 'normal' and what 'abnormal' will be hard to define).
On the horizon, intelligence, happiness, weight loss and sex in a pill.

Iconography:
- Life in the fast lane: gregarious city stock brokers, advertising & TV execs and celebs
- Music: on tour with rock stars and supermodels
- Club culture: the rave scene, Ibiza, sex in the sun
- Fashion and beauty: drug chic – young, beautiful, all fucked up
- Gay: crystal meth, 48-hour club scene
- Glamorized crime: fast cars, yachts, bodyguards, guns, strippers, beaches

Style/Aesthetic:
- Glitz and glamour; association with hedonism and the high life
- The tag 'recreational' gives drugs a semblance of normality, like having a swing in the park

Reality check:
- The 'high' life of rock stars and fashion models is now available for all. 'Partying' has become a euphemism for taking drugs. From New York to London, cocaine, as much as legally available alcohol, is becoming accepted as a conventional stimulant.
- Though we associate 'the high life' with the city, drug taking has become socially acceptable, even fashionable, in middle-class suburbia and the country. Viewed in the context of our fast-forward society, – see more, do more, work more, experience more – drugs have become a necessary ingredient within the aspirational mix.

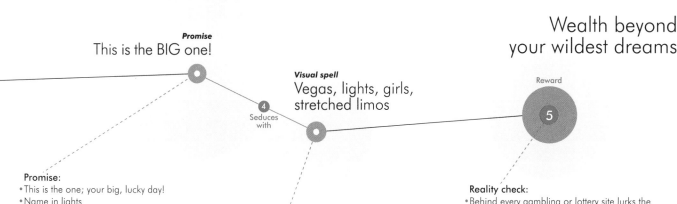

Promise
This is the BIG one!

Visual spell
Vegas, lights, girls, stretched limos

4
Seduces with

Reward
5

Promise:
- This is the one; your big, lucky day!
- Name in lights
- Sudden mega wealth
- Nothing can stop you now
- The tension, thrill of success
- Who says you can't beat the system?
- Big houses, fast cars, pretty girls, drop-dead-gorgeous pool attendants
- Never work again; life of leisure
- The world will be your oyster

Future Vision:
- The increasing dominance of online gambling on the internet, with ever more extravagant rewards for the lucky few will mean more people chasing the dream and a greater percentage of the population hooked and addicted to the game.

Iconography:
- The hot winning number, ticket, roll of the dice, spin of the wheel
- Dollar signs, diamonds, mountains of gold
- Glitter, neon lights, glamour
- Dancing girls, playboy bunnies
- Pink stretched limos, champagne on ice
- Vegas lights, fantasy architecture, fountains

Style/Aesthetic:
- Glam, glitter, gold, girls
- Spend, spend, spend
- Mega millions reward

Reality check:
- Behind every gambling or lottery site lurks the number crunching maths; the algorithm that dictates that you can never beat the system. Such software is designed to ensure that the system consistently takes the lion's share of the haul. Despite this, gamblers are not deterred. Logic doesn't win, luck does. And luck, like fate, can happen to us all – let the mugs take the losses.
- Self-delusion and selective memory (recollection of wins not losses) explains the rest.

SE

SPE

BLONDES & BIMBOS
BASIC INSTINCTS

GIRL POWER
ME-GENERATION

FETISH
FORBIDDEN PLEASURE

CYBER PORN
SUPER SEX HIGHWAY

LADS CULTURE
*F*CK THE WORLD*

Blondes & Bimbos

Despite Raquel Welch's memorable bikini-clad appearance in the film, *1 Million Years BC*, blondes actually first appeared on the scene about 10,000 years ago. Hair grooming in primitive societies was one of the earliest skills. Blonde hair was self-promotion, a 'fitness indicator' (and remarkably, still is…). Since then the association of blonde hair with beauty and pleasure has been engrained by centuries of art and imagery. From Botticelli's Venus, to the 60's icons, Brigitte Bardot and Marilyn Monroe, this is an allure that has remained remarkably resilient to changing fashions. Today, kids are conditioned at an early age. Research has shown that Barbie dolls and the more provocative, Bratz dolls, make young girls aspire to unrealistic images of themselves, their weight and appearance. Though 50 years of feminist campaigning has tried hard to dislodge such sexual stereotypes, more radical action only eroded the cause. Lad's culture bit back with a vengeance. The blonde has returned ever stronger, over populating our media, magazines and billboards. And with peroxide, lip enhancements and silicon implants readily available, this is a look that can be bought by all.

US TV dramas might be well respected for their 'gritty realism', yet even here we find the hospitals, police departments and law courts of America staffed with stunningly capable beautiful blondes.

From garden products to automotive parts, the blonde is selling a vision of something. Even classical music and high-brow opera are exploiting the strategies of pop culture to shift seats. Uncensored media, such as the internet, cyberworlds and mobile entertainment will only multiply this prominence.

Blondes & Bimbos

Basic Instincts

1. Values

Survival of the prettiest

2. Target

Men Only

3. Exploits

Emotions

'I Want'
primordial lust

Fears

A dream that
is unobtainable
(highlights inadequacy)

Obedience To
- World of pleasure and sexual fantasy
- Hedonistic playboy, bad-boy lifestyle
- Blondes are more fun; i.e. 'Up for it'
- Blondes as plaything, entertainment –
  sexually promiscuous and air-headed
- The established western ideal of feminine beauty:
  golden hair, big breasts, size '0' waist
- Lads' world: women created for the
  gratification of men
- Blondes as lifestyle accessory: fawning over bald-
  headed executives, billionaires and wealthy footballers
- Female empowerment (if that means writhing on a
  stage in lurex bikinis)

Rejection of
- Beauty is on the 'inside': people will appreciate
  you for your mind not just your looks
- Natural beauty
- Political correctness and whingeing feminists
- Moral censure and restraint

Emotions
- Powerful, successful men get where they are by
  being sharp-witted, cunning and ever vigilant.
  So what is it about the timeless allure of the blonde
  that makes even the shrewdest spies, most ruthless
  politicians and hard-headed entrepreneurs, drop all
  their defences and risk everything for a tussle between
  the sheets or relief under the table? Lust, the most
  primitive of our emotions, shuts out all rational thought
  and restraint.

Personal Fears
- Blondes come at us with conflicting emotions:
  The unobtainable fantasy – you're inadequate,
  way out of your league
- The sex goddess – danger of the forbidden
- Blonde babes – you're old, she'll only love you
  for your money
- The Femme Fatale – she'll ruin you
- The mistress – scandal in the making

World Fears
- World shortage of peroxide.

4.Seduces with

Promise

Visual Spell

*Playboy lifestyle,
girls, fast-cars,
sex & fun*

Live
the
Fantasy

5.Result

World
of Pleasure

Reality Check
Saturating all forms of contemporary media, the appeal of the blonde
remains undiminished, a dominance that has now moved from the
real world into the virtual.

As concepts of 'female empowerment' crept into the vacuum left over
by the rout of the feminist movement, the freedom to express female
sexuality in Madonna, Christina Aguilera-style erotic stage acts (intended
to challenge the idea of women as passive sex objects), only reinforced
the image of the blonde as sex toy. And girls are toying with such
looks from ever younger ages. The sex-kitten look (fishnet stockings
and pencil-thin shirts), even Peekaboo Pole Dancing kits, have added
to the perception among the new-generation of the erotic industry as
being glamourous and aspirational.

Promise
- For men a life of constant excitement
  and sexual adventure
- Symbol of success, wealth, power: 'you've arrived'
- Status enhancing
- Youth, virility, machismo
- Share in a fantasy world of glamour, hot tubs,
  sunseeker power boats and boys' toys
- Live life to the max – why listen to the voice
  of dull restraint?
- You'll be the envy of your mates, your peers
  and your family
- 'Call me' availability
- What ever is wrapped between my legs you're
  going to buy irrespective of its need, because you're
  gullible and will surrender to your base emotions

Future View
- Blondes are big business. Less than 10% of US women
  are naturally blonde. Girls worldwide aspire to the
  Playboy look. Hair colouring products account for
  an annual $3 billion in sales. Science, both with
  cosmetic surgery and genetic advances, has within
  its sights the ability to create the perfect beauty.
  And in the virtual world, of cyberspace and online
  porn, the Blonde will further increase her global
  hold over the male psyche.

Imagery/Style
- Aspirational ideal of feminine perfection
- Object of worship (sex goddess), object of ridicule
  (pop-tart), object of lust (angelic slut)
- Wannabee celeb, 'do anything for fame'
- Fantasy sex toy, blow-up doll
- Cheerleaders and pop star groupies
- Pole dancers, lap-dancers, wet t-shirt contestants
- Playboy lifestyle, hot-tubs, sunbathing by the pool
- Footballers' wives, Russian gangster molls
- 'Babes' languishing on the sundeck
  of millionaire's yacht
- Staring out of the passenger seat of
  fast open-top sports car
- Californian beach babe: perfect beauty
  with the perfect tan

Dolly Parton

I'm not offended by all the dumb blonde jokes because I know, I'm not dumb. I'm also not blonde.

Andrew Clark
FT Magazine

She looks glamorous, sexy, the dress reeks of haute couture, the pose is alluring. But this is not the latest face of consumer culture: it's Anna Netrebko, starlet of classical music.

Like Vanessa-Mae and Church, Netrebko is being marketed to a mass audience on the strength of her youthful appeal.

Susan Blackmore
The Meme Machine

According to the Amercian author Richard Brodie, memes that deal with sex, food and power all press powerful 'buttons' because of the importance of these topics in our evolutionary past. And memes that press buttons are successful memes.

Mimi Spencer
(asks why women are so fascinated by other women's bodies in Heat and Hello)

Dr Kerry McPherson, offers two explanations for this invasion of body watchers. 'There's the classic sociocultural reasoning – that we are bombarded by images of perfect bodies and we internalise them to the extent that we're assessing everything against that standard. So we're in a constant state of judgement. But also at the heart of everything we do is the drive for perfection. What women are striving for is to look better than the next person; we are all in competition with each other – far more so than with Nicole Kidman. The majority of us realise that we'll never look as good as celebrities, so we choose to outshine our nearest rivals.

George Walden
The New Elites

Diana managed to have it all ways: somehow she persuaded the public to pity her for being stuck in the richest and most prestigious hierarchy in the land, and to pity her for running away with the star-struck son of a billionaire.

Guardian
G2 Magazine

From the pornography women share with their partners, to the way we are sold cars, the exotic landscape is overwhelmingly male. Our culture is suffused with the homogenous imagery that has come to represent what turns men on.

Geoffrey Miller
The Mating Mind
(on the relevance of appearance in sexual selection)

The amplification of female human breast size beyond what was useful for milk production reveals the importance of male mate choice in human evolution. If males had not been picky about their sexual partners, female humans would be as flat chested as chimpanzees.

GirlPower

Ariel Levy
*Female Chauvinist Pigs: Women and
the rise of Raunch Culture*

The women who are really being
emulated and obsessed over in our
culture right now — strippers, pornstars,
pinups — arn't even people. They are
merely sexual personae, exotic dollies
from the land of make believe. In their
performances, which is the only capacity
in which we see these women we
so fetishsize, they don't even speak.
As far as we know, they have no ideas,
no feelings, no political beliefs,
no relationships, no past, no future,
no humanity. Is this really the best
we can do?

Provocative stage acts, where stars aggressively assert their sexuality under the
guise of girl power and new wave feminism, have become a common staple
of girl pop bands and high profile celebs. And for the Madonnas, Britney Spears
and Christina Aguileras of our contemporary music scene, writhing on stage
in a gold latex bikini is empowerment of sorts — a power evidenced by a small
army of cowering sycophantic tour managers, personal assistants, hairdressers,
stylists and bodyguards bending to their every command. But empowerment
for one is an impossible dream for millions. Hopelessly aping their icons by
buying into the raunch culture, pimp chic aesthetic, such dreamy wannabee
aspirants only find themselves as fodder for the great exploitation machine:
internet sites, sex joints, pole dancing clubs and cheap lads magazines, and
its darker side, human trafficking and child prostitution. There's nothing ironic
in sex street.

Me-Generation

Personal Fears:
- Spots, pimples, cold sores
- Bad hair day
- Cellulite, stretch marks
- Mums behaving badly
- Cyber-bullying (social networking sites damning one as a loser)
- Not being recognised
- Being left on the shelf

World Fears:
- What's there to worry about?

1. Values

2. Target

Impressionable *teenage girls*

3. Exploits

Fears

Emotions

Horror of growing dull and old **like one's** **embarrassing parents**

thin sexy cool

self- seeking

Obedience to:
- Having it all: beauty, fame, success, sex
- New found attitude and assertiveness
- Girls are much better than boys
- Self love, vanity, compulsive need for public attention
- Fast track to stardom (*Pop Idol*, *Big Brother*)
- Top rated site on MySpace
- Addiction to glamour and celebrity, (famous for being famous): Paris Hilton, Jordan, Chantelle
- Raunch culture and the new sexual revolution
- Shameless self-seeking and coverage in the gossip columns
- Wanabee rich, wanabee beautiful
- Glamour modelling: *Maxim*, *FHM*, *Heat*, Page 3 in *The Sun*
- Do anything for fame; shagging footballers & stars
- Clubbing, binge drinking
- A new identity every five minutes

Rejection of:
- Failure
- Mummy's girl
- Following in 'goody sisters' footsteps
- Getting a serious education
- Having to work hard for a living
- Life of drudgery, doing the housework
- Traditional romance, marriage and dependence on the 'breadwinner'
- Exploitation; pandering to the male gaze

Emotional Context:
- For young, easily impressionable girls, sometimes from broken families, the promise of instant fame is irresistible as a fast track out of total obscurity to sudden wealth and success. Ability, academic prowess, or intelligence doesn't enter the picture. Neither does the unpalatable reality – 99% will end up as bar girls, waitresses and call girls.

Social context:
- On several fronts, girl power assertiveness is making an impact. In a recent survey of young girls questioned as to their ideal careers, 88% went for either glamour model or pole dancer, as opposed to 6% for doctors or teachers.
- Social competition at school, sexy clothing, toys (Bratz dolls), marketing and MTV combine into a potent cocktail, encouraging small girls to be older younger.
- From computer game heroines such as Laura Croft, to tough man-kicking stars like *Kill Bill's*, Uma Thurman, such tough girl stereotypes have led to a rise in violent teenage girl gangs.
- On the internet, cyber-bullying is on the increase. Young girls can find themselves the victim of a campaign of vitriolic abuse from people they don't even know.

Promise:
- Girls kick ass
- Fast track to success
- Anyone can do it
- Follow your dream
- Don't give up on yourself
- Every girl is a sexy supermodel waiting to get out
- Dressing up as a tart is kind of cool

Future Vision:
Proponents of Girl Power look to a future where women are more independent, can do anything, say anything and be anyone. But are the values of raunch feminism the answer? Binge drinking, girl violence, recreational drug use and underage pregnancies are all on the increase. If this is empowerment, the future of youth is in trouble.

4.Seduces with

5.Reward

Promise

I'm bitchin, I'm *sexy*, I'm cute

Visual spell

Blonde hair, silicone breasts, spray on tan chic mobile

In your Face Empowerment

Reality check
The emotional and commercial pressures on teenage girls are intense. Girl Power provides a way for young women to feel good about themselves and brings a degree of empowerment and independence. But it is also an assertiveness in which raunch culture and provocative clothing are a potent part of the mix.

Exploitation or empowerment? Girl Power thrives on such blatant contradictions. But the central question remains: Is the new pole dancing, porn star chic, real liberation, or a cynical con created by big business (from magazine publishing, TV, fashion and music) to co-opt the whole idea of empowerment for commercial gain?

Iconography:
- Barbie doll blonde hair, silicone breasts, bronze spray on tan
- Vodka cocktails
- Lip gloss, mascara, blusher, tattoos, piercings
- G-String, thong; one time garment of choice of the sex club now mainstream fashion accessory
- Pussycat Dolls video
- Personal webpage – 'I'm bitchin, I'm sexy, I'm cute'
- Tabloid 'shagging footballers' sex scandal
- Flashing your knickers for the paparazzi
- Legless in the doorway of a stretched limo
- VIP room in Chinawhite
- Provocative, ultra-revealing dress that will secure a picture in the tabloids

Style/Aesthetic:
- Glamour gloss
- Raunchy dance routines
- The new face, body on the block
- Hollywood porn-style fame

Fetish

2.Target

Sexual extremists

1.Values

The *wicked* & the *taboo*

Emotional Context:
•Childhood experiences, trauma, even humiliation, have a large impact on the imprinting of future fetishes; the sight of a forbidden stocking leading to a fetish for burlesque; an early infatuation with the TV series, *The Avengers*, may seed a desire for leather catsuits. Photographers such as Helmut Newton and Carlos Clarke stylised and made culturally acceptable, images of bondage, S&M and spanking. Madonna videos made it mainstream, high-street fashion.

Social context:
•One of Freud's earliest patients was 'excited' on seeing a 'certain shine' on the side of somebody's nose. This supports current neurological theory that anything can be endowed with sexual values – from shoes and shampoo bottles, to furry cartoon jumpsuits, even diapers (advertising has long attached emotional tags to products to fetishize commodities). And for those consumed with guilt over the weirdness of their obsession, the internet brought comfort that they were not alone – thousands, if not millions shared their illicit passion.

Emotions

Hedonistic *pleasure*

Fears

Discovery *of dark secrets*

3.Exploits

Obedience to:
•The wicked and the forbidden
•Guiltless, hedonistic pleasure seeking
•Sexual arousal and excitement
•Kinky fashion: rubber, leather, lingerie, high heels, handcuffs, bondage, ropes, body adornment
•Fetish fashionistas and perveratti
•Transvestites and cross dressers
•World of dungeons and torture clubs
•Freedom of expression; in private life, anything goes
•The association of sometimes ordinary objects with obsessive, sexual qualities
•The internet: never-ending super-sex highway

Rejection of:
•Conventional moral values
•Conservative outrage (only betraying guilt over their own sexual conflicts)
•Media censorship
•The bland ubiquity of modern life; safe high-street fashion and dull social behaviour
•Prissy middle-class sensibilities
•Religious censorship (which sees such acts as further evidence of western decadence, moral decline, depravity and sin)

Personal Fears:
•Being considered an oddball, outcast, a pervert
•A life tied to convention
•Dark secrets will be discovered
•Obsessions becoming addictive
•Shame

Promise:
- World of forbidden, erotic, excitement
- Punishment; pleasure through pain
- Wicked, naughty world
- Fun-loving hedonism

Future Vision:
- The world of fetishism will escalate. The internet has given it the perfect medium to proliferate worldwide. Further advances in technology married to new media will strengthen its hold.

5.Reward

Promise

Live out your
wildest fantasies

Forbidden pleasure

Reality check:
Fetish culture has moved from the underground to the mainstream. Previously kinky leather and rubber are now commonplace on the Paris catwalk. Hollywood movies such as Cronenberg's *Crash* introduced the bizarre fetishes mixing technology and pain. Once the imagery of the forbidden has become yet another ingredient in the popular culture mix it loses its currency. And the fetish scene moves on. What's taboo anymore? Who's left to shock?

Visual spell

From dominatrix & bondage
to dogging & furverts

4.Seduces with

Iconography:
- Mainstream fetishes: leather, PVC, bondage, spanking, the dominatrix.
- Freaky fetishes: mutilation, piercing, bestiality, dogging, necrophilia.
- Whacky fetishes: Japanese robot, doll fetishes, furverts (who get aroused dressed up as furry cartoon characters)
- Weird fetishes: Diaper wearing, crush fetishes (deriving sexual pleasure from seeing small creatures being crushed underfoot).

Style/Aesthetic:
- Dark, forbidden
- Underground clubs
- The dominatrix
- Seedy suburbia; the basement torture chamber

CYBERPORN
SUPER SEX HIGHWAY

2.Target

ADULTS
male and female

1.Values

SEXUAL FREEDOM, UNMEDIATED, UNCHECKED, UNCENSORED

Emotions

SEXUAL EXCITEMENT

Personal Fears:
- Guilt
- Fear of discovery
- Porn addiction
- A propensity for something so weird that no one shares my fantasy

World Fears:
- Censorship

Fears

✿ PORN ✿ ADDICTION

3.Exploits

Obedience to:
- It's free
- Anonymity; no shame of a trip to the newsagents
- From car-sex to cartoon sex, it's all on view
- The freedom to explore suppressed desires and hidden interests
- Instant, 'always on' gratification
- Erotic material enhances one's sex life
- Tech liberation: broadband, adult chatrooms, webcams, downloadable media has opened up unlimited opportunities for delivery
- An international language; it's worldwide

Rejection of:
- Nanny state
- Moral censure (those who condemn porn are hypocritical, in denial of their own fantasies)
- Religious condemnation – it will send you blind
- Work friendly software (barring access to x-rated sites)

Emotional Context:
- Deals with a primary emotion – sexual excitement, lust
- The internet, being international and highly popular, delivers sex without judgement; why should I feel guilty if millions share my sexual fantasies?

Social context:
- Although accounting for less than two percent of the internet, sex sites are viewed by more than a third of the adult population, men and women, making it more than a $3 billion-dollar industry. Every year these numbers exponentially increase. Few are prepared to admit their addiction
- In a survey produced by the University of New Hampshire, 42% of US teens had been exposed to porn.
- Not all is negative about porn. The fastest growing audience is women. Some single women feel that the 'pornosphere', together with online dating, is improving their sex lives, empowering them to instigate contacts and explore their sexual fantasies.

Promise:
- One click from sexual excitement
- A world of pleasure, where every fantasy, every fetish, is catered for
- Naughty, exciting, 24/7
- Never ending; something new every minute
- Give us your credit card and it's yours

Future Vision:
- The technology of cyberporn and virtual sex is still in its infancy. A convergence of recreational drugs (sex in a spray), the increased realism of virtual partners and avatars, of any shape and form, together with advances in multi-sensual interactive stimulation (teledildonics), are converging on the perfect sexual experience (the orgasmatron). Neurologists are currently exploring the ability to directly stimulate the brain to create states of sexual pleasure

Promise

ANYWHERE, ANYPLACE, ANYHOW

5. Reward

SUPERSEX HIGHWAY

Reality check
- The full implications of Cybersex have yet to make an impact. This is only the beginning. Sophisticated advances in technology and the internet, combined with powerful commercial interests and an ever-hungry audience are making the industry a runaway juggernaut. Future virtual environments will offer personalised fantasies that will prove irresistibly attractive to individuals either living alone, or locked in uninspiring relationships. But as more people surrender their emotional and sexual selves to cyberspace (where no one says no or suffers from a headache), will individuals lose the need to relate with others and thus the ability to form meaningful relationships with real partners in ordinary life?

Visual spell

MODELS, NURSES, SEX MACHINES, ANIME TOONS

4. Seduces with

Iconography:
- From sexy models, to naughty nurses and dominatrixes
- Sex machines, and bizarre Japanese bondage
- Mobile porn; anywhere, anyplace
- And for women, porn chic empowerment – raunch culture, lap dancing and pole dancing
- Sex den in Second Life
- Toon sex: Hentai, Anime
- Fashion porn: bedroom fantasies
- Kinky sex toys: rabbits, vibrators, fleshlight

Style/Aesthetic:
- Kinky, voyeuristic
- High-class, high-gloss art-house porn
- Amateur (one night in Paris)
- Gonzo porn (extreme adult content with zero plot)

LADS CULTURE

F* the World**

Joseph LeDoux
The Emotional Brain

James Averill describes a behaviour pattern called 'being a wild pig', that is quite unusual by western standards, but is common even 'normal' among the Gururumba, a horticultural people living in the highlands of New Zealand. The behaviour gets its name by analogy. There are no undomesticated pigs in this culture, but occasionally, and for unknown reasons, a domesticated one will go through a temporary condition when it will run wild. But the pig can, with appropriate measures, be redomesticated and returned to the normal pig life among the villagers. And in a similar vein, Gururumba people can act in this way, becoming violent, aggressive, looting and stealing, but seldom causing harm, and eventually returning to routine life after with no memory of the experience and is never reminded of the event by the villagers. – westerners are prone to think of this as psychotic abnormal behaviour, but for the Gururumba it is instead a way of relieving stress and maintaining community health in the village.

Jonathan Margolis
The Guardian G2,
November 2002

Jones gave evidence last year that helped Kenneth Kinnard of Glasgow successfully appeal against a breach of the peace conviction after Kinnard told an Edinburgh traffic policeman to fuck off. Lord Prosser agreed that Kinnard, 43, was only using the 'language of his generation'.

We all have inner defense strategies to hide or shield our insecurities and anxieties. For lads, daily besieged by conflicts and concerns, they shroud their defeats, conflicts and humiliations in relation to the rest of the world in drink and acts of aggression to those who they deem responsible for their condition: authority, middle managers, poncey intellectuals, parents, school teachers, gays and feminists.

Fuelled by cheap girlie magazines, such as *Maxim*, *Loaded* and *Nuts*, lads are not just sold a distortion of what women are and what they want, but an equally pernicious and damaging distortion of what maleness and masculinity is all about; that you have to drown yourself in alcohol, laugh at every fart and engage in acts of mindless machismo to be a 'real' man.

It is the sentiment that their ills are caused by others that makes this social class an easy target for political extremists, bigots and racists. Politicians will often decry the disruptive antics of yob culture undermining the social fabric of the country. But come election time, no party is beyond making an appeal to 'core support' by taking a stand on issues such as immigration or stoking nationalism with anti-Europe rhetoric.

LADS F*CK THE WORLD CULTURE

1. Values

ACTING THE PIG

2. Target

THE MOB

Emotions

LIVE IT UP WHILE YOU CAN

3. Exploits

Fears

PENALTY SHOOT-OUTS CLOSING TIME

Obedience to:
- Old school machismo; blokey, bullish, belligerent
- Tribalism; identifying with the pack
- 'Acting the pig', 'Living it large', 'men behaving badly'
- Attention seeking
- Just having a laugh
- Self-gratification
- Adrenalin of confrontation and aggression
- Provocative, abusive language
- Zapoi: the Russian art of getting pissed and unconscious as rapidly as possible
- Women as sex objects: 'show us your tits'
- 'The beautiful game' (sports, football etc)
- No nonsense guy – 100 percent authentic bloke

Rejection of:
- Conservative wankers
- Boring, nagging parents
- Gays and ponces
- Upper-class twits
- Grey suits, bureaucratic bullshit and authority
- Spineless middle management
- Johnny foreigners
- Liberal, holier-than-thou, limp, intellectual lefties
- Fat slag feminists
- Political correctness
- Crying or showing emotions (for wimps and ladyboys)
- Moral prudes; in denial of their 'true' instincts
- Low-fat malarkey

Emotional Context:
- The soullessness and monotony of unrewarding work and home life can cause loss of motivation, lack of pride, and low self-esteem. Personal failings and frustrations find release in irresponsible behaviour and acts of mindless violence and aggression. Getting drunk with the mates, a scuffle in the streets and chanting abuse at the big game provide the solidarity and a sense of belonging so missing in tame, conventional life.

Social context:
- A lot of the anger is engendered by disadvantage; unaffectionate family upbringing, lack of male authority figures, violent parents and career exclusion through lack of qualifications.
- The social science view lays responsibility for the actions of rebellious young people upon society, blaming failures in the educational system, lack of opportunity and an over-competitive career environment.
- Fearing the showing of emotion as weakness, 'lads' are often shutting out the social support that can sometimes prevent disruptive behaviour.

Iconography:
- *Loaded* magazine
- Kebabs, curries, beer and lager
- Friday night on the piss
- Mooning
- Porn/internet/top-shelf mags
- Big tits, big arses
- Wet t-shirts, pole dancing and lap dancing
- Shagging
- Real blokes
- The beautiful game
- Big bikes and cars

Style/Aesthetic:
- Provocative, loud, abusive
- Brash, in-your-face graphics, lack of style
- Corny chat-up lines
- Gratuitous sexual imagery
- Fuck the world, live for the moment

4.Seduces with

Visual spell

LIFE'S ONE BIG PISS UP

5.Reward

REAL MAN
NOT FAUX MAN

Reality check
Lads Culture is a label primarily created by lads' magazines, *Loaded* and *FHM*, who believe lads culture, though crude and crass, to be harmless fun, just having a laugh, and an honest reflection of male attitudes, as opposed to the limp spectre of 'metrosexual man', propagated by *Guardian* readers. In part Lads Culture is a reaction against new wave feminism and what were perceived as 'double standards'. It was ok for girls to talk dirty about men, but men would be bitched about for relatively minor transgressions such as leaving the loo seat up.

Promise

THE WORLDS RUN BY PONCES, SUITS, POLITICALLY CORRECT CRAP. THEY'VE NO RIGHT TO TELL YOU WHAT TO DO

Personal Fears:
- Social inadequacy
- Academic underachievement
- Peer pressure – run with the mob
- Job insecurity
- Debt
- Threatened by the success of women and those from ethnic minorities
- Fear of showing weakness or excessive emotion
- Not getting enough – a sad loser in the sexual rat race
- Latent homosexual tendencies – forcing greater displays of overt machismo

World Fears:
- Closing time
- Penalty shoot-outs
- Being tamed by political correctness

Promise:
- Tough guy number one
- Allegiance to the group: run with the pack – run with the mob
- In a world dominated by health and safety officials, political correctness and feminism (that created the stay-at-home, diaper-changing metrosexual man), lads' culture, of having a laugh, going on the piss, living it large, provides the only outlet for the real man. The ideal of asserting one's own manly ideas against the small mindedness of middle-classdom – obediently washing their cars on a Sunday or chatting round wood-burning stoves – is as compulsive as ever.

Future Vision:
- The real world is under seige; live for the moment

FEEL G

SPE

YOU'RE BEAUTIFUL
BUYING HAPPINESS

UNDER THE KNIFE
SURVIVAL OF THE PRETTIEST

BODY & SOUL
STYLE NIRVANA

GOOD

LLS

CLICK FOR LOVE
BITE-SIZED ROMANCE

HAPPINESS INDEX
PERFECT JOY STATE

NEW AGE CULTS
THE GUIDING LIGHT

YOU'RE
BEAUTIFUL

Buying Happiness

It's well known that we are hard wired for good looks. Pretty women, firm breasts, healthy hair and symmetrical faces all provide clues to those who have a better chance of rearing healthy children. Tall, muscle-bound men promote equally dependable attributes. So it's not surprising that away from the harsh plains of our ancestors that our contemporary society, despite the feminist movement of the 60's, is as lookist as ever.

On a recent ABC programme 20/20 in the US, two actresses were hired to investigate if great looks gave the prettiest preferential treatment. In the 'girl in distress' scenario, having to change a tyre at the side of a motorway, the blonde received 12 times more attention than the plain girl. Inside a charity fund-raising event, again the blonde was able to shift 50% more product than her less attractive counterpart.

Such shallow favouritism can only further benefit the beauty industry, who argue that beauty remains a woman's most tangible asset. An asset that can be used to secure a great job as much as a great husband.

It's quite clear how beauty advertising works. A daily diet of the rich and beautiful creates a state of insecurity in us all — implying that we don't measure up — then it dazzles us with a range of products with which to achieve this goal. To conceal the fact that it's vanity, they make it fun, hip and cool.

What's new, big biz will say — women have been adorning themselves for three thousand years. Fair enough if we are talking about the occasional luxury. But the beauty products fix amounts to an average spend in the UK of more than £200,000 over a lifetime (enough to buy a small house). A single dermatology treatment in New York can sell for as much as $20,000. French manufacturer, Clarins, has warned women not to wash in tap water. Naturally they sell 'pure' water blended with mint and peach for $20 a bottle. More extreme measures like botox, liposuction and cosmetic surgery, now becoming mainstream, may more than double this 'lifetime' spend.

YOU'RE BEAUTIFUL
THE BUYING OF HAPPINESS

girls,
women,
(and now men...)

1. Values

beauty liberates,
EMPOWERS

2. Target

LOOK AT ME
GLAMOUR

Emotions

Fears

I LOOK TOTALLY SHIT
NOBODY LOVES ME

3. Exploits

Obedience to:
- Glamour, sex, success, eternal youth
- Beauty liberates, empowers
- It's a lookist world; beauty gets the job, the man and the money
- Perfection is attainable (at a price)
- Turn heads, attract attention, get your man
- Who needs reality?; live life like the stars/celebs
- Go for it, glamour and fun
- Draconian diets and fitness regimes
- A fantasy world; liberation from the mundane, a promise of perfectibility – always make the most of yourself – you deserve it
- (With rock chicks to movie stars rushing to endorse products, from lipstick to miracle creams, the beauty spell of sex, fame and fun is hard to resist; be plain Jane or glamour queen)

Rejection of:
- Natural beauty
- Getting old gracefully (nothing graceful about wrinkles)
- Modesty and restraint
- Grunge, anti-style
- Men will like you for who you are (a delusion – men are genetically attuned to luscious lips, blonde hair and big breasts – you'll need all the help you can get)
- Unflattering brightly-lit interiors or restaurants

Emotional Context:
- The emotional appeal of beauty remains the same: to be drop-dead gorgeous, stand out in a crowd, be desired, have strong sex appeal, be envied, have handsome suitors fighting for your attention

Social context:
- Peer pressure and a competitive youth environment (school) introduces beauty products at an ever younger age. The new aspirational size zero body shape is responsible for a rise in eating disorders and anorexia.
- TV media, together with style, fashion and gossip magazines, endorse the association of youth and beauty with excitement, happiness and popularity. Running in parallel, a portrayal of older people as being infirm, of being a social burden, sad, grumpy and lonely, induces a negative view of old age.
- Much of the consumption of beauty products is by middle-aged women fighting to maintain fragile youth – from anti-aging creams and make-up, to face lifts and botox. This is as much to maintain competitive looks at the office (with bright new things joining the payroll) as to please husbands at home.

Personal Fears:
- 'I look awful – no one gives me a second glance'
- Looking plain, losing one's looks, being unnoticed
- Being left on the shelf, abandoned, forgotten
- Appearing dull, boring, uncool, unfashionable
- Being alone, not belonging, excluded from the 'cool gang', considered a social failure
- Having low self-esteem, no confidence
- Feelings of sexual inadequacy
- 'Nobody loves me', 'nobody fancies me'
- (With the rich and beautiful brought into the intimacy of our homes though Reality TV and lifestyle magazines, concerns that we don't measure up, that we are always overshadowed by others who are better, become that much more acute.)

World Fears:
Only young once

Iconography:
- Centre of attention
- Beautiful, happy, sexy, young, successful girls
- A world of physical perfection; well-toned bodies, glistening hair, all-over tan
- Glamorous locations, film sets, white beaches, loft apartments, mansions on the Riviera
- Italian photographers/paparazzi
- Playboy lifestyle, sports cars, private jets, limos
- Lingerie/swimsuits, cocktails by the infinity pool
- LA girl size 'O' body shape

Style/Aesthetic:
- I'm a successful movie star/model, but I owe my success to…
- On the move, on the go, carefree, living life to the max – gawping men in my wake
- Seductive colours and tones
- High-gloss photography

Visual spell

LIFE AS
ONE LONG COMMERCIAL
PERFECT LIFE,
PERFECT LOOKS

Promise

IMAGINE A WORLD
IN WHICH YOU'RE
DROP-DEAD
gorgeous

4.Seduces with

5.Reward

Centre . of the
universe

Reality check:
Playing off fears of inadequacy and self-esteem, the beauty industry (from the manufacturers to the publishing empires that depend on them for advertising) escalates competition between women. Its message is stark: in the race to become attractive, you can't be left behind. The question is, how obsessive can such concerns become, as 'Barbie' drugs, and cosmetic surgery become the front line in the battle for perfection.

Promise:
- Novelty, 'the new new', the must-have 'look'
- Transform yourself from plain Jane to sexy siren
- Reinvent your mundane life
- Be loved, appreciated and adored
- Alleviate suffering/dispel the blues
- Indulge in guilty pleasures
- Beauty brings success and popularity
- Hip to be thin

Future Vision:
- The cosmetics industry is aiming at the Barbie drug – not only do you lose weight, you also look great, and feel sexy. Cosmetic surgery, previously the domain of the jet set, is becoming common practice. It is also having an impact on ever younger girls, begging their mums for the nose jobs, breast implants and lip enhancements that will bring happiness and love for the rest of their days.

The Economist
(Americans spend more on beauty than they do on education.)

Nancy Etcoff, a psychologist and author of *Survival of the Prettiest*, argues that 'good looks are a women's most tangible asset, exchangeable for social position, money, even love. But, dependent on a body that ages, it is an asset that a woman uses or loses.'

The emerging beauty industry played on the fear of looking ugly as much as on the pleasure of looking beautiful, drawing on the science of psychology to convince women that an inferiority complex could be cured by a dab of lipstick.

Vanessa Wilde
(Harrods Beauty devotee, takes issue against the critics of beauty), *Sunday Times Style*

Actually they're the ones who are seriously vain – all those disapproving types who look down on body maintenance and make you feel that low-lighting is a sin against the holy ghost, for God's sake. I think it's unbelievably vain of anyone to think they're so fantastic they can be accepted as they are.

As far as I'm concerned, vanity is just another word for perfectionism. And perfectionism means obsession. Nobody seems to think it's wrong being obsessed with work or organic food or sex or status or achievement, so what's wrong with being seriously into how you look?

Geoffrey Miller
The Mating Mind

Our sense of beauty was shaped by evolution to embody an awareness of what is difficult as opposed to easy, rare as opposed to common, costly as opposed to cheap, skilful as opposed to talentless, and fit as opposed to unfit.

Robert Adler
The New Scientist, The Pigeonholed

Paul Davies of the University of Waterloo in Ontario, which is known for its science and engineering programme, examined the impact of stereotype loaded advertising on young women studying maths there. They had all described themselves as being good at maths, and that this was important to them. But Davies found that watching two sexist television commercials quashed the ability of female, but not male, under-graduates to solve difficult maths problems. In a second experiment, female undergraduates shifted the subject they said they would like to specialise in away from the sciences after viewing the advertisements. The same ads also caused these highly motivated young women to avoid the leadership role in a two-person task.

Michael Stebbins
Sex Drugs and DNA

Studies have shown that men are more attracted to women with a hip to waist ratio of 0.7. This is a weird concept, but it holds up across cultures and time. Even as trends in weight differ over time, the most attractive women generally are the 0.7s. Skinny women, voluptuous women – it doesn't matter, the 0.7 wins. This is likely a reflection of our innate perception of fertility, as prepubescent girls do not form hips and thus do not have 0.7 ratios. The same is true for post-menopausal women who lose their hour-glass shape.

John Emsley
Vanity, Vitality, and Virility

As we get older, the boom of youth fades. Our skin gets thinner, loses its elasticity, becomes dryer, and develops wrinkles. What we want is something to rub on it that will restore its smoothness, add tautness, and remove the lines of age. Every year, new products are launched claiming to do just that, and sales of cosmetics and toiletries now exceed $30 billion a year in the United States, and probably more than twice that world-wide, their sales increasing in line with the world's ageing population. The cynics will say that this is mostly money wasted, that nothing can reverse the slow duration of the skin. They would be surprised to learn, however, that some anti-ageing creams really do work, albeit to a limited extent.

under the ✂ knife

2.Target

vain young
and
old things

1.Values

survival of the
prettiest

Emotions

beauty
'buzz'

Fears

bitch friend
getting a better
boob job

3.Exploits

Obedience to:
- Beauty: how you look, the shape of your body, is one of your greatest assets; use it, or lose it
- Shameless narcissism (why not feel great about yourself?)
- You don't have to accept the looks your were born with – perfection is possible
- Turn back the clock; rejuvenation, self-enhancement
- Barbie, Playboy perfection
- Aspirational world; make the most of yourself
- If you don't believe it see the before and after shots (though careful positioning of the lights can achieve the same wrinkle-free look)
- Getting them young; internet game, Missbimbo.com, where young girls can 'buy' virtual breasts and facelifts to compete to become the coolest bimbo on the planet

Rejection of:
- Natural beauty (ok to say if you are blessed with great looks – but most of us are not)
- People will love you for your mind (yeah, sure)
- Aging gracefully (anathema)
- Beauty is only skin deep (no: it's hard wired into hunter gatherers – and now they drive Porsches)
- Don't mess with nature – you are the way God made you (and God gave us the ability with which to develop cosmetic surgery)

Emotional Context:
- With the retreat of feminism, its nemesis, lookism, has transformed contemporary values. Our society rewards beauty, and we are prejudiced against those who aren't beautiful. Those who look good, look young, are chosen over those who do not. This is as true for jobs as it is for relationships.
- No longer the shameful secret that it once was, cosmetic surgery has become part of mainstream beauty. Those fixated on such procedures get a 'buzz' from their new looks – like getting a new hairstyle. And like a new hairstyle, it's a buzz that fades, leading to a desire for ever more enhancement.

Social context:
- Celebs and pop culture, remind us every day to use our assets – great looks, and a great body, will find you fame and wealth. But it's not just an advantage in career life. One's looks have a significant effect on performance at school. Research has shown that both teachers and parents pay more attention to better-looking children, thereby raising their confidence and thus their ability to deliver better results. No surprise then that more teenagers are getting self-esteem boosting surgery as part of their birthday presents.

Promise:
- Transform your humdrum life
- Youth; roll back the years
- Barbie-girl looks
- Buy beauty: botox, liposuction, face lifts and implants
- Turn heads on the beach
- Be the envy of your friends
- Get the man of your dreams
- Cosmetic op holiday (surgery in the sun)
- And for men: cut the fat, brow lifting, penis enlargements

Future Vision:
- The number of those undergoing cosmetic surgery is accelerating at record speed. Advances in technology will mean faster, cheaper, more sophisticated and less painful operations. With the ability of the majority to alter their looks, will beauty become homogenised, leading to a world populated with blonde, saccharine lookalikes?
- To compliment your new looks, future drugs will not only make you feel happy, but sexy too.

Personal Fears:
- Looking shit
- Feeling inferior, loss of self-esteem
- Looking unsexy
- Being unloved
- Social competition – at school and at work
- Old age; another birthday on the horizon
  (letter to an agony aunt in the *Observer* newspaper:
  "My 18th birthday is approaching, I feel hideously old as if my life is at an end")

5.Reward

young
until you die

Reality check:

To transform one's looks has always been a fantasy for women. Now cosmetic surgery makes it possible. Why, they ask, if you are ugly, condemn yourself to a lifetime of setbacks when cosmetic surgery can transform your prospects and thus your future happiness? Popularized by the media, cosmetic surgery, once a luxury, is now mainstream, as natural as going to the hygenist. In a BBC Radio 1 programme, Newsbeat, 51% of young women said they would have surgery to improve their looks. The net result, more young girls and women will be spending a higher proportion of their income in the new race for beauty – one of the prime addictions of the 21st century.

Promise

celeb lifestyle

4.Seduces with

Visual spell

barbie girl
in a bikini

Iconography:
- Sexy surgeries, doctors and nurses
- Gorgeous, beautiful, perfectly-formed celebs, rock musicians, films stars, supermodels
- Playboy lifestyle; fast cars, stunning babes, hunky men, yachts and beach culture

Style/Aesthetic:
- Fame, wealth, sex and success
- High-gloss cool

Body & Soul
Spiritual Sustenance

Personal Fears:
- I'm unfit, over stressed, putting on weight, getting old, looking shit, nobody loves me
- Worn down by the pressures of modern life, I feel 'empty' inside
- Like a holiday tan – the benefits of a spiritual detox fade as soon as you get back to the office

World Fears:
- Population explosion; overcrowded world, see it while you can

2.Target

1.Values

3.Exploits

Fears

Stressed,
young professionals

Soothing seclusion

Modern life crushes the sprirt

Emotions

Leave it all behind

Obedience to:
- The inner you; peace of mind, stress-free calm, tranquillity
- A life-changing experience
- Balance with nature
- Zen, eastern philosophy; restore your spiritual equilibrium
- Food for the soul
- Vitality, rejuvenation
- Detox; your body is a temple
- The ultimate escape: exotic private sanctuary, crowd-free exclusivity
- For once, indulge your senses; be loved, cared for, spoilt and pampered

Rejection of:
- Mass tourism; crowds, coach tours, noise and cars
- Pressure of work/modern life
- Family stress – looking after the kids (school run, homework)
- Polluted cities and congestion
- The corrupting power of society, government and mass culture
- Financial and emotional anxieties

Emotional Context:
- The spa proposition uses disarming language; you're stressed, overworked – kids, husbands, boyfriends demand your time. Leave it all behind, spoil yourself, you deserve it. Look after number one – be cared for, be loved.
- For a life-changing experience the cost should not be a consideration (you've got the rest of the year to pay off the extravagance).

Social context:
- The spiritual message of Eastern philosophy was simplicity – to transcend egotism, status seeking and the pursuit of sensual pleasures.
- Ok, no one would pretend that the luxury spa is going to be monastic in discipline. So why the mumbo jumbo, the monks chanting, the silly undecipherable treatment names? It's theatre, a smoke screen, a veneer of exoticism to conceal what is essentially, extravagant old school pandering. Real solitude and inner peace is a night on the beach.

Iconography:
- Celeb, supermodel clientele
- Designer yoga pyjamas
- Yoga and Tai Chi on the beach at sunset
- Remote island retreat, white sand beaches, azure seas, infinity pools, palm-thatched villas
- Muslin curtains, candles, tinkle of bamboo chimes, Buddha images, chakras, incense, marble baths strewn with rose petals
- Neat shelves of massage and aromatherapy oils
- Asian fusion cooking
- Indecipherable Asian manuscripts and charts

Style/Aesthetic:
- Where east meets west
- Muted earth tones, ethnic sculpture, natural materials
- Soft golden light, dreamy solitude, distant world music

Visual spell

Tai Chi at sunset

Promise

Detox for body & soul

4.Seduces with

5.Reward

Style Nirvana

Reality check:

Originally the province of cheap, hippy, ashrams, modern spa retreats and wellness centres have become a highly effective revenue generation formula for the international five-star hotel industry. Its architects and designers have plundered the east for its visual style book, happily mixing images of the Buddha with those of Chairman Mao. This is the hippy trail reinvented for $850 a night, with a superficial sprinkling of spirituality and mysticism (available as an exclusive range of special potions and creams at reception).

Promise:
- Love yourself
- Find the 'real' you
- Reawaken the senses; balance your mind and body
- Be purified; detox for the body and soul
- Regenerate your spirit (chi)
- Feel like a goddess
- Sensuous pleasure, wellness and blissful relaxation
- Back to the womb comfort
- Leave the 'noise' of modern life behind

Future Vision:
- As the work world becomes more stressful, the promise of health, youth and the soul, becomes more attractive. Now offered as part of the corporate package for over worked executives, the wellness industry, propelled by an army of management gurus and PR, will be perfecting their strategy for the future; luxury 'green' spas, fractional ownership clubs, retirement paradises for the baby boom generation (well it sounds better than old people's homes…)

Click for Love

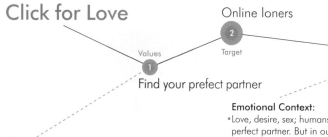

Online loners
2
Target

Emotions
Romance, love, lust

Fears
Connection failure

1
Values

Find your prefect partner

3
Exploits

Obedience to:
- Love in the tech age: online dating, chatrooms, social networking sites
- Ease of use: log on, type your name, start dating
- Bite-sized romance — log off when you want to
- It's impersonal — on the Internet no one knows you're a dog
- Future love; alter ego in Second Life. Hang out with your 'real' friends
- Power of the word; text and e-mail allow you to express your truer feelings and emotions. You're in control
- Socialisation, rather than data, is emerging as the primary use of the web

Rejection of:
- Formal dating (too slow…)
- Mother knows best (yeah, right…)
- Waiting for the right one (I could wait until my dying day…)

Emotional Context:
- Love, desire, sex; humans are hard wired to find their perfect partner. But in our goal-oriented workplace where it's difficult to find the time for romance, more people in the West are staying single for longer. Online dating fulfils the need for time efficient 'click on off' relationships. Rather than waiting anxiously by the telephone, or for the early morning post, the computer becomes the focus of our emotional anxieties — "you've got mail".

Social context:
- From an activity that was nonexistent ten years ago, Internet dating impacts on more than 70% of single Internet users in the US. Of course it has its drawbacks. Online you can only type and message, you can't judge people by their looks. Those who have found love online argue that this can be an advantage; it's cheaper and safer to assess someone by personality, interests and sense of humour first, without being distracted by appearances. Women especially feel more in control of the process and less threatened.

Personal Fears:
- Home alone (by 2025, 50% more people will live alone)
- No e-mail, no love (millions of people are spending more of their lives in front of a computer — and many will be wishing they weren't alone)
- Meeting nutters, psychos, and freaks
- When the fateful meeting does occur — 'let's get together for real', the reality may fail to match up to the online fantasy of bronzed Adonis or drop-dead gorgeous blonde

World Fears:
- Connection failure

Happiness Index

1
Values

Quality of life, of wellbeing

2
Target

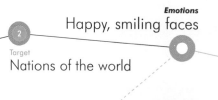

Nations of the world

Emotions
Happy, smiling faces

Fears
No money, no mates, no love

3
Exploits

Obedience to:
- The search for the allusive happiness equation: an optimum state of health, wealth, comfort and friends
- Such a formula when applied to a country produces 'gross national happiness', as rated by the happiness index
- Accordingly, nations should look beyond economic success and work to improve the contentment of their people (Victorian philosopher, Jeremy Bentham, posited a theory on moral action which provided for 'the most happiness to the most people')
- Happiness can be taught: the happiness formula
- Happiness can be bought — finding contentment in material possessions and luxury
- Happiness can be induced — new designer drugs like Prozac and the growth of cosmetic pharmacology

Rejection of:
- Anxiety, stress, excessive labour and work
- Conflict, anger, antagonism, hatred
- Discomfort
- Financial concerns, debt

Emotional Context:
- Most of the decisions we make in life are guided by trying to optimize our happiness. An industry of self-help manuals and magazines offer diverse paths towards contentment, or ways to suppress the 'trouble makers of our mind': anxiety, stress and discomfort. Author Alain De Botton argues that we might be better off being productively unhappy. A sentiment echoed by Nietzsche who decried our obsession with comfort, arguing that unhappiness is a state that gives happiness its meaning.

Social context:
- Even in the most remote village, Western entertainment, its soaps and advertising, convince people that the secrets of happiness lie in aping modern standards of living. It is the West's most successful and addictive influence. Yet an endless portrayal of beautiful smiling people, popular culture and advertising has perversely become a driving source of global dissatisfaction. By diminishing our innate sense of well-being, the aspirational world has directly contributed to an increase in gross international unhappiness.

Personal Fears:
- No direction: life going nowhere
- Job uncertainties, status, financial security
- No money, no mates, no love
- Positional worth; measured by material possessions — home, car, TV
- I am woefully inadequate. (Advertising exploits such anxieties by its portrayals of the cool and comfortable, seeding feelings of inadequacy in the majority who fail to live up to these standards)
- No family, no friends — our present-day obsession with individuality and personal success has only increased loneliness, shutting out the 'wealth' and benefits of community

World Fears:
- Global misery (terrorism, poverty, climate change)
- Conflict and War

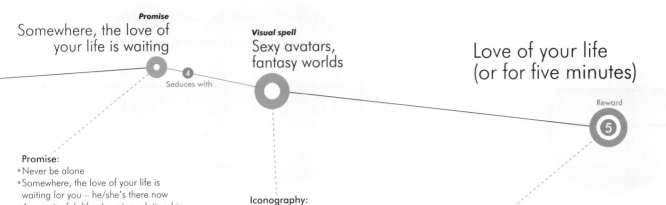

Somewhere, the love of your life is waiting

4
Seduces with

Sexy avatars, fantasy worlds

Love of your life (or for five minutes)

Reward
5

Promise:
- Never be alone
- Somewhere, the love of your life is waiting for you – he/she's there now
- A meaningful, life-changing relationship is but a mouse click away
- It's fun, exciting, sexy
- Live out your fantasies

Future Vision:
- With more online communities, interest groups and virtual worlds opening for business, the landscape for romance is going to multiply. Animated avatars, and the ability to engage in cybersex, will expand the experience of these virtual worlds. Technology will ensure that one's emotional engagement online will become more sophisticated and realistic. But with so much instantly on offer online, will people feel less inclined to put up with the complexity of a relationship in 'real' life?

Iconography:
- Jaw droppingly gorgeous male and female avatars in Second Life
- Pure escapism: every fantasy catered for, fairy-tale castles, cool discos and bars, futuristic cities, romantic landscapes
- Note the new terminology:
"Fun loving" = sex maniac
"Professional" = fat and balding
"Young in spirit" = granddad

Style/Aesthetic:
- Vast diversity: from cold, mechanical match-making databases, to surfing communities, cartoon badlands, even Christian interest groups.

Reality check:
- In several cultures world-wide, parents decide future husbands and brides. Now you trust your love life and happiness to an algorithm. Online chat rooms and games are often built around shared interests and themes. Dating services claim that because of the huge numbers involved (more people than you would ever meet in a lifetime of trawling the local bars) you are more likely to find the love of your life online. And the search is global.

Goodbye to misery

The sun always shines

4
Seduces with

Perfect joy-state for all

Reward
5

Promise:
- Smile on your face
- The sun always shines
- Jumping for joy
- Life of fun and relaxation
- Leave your troubles (fear, stress, anxiety) behind

Future Vision:
- Ever since the 'soma' of *Brave New World*, chemists have searched for the happiness drug. Products like Prozac acts on neurotransmitters and led the way in treating disorders such as depression and anxiety. But beyond the therapeutic benefits, normal healthy users are turning to the drug to make them 'feel better than good'. And if certain drugs boost self-confidence and contentment, who wouldn't want to try them?

Iconography:
- Happy, smiling, contented families, dogs and small babies
- Happy, smiling, contended locals
- The perfect home, every material, designer comfort, kitchen appliance and time-saving gadget
- SUV, sports car, parked on the forecourt
- Happiness in a pill

Style/Aesthetic:
- Whether at the kitchen sink, a high-street bank, or weeding the patio, popular culture's 'joy state' is ubiquitous. From cars to personal electronics to lavatory cleaners and beauty creams, our products promise contentment, fulfilment and (dare we say it) happiness.

Reality check:
- Has the weight of popular commercial culture so distorted our understanding of well-being that we have confused happiness with lifestyle and its symbols of luxury? Daily tempted by the latest novelties, we work harder to afford the things we believe will improve our lives. Once secured and made commonplace, they lose their special caché and thus their appeal. Thus we become trapped in an acquisitive spiral, in which we compete with others to achieve higher status. In the end, everyone loses.

NEW AGE CULTS

Felipe Fernandez Armesto
Truth

A modified version of Father Brown's curse, however, seems to be coming true: when people stop believing in something, they do not believe in nothing, they believe in anything. Crackpot cults prosper.

Patrick French
Younghusband

At least one Tibet-inspired mystical work had proved to be fraudulent: the clairvoyant Tibetan Lama Lobsang Ranya, author of the highly successful 'The Third Eye', turns out to have been a Cornish plumber called Cyril Hoskins.

The intention of *Mesmerization* was to highlight the most persuasive and dominant cultural spells that impact on our lives. But seen in another light, this book is also a catalogue of states that frame fears and anxieties. The big global mind-numbing concerns – Frankenstein science, GM food, global warming and terrorism – sit side by side with a relentless stream of dream imagery from the lifestyle world. Measured against this daily diet of the most wonderful, the wealthiest, the sexiest and the most beautiful, it is easy to feel small, diminished, a total loser.

The evils of 'mindless materialism' and the relentless pursuit of power, comfort and money, feature prominently on the websites of the thousands of new wave cults that have spread over the internet. Each peddles their own variant of the true way, the spiritual path and the new enlightenment.

Francis Wheen, author of 'How Mumbo Jumbo Conquered the World – A Short History of Modern Delusions', writes about the rise of New Age cults in the modern age: "The new irrationalism is an expression of despair by people who feel impotent to improve their lives and suspect that they are at the mercy of secretive, impersonal forces, whether these be the Pentagon or invaders from Mars. Political leaders accept it as a safe outlet for dissent, fulfilling much the same function that Marx attributed to religion – the heart of a heartless world, the opium of the people. Far better for the powerless to seek solace in crystals, ley lines and the myth of Abraham than in actually challenging the rulers, or the social and economic system over which they preside. Ever since idealist philosophers such as Hegel and Schöpenhauer denounced the demythologising spirit of modernity, empirical analysis has always been opposed by those who fear that the stripping away of illusions can only end in miserable disillusion."

Personal Fears:
- Sense of loneliness, of being unloved
- Spiritual void inside
- Disillusionment with life
- Sense of abandonment
- Emotional conflicts (parents/boyfriend)
- Depression

World Fears:
- Judgement Day
- The new coming
- Global conflict and the coming Apocalypse

2.Target

THOSE DISILLUSIONED
AND WORN DOWN BY
MODERN LIFE

Fears

EMPTINESS INSIDE

1.Values

REDISCOVER
YOUR
INNER SELF

Emotions

TO BE SAVED,
TO BE LOVED,
TO FIND
SPIRITUAL FULFILLMENT

3.Exploits

Obedience to:
- Guiding light in the darkness
- Rediscover your soul
- Attain spiritual wisdom, knowledge, understanding
- You are born with special gifts, unrealised talents and abilities
- Let go of negative thoughts – anger, envy, hatred
- Self-fulfillment, self-expression
- Mystical ideology, eastern symbols and cryptic scripts
- Animism and superstition
- Balance with nature and the environment
- Holistic, faith cures
- Horoscopes and astrology: your fate is in the stars
- Other enlightened worlds are out there
- Faiths are beyond criticism
- Conspiracy theories: The Da Vinci Code, Nostradamus
- Ley lines and stone circles

Rejection of:
- Money, materialism and the comforts of consumerism
- Pain and suffering of the modern world
- The decadence and mindlessness of contemporary mass culture
- The established 'old school' faiths
- Self-seeking society
- Doubt or scepticism (betrays weakness, immaturity, you are not ready to be chosen)
- Rationalists, scientists, atheists, or accusations of brain washing

Emotional Context:
- Though the very idea that belief might have a neurological basis is anathema to religious people, there is mounting evidence that this might be so. Recent advances in mind science lead credence to the theory that your propensity to subscribe to irrational ideas, may be due in part to your brain chemistry. People with high levels of dopamine are more likely to ascribe profound meaning to what are in reality insignificant events and to see narratives where there are none.

Social context:
- Many things have contributed to the new irrationalism. Quantum physics has made science indecipherable. Eastern mysticism baffles us – 'everything can be said to be true, you just have to find the sense in which it is true.' The academic vogue for relativism and non-judgementalism, undermines our faith in the empirical nature of truth. Together with the decline of secular values the road lay open for a mass of charlatans and fake gurus, all peddling their own variants of salvation and the 'inner' truth. And 'modern life', constantly overloaded with global fears, niggling anxieties and daily assaults on our self-esteem, provided the essential humus.
- Cults are cash, making money out of our fear of abandonment.

Iconography:
- You at the centre of powerful cosmic forces
- Guiding light in the growing darkness
- Ever-present image of the mesmerising, charismatic, benevolent being
- A juxtaposition of the positive – sun, serenity, nature, trees, small animals (under the gaze of the omnipotent one) – with destructive earth-bound evils – big business, the power of money, sex and sin, pollution, wars and suffering

Style/Aesthetic:
- Guiding light
- Future paradise and redemption
- Peace and inner harmony
- Sustenance and salvation for the soul
- The gathering storm is coming – be saved before it is too late

Promise:
- Transform your miserable life
- Bubble bath for the Soul (Francis Wheen)
- Be part of an exclusive inner circle
- Cure for suffering and unhappiness
- Purpose and self-fulfillment
- Recognition of your worth
- The inner truth
- Salvation and redemption
- Comfort in community
- Love and peace for the chosen few

Future Vision:
- With the worldwide spread and dominance of the misinformation highway, where content has neither been verified or mediated by editors, experts or academics, conspiracy theories and crap cults abound. Blogs and community network sites will add to the drift towards sensationalism and the new irrationalism.

Promise

BE PART OF THE
EXCLUSIVE
INNER CIRCLE

5. Reward

SOMEONE TO WATCH OVER YOU

PROTECTION
UNDER THE GAZE OF THE ALL-SEEING BENEVOLENT ONE

Visual spell

4. Seduces with

THE
CHOSEN
FEW

Reality check
From the White House to Number 10 Downing Street, our age is marked by a new irrationalism. In the vacuum created by the demise of mainstream religion in the western world, even the most mind-bogglingly absurd narratives can take hold (The Moonies, and the teachings of Deepak Chopra come to mind). Such creeds might argue that their narratives are no more absurd than Hindu beliefs (the churning of the sea of milk), or even Christian beliefs (Elisha's great Chariot of Fire). If you deny the rights of existence of one you deny them all.

NEW
AGE CULTS
THE GUIDING LIGHT

THE BEACH
THE FANTASY THAT SUSTAINS US

SUNSHINE
ITS A WONDERFUL LIFE
FLIGHT FRENZY
COME FLY WITH ME

LONELY PLANET CROWD
RACE FOR EXPERIENCE

THE GREAT OUTDOORS
FREE SPIRIT

The
Beach

Kerry Lorimer
Code Green

Every seasoned traveller has a story about a magical place they knew 20 years ago – the deserted beach, the remote mountain village, that has succumbed to rampaging development or has been ruined by too many backpackers and package tourists.

Contrary to popular belief, we haven't always felt at ease on the beach. Haunt of debauched pirates, smugglers, rapists and brigands, it wasn't the ideal place for a family picnic. Even our 'healthy' celeb look, with the all-over perma-tan, was regarded as a sign of being common, of having to toil in the fields for a living. Little did the first eccentric bathers of Victorian seaside towns realise that their unorthodox pursuits would become so global and ubiquitous. The world travel industry today is a $500 billion business – and much of that is a rush to the sun.

Powerful Hollywood movie imagery of Burt Lancaster rolling in the surf with Deborah Kerr in *From Here to Eternity,* the iconic bikini-clad Ursula Andress emerging from the seas of the Caribbean and Pamela Anderson running in gratuitous slow motion through the waves in *Baywatch* cemented the allure of the beach into the global psyche. Such fantasies are daily mass produced in thousands of travel magazines, online sites and books. The promise of the beach is compelling – the virgin purity of the sand (conveniently washed clean by the midnight tide), nonchalant palm trees, languid branches dipping in the water, aquamarine skies and turquoise seas, all unspoiled, serene and yet to be discovered. Such images suggest the availability of this perfect exotic escape to the world's travellers. And every year, tens of millions will set out on their quest of discovery.

The Beach

The Fantasy that Sustains Us

Personal Fears:
- Personal well-being and health
- Stress of balancing family and work
- Disillusionment with work, anxiety over future direction, status and self-worth
- Self-doubt; there must be more to life
- No room on the beach
- Storm at sea
- Sharks, sea snakes, jellyfish
- Tsunamis
- Being ill on holiday

World Fears:
- The world is becoming overpopulated and overexploited
- Global warming
- See it while you can
- World terrorism
- Global epidemics
- Natural disasters: tsunamis, earthquakes, hurricanes

1.Values

Instant Getaway

2.Target

Sun-seeking
Hedonists

3.Exploits

Fears

Dreary monotony
of work and city life

Emotions

Solitude,
time to reflect,
unwind,
let yourself go…

Obedience to:
An escape from the monotony of real life
Just reward for a year's hard graft
The romantic, exotic getaway
Total indulgence; the luxury beach villa
Live-it-up hedonism; sun, sea and sex
Discovery, adventure and (the promise of) uncharted territory
Meet new people and places
Spiritual journey of self-discovery, a quest for the authentic, lonely planet nirvana
Breathing space; chance to re-evaluate one's life

Rejection of:
The soul-destroying drudgery of 9-5 work
Being chained to your desk and computer terminal
City life, the rat race, competitive consumption
Financial stress, debt and the complexity of modern living
City life and pollution
Grey, gloomy, depressing skies

Emotional Context:
The beach holiday was invented as a retreat from the fast-forward stress of city life. It was a time to do nothing, slow down, drift and be aimless. But even such rare moments of solitude have come under seige. Promotions, shopping bargains, bungee jumps and jet skis, now vie for our attention; the beach as playground guarantees that you will never have a dull moment.

Social context:
The sea has always held an emotional resonance; from classical culture (the Iliad), to romantic painting (Turner, Caspar David Friedrich). The sea symbolises purity, escape, new horizons and opportunities. Contemporary culture promotes the beach as a world that is unspoiled, untouched and unpopulated. The 18-30's culture, of blokes, girls in bikinis, wet t-shirts and all night clubbing, changed all that. Sex and hedonism became a potent part of the aspirational mix. And as small island airports stretched to accomodate the wide-bodied 747's, previously remote locations opened their doors to the swelling crowds.

5. Reward

A glimpse of paradise

Reality check:
The world's most enduring cliché never loses its power to seduce. It's an image that populates travel and lifestyle magazines, television shows, retirement brochures, insurance literature, sales promotions and fashion centre spreads. But the beach is an illusion -- the ideal rarely exists. It is a fantasy, a metaphor for a perfect state, a glimpse of paradise, that keeps us hopeful and sustains us through the daily 9 to 5, a modest dividend for a year of conformity, obedience and graft.

4. Seduces with

Promise

Live it up:
sun, sea, sand, sex

Visual spell

Virgin sand,
palm trees,
cloudless skies,
beauty in a bikini

Promise:
Escape to the sun
Live it up: sex, sun, sand, alcohol
Spiritual high; recharge your soul
Back to nature: ethnic villas, swimming with fishes,
sea-shells as currency
A metaphor for life – perfection awaits us

Future Vision:
With the rise of affluence, worldwide millions will imitate this originally Victorian leisure pursuit and beat a path to the sea. As a result, the human race has never travelled so far and so cheaply. And they are all heading to the one perfect beach. Reserve your space on the sun lounger now…

Iconography:
• Palm trees, cloudless skies, perfect virgin sands
• Turquoise seas, coral islands and reefs
• Californian beach culture; perfect tanned beauties, windswept hair, sunglasses
• White umbrellas, whitewashed villas, infinity pools
• Exotic locals, simple fishermen, colourful boats and bamboo huts
• Grilled seafood on the barbeque, cocktails and ethnic music
• Rush to the shops; the latest holiday fashions, sandals, wraps (in the UK alone, £7bn is spend on beach fashion)

Style/Aesthetic:
• The perfect beach
• Soft, seductive light
• High-gloss imagery
• Bright saturated colour
• Deserted landscapes
• Unspoilt environments

Sunshine

It's a wonderful happy life

① Values

Holiday makers

② Target

Emotions
Feel great

③ Exploits

Fears
Grey, gloomy cloud on the horizon

Obedience to:
- Beautiful, warm, life-affirming sunshine
- Happy state
- Fun, outdoor lifestyle
- Sunbathing/all-over tan, all of the time
- Feel great
- Looking beautiful and sexy
- Relaxation, warmth, total bliss and happiness
- Line up for the 'perfect' photo opportunity
- Sun lounger by the pool, trash chic novel
- Suddenly life has meaning, purpose

Rejection of:
- Grey, lifeless, gloomy skies and the despondency that it brings
- Clouds on the horizon spoiling the moment
- Cold front, rain, falling temperatures
- Staying indoors
- Being stuck in the office

Emotional Context:
- A scientific basis underlies the way sunshine affects our mood. Sunshine stimulates the pineal gland in the brain triggering the release of tryptamines, feel-good hormones.
- Sunshine also effects our health; Vitamin D is essential for building up the strength of our bones and muscles. Lack of sunshine has even profounder effects: feelings of depression, 'the winter blues', a sense of misery, the cause of conditions such as SAD.

Social context:
- Our world-wide obsession with the sunshine state is relatively recent in our social history. In the past having tanned skin was considered to be a mark of being a peasant. Today such values have been turned on their head. To look pale is to look like someone who is deskbound, too poor to enjoy the good life.
- The frequency and weight of media imagery in TV, films and advertising, links sunshine to a state of happiness, of status, wealth, beauty and health. These values are now becoming global and ubiquitous.

Personal Fears:
- Looking tired, looking worn
- Having an unhealthy appearance
- Missing out on the goodlife

Rational Fears:
- Link with sunshine and skin cancer (50% of Australians will develop some form of cancer during their lifetime)
- Exposure to sunlight risks the development of cataracts in the eye
- Sunstroke and dehydration

World Fears:
- Global warming
- Rising sea levels

Flight Frenzy

Come fly with me

① Values

② Target
World traveller

Emotions
New life, experiences, things to see

③ Exploits

Fears
Catastrophic engine failure

Obedience to:
- Fly anywhere, any time
- Escape to the sun
- Last-minute weekend getaway
- Do something extraordinary, go somewhere new
- Leave it all behind, hop on a plane
- Spirit of adventure, do something exciting
- Romance of flight (exotic capitals, mountains of Nepal, Serengeti Plain)
- Take home memories (100s of holiday snaps and mind-numbing anecdotes to bore people at dinner parties)

Rejection of:
- Flying is dangerous (per passenger mile safer than other modes of transport)
- Airlines are big polluters (why pick on us – merchant ships put out a third more carbon than planes)

Emotional Context:
- Travel has always been one of life's great pleasures: the excitement and novelty of flight, the escape from routine, the exposure to new experiences, cultures and people. Now it has become ubiquitous the novelty has worn thin. Different emotions surface: impatience, anger, fear, discomfort, boredom, more of the same… luggage in Estonia.

Social context:
- The aeroplane is one of mankind's most extraordinary inventions. Air travel has transformed the globe. No longer the domain of the elite, ordinary people can move around the world when they want, where they want. The travel industry is now a massive 500 billion dollar business. And with China and India joining the rush for a place in the sun, holiday travel looks set to explode.

Personal Fears:
- Flight delayed/cancelled
- Seats overbooked
- Passport expired
- Storms, sudden air turbulence
- Engine failure
- Oxygen masks; 'brace, brace'…
- Luggage gone astray
- Sitting next to a very large person/crying child

World Fears:
- Hi-jacking
- Global terrorism
- Climate change
- Horrific air crash

Promise
Come out to smile

Seduces with — 4

Visual spell
A life outdoors, sun-cream, ice cream, daydream

Symbol of happiness

Reward — 5

Promise:
- Perfect state of happiness and contentment
- Live for the moment (while the sun shines)
- All-over tan; youth, vitality and health
- The appearance of success, status and wealth
- Future hope, optimism
- Glamour and the playboy lifestyle: supermodels, celebs, Hollywood starlets and studs

Future Vision:
- Increased global wealth, in particular in China and India, will mean we will travel more, to the same places, at the same time of year. Join the crowds.
- Though sunshine promises escape and relaxation the reality is flight delays, lost luggage, broken-down coaches, traffic congestion, tourists herded like cattle, the queasy aroma of sweat and suncream: global swarming.

Iconography:
- Sex, sand, sun
- White beaches, tropical islands, palm trees
- Beautiful people
- The Mediterranean jet-set lifestyle: yachts, café life, beaches
- Celeb style: sunbeds and fake sun-tans
- The outdoor life: games, gardening, sundeck and patios, barbecues

Style/Aesthetic:
- A life of luxury, fun and leisure
- Cloudless, perfect skies
- Optimum state of happiness

Reality check:
- Have we become so conditioned by modern media's association of sunshine and the good life that our ability to experience the world, appreciate beauty, take smiling photo snaps, feel content and happy has become governed solely by the state of the weather? Will the first signs of rain make us rush for the Prozac?

Promise
Destination fun; when you want to go, where you want to go

Seduces with — 4

Visual spell
Smooth, cloud free skies, smiling, blonde air stewardesses

The world is your oyster

Reward — 5

Promise:
- Carefree travel; comfort, peace, dream and doze
- Your home in the sky
- We'll care and look after you
- Reunite you with your loved ones
- Arrive refreshed and ready for business
- Pampering; luxury that reflects your high status
- The world is your oyster

Future Vision:
- The building of bigger planes (the 600-seater Airbus 380) and larger airport hubs, have already anticipated the massive rise in future air travel. But clouds are on the horizon; the environmental lobby are rightly focusing on high carbon emissions from air travel. A year's worth of virtuous activity – recycling, bicycling, buying eco products and turning off the lights – can be blown away in a single international flight. The hard truth is, we need to fly less, flying needs to be more expensive and polluters must pay.

Iconography:
- Cloud-free skies
- Smiling, beautiful, capable, air stewardesses
- Captain dependable at the helm
- Comfy, do-anything seats
- Gourmet meals
- Airmiles

Style/Aesthetic:
- Speed
- Stress-free
- Smooth as silk travel
- Peace, comfort, tranquillity
- Planes as things of beauty

Reality check:
- The image airlines like to portray is of the serenity, calm, comfort and beauty of flight. Contemporary air travel is anything but – the hectic rush to the airport, parking, queues at baggage check in, grumpy passport officials, lengthy security searches, fighting for seats, cramped conditions, boot camp rations, air traffic delays and lost luggage. And that's before you get to the beach…

Lonely **Planet** Crowd

Primo Levi
The Periodic Table

What was the point of being twenty if you couldn't permit yourself the luxury of taking the wrong route.

Orhan Pamuk
Istanbul: Memories of a city

(on our western obsession with finding beauty in old buildings and decay) None of these things look beautiful to the people who live amongst them; they speak instead of squalor, helpless, hopeless neglect. Those who take pleasure in the accidental beauty of poverty and historical decay, those of us who see the picturesque in ruins — invariably, we're people who come from the outside. (It was much the same for the northern Europeans who lovingly drew the Roman ruins while the Romans themselves ignored them.)

Alain De Botton
The Art of Travel

From 1799 to 1804, Alexander von Humboldt undertook a journey around South America, later entitling the account of what he had seen *Journey to the Equinoctial Regions of the New Continent*. Nine years earlier, in the spring of 1790, a twenty-seven-year old Frenchmen, Xavier de Maistre, undertook a journey around his bedroom, later entitling the account of that he had seen *Journey around my Bedroom*. Gratified by his experiences, in 1798, De Maistre undertook a second journey. This time, he travelled by night and ventured out as far as the window-ledge, later entitling his account *Nocturnal Expedition around my Bedroom*.

The temple of Angkor Wat in Cambodia, by virtue of the fact that it lay locked in a war zone since the 1970's, has come relatively late to the travellers agenda. It fufills all the demands for the experience-seeking world traveller; exotic ambience, ancient mythology and culture, together with photogenic ruins and people. Watching the sunset from the top of the Phnom Bakheng temple was one of those 'small' moments of solitude experienced by a handful of the first visitors to the site, just after it reopened its doors to the outside world.

It was a whisper that became a flood. Amplified and duplicated across hundreds of guides and online sites (a Google search brings up eight hundred thousand results), this previously solitary experience has now become a 'must see' part of the Great Angkor experience. Coaches deliver their daily compliment of tourists, and the thousands now jostle for position on the slippery steep steps leading to the top of the temple, digital cameras at the ready.

Rare experiences have become like a checklist of life's essentials: the son et lumière at Giza, the trek up Machu Picchu, or photographing the elephants on the Serengeti. As the world's tourists surge through these exotic destinations, photograph the quaint locals in their decrepit, run-down huts, race through their food and snap up the ethnic gifts on the rush back to the airport, how much of what we encounter makes any sizeable impact on our lives or holds any meaning? Do we see more but end up seeing less?

Lonely Planet Crowd

Race for experience

1.Values

Voyage of discovery, spirit of adventure

3.Exploits

Fears

The 'soul-destroying' MODERN WORLD

2.Target

20–50 somethings

Emotions

See it before work, wife, kids and mortage steal your life

Obedience to:
- See the real world
- Exotic travel, romance, adventure, exploration
- Find yourself; a spiritual, mystical experience
- The hippy trail
- Hangout, trust to fate, chance encounters
- Happy-go-lucky; hitchhike around the world
- World music and local art and culture
- Gap year (18-something), sabbatical (30-something), mid-life crisis (50-something)
- Well-thumbed edition of Kerouac, Ginsberg, Steinbeck

Rejection of:
- Crowds and mass tourism
- Coach parties
- Package, organised tours
- Family holidays
- Job for life
- Deskbound work
- Cities, pollution, congestion

Emotional Context:
- The emotional allure of the hippy trail was both the promise of adventure and rebellion. It was freedom from nagging, concerned parents, officious school lecturers and middle managers. To travel the world was to reject the straightjacket of conventional society for the independence of the open road; go anywhere, do anything, be yourself, be free, escape.

Social context:
- It was the intrepid explorers such as Wilfred Thesigner and Laurens van der Post, followed by the 60's hippies, who came back with images of the beauty, nobility and simplicity of ethnic life in exotic destinations. Today such images have become the symbols that we, as global nomads, seek out. The grass hut, the dusty village kids, the old ox carts, the decrepit buildings have become a backdrop for a thousand digital photos recording the 'purity' and 'innocence' of traditional cultures. This is a romantic interpretation of the landscape. Its harsh reality is poverty, helplessness, corruption, lack of medical care and clean water.

Personal Fears:
• Mass tourism and crowds
• Western brands and culture crowding out the local
• Money being stolen
• The return ticket
• Parents turning up
• Debilitating illness
• Killer snakes, fish and spiders

World Fears:
Global terrorism
The march of globalisation smothering
indigenous cultures
Global warming (see it while you still can)

5.Reward

The great escape

Reality check
As we jet off to the former hippy retreats of South America,
India and South-East Asia in the search for the exotic and the
undiscovered, we will follow in the footsteps of thousands who
have bought the same guidebooks, booked into expensive faux
ethnic villas, sat through interminable tribal dances and rushed
to join the queue for the 'must see' essentials – the most beautiful,
the oldest, the largest – whilst the smaller insights remain ignored,
negating any real engagement with the culture or people.
In the race for rarer more exclusive experiences we have
never travelled so far and so frequently, directly contributing
to the endangerment of the natural and ethnic diversity we
profess to protect.

4.Seduces with

Promise

REMOTE PLACES,
PEOPLES, CULTURES;
the experience of a lifetime

Visual spell

Small children,
wizened ancient people,
dilapidated old wooden huts

Promise:
• Escape
• Chance on the undiscovered
• Off the beaten track
• Experience of a lifetime
• Memories that will stay with you forever
• New cultures, remote places, unspoilt beaches
  and villages
• Peace, solitude and nirvana for $5 a night
• Spiritual enlightenment

Future Vision:
• Lonely planet no more

Iconography:
• Jungles, deserts and mountains
• Magic Bus
• Indigenous people (Indian, Masai, Thai hill tribe)
• Anything remote: Patagonia, Kathmandu,
  Machu Picchu, Marrakech, Rajasthan, Goa,
  Thailand, Mongolia
• Age of Aquarius
• Exotic wildlife and environments
• Picturesque poverty; dilapidated wooden huts,
  ramshackle buildings, run down interiors and
  ancient rusty cars
• Local produce and markets

Style/Aesthetic:
• Escape from modern life
• Return to simplicity and the innocence
  of primitive and traditional cultures

The Great Outdoors

Free spirit; live for the moment

Obedience to:
- Ditch city life for adventure & discovery
- Go with the flow, be a 'free' spirit, live for the moment
- Authentic, simple living
- Self-discovery
- Respect for nature
- Freedom from commitment
- Fulfilment; express your true creativity
- Foraging for mushrooms; live off the land
- Old ways were better
- The emotional versus the rational
- Mobile phone free

Rejection of:
- Ownership
- 9-5 work ethic
- Status & wealth
- Materialism & consumerism
- Grey suits & bureaucracy
- Corporations & the rat race
- Modern life/technology
- Cities & pollution
- Mass production
- Processed food

2. Target

YOUNG,
disillusioned with the
empty values of
contemporary lifestyle

Fears

LOSS OF IDENTITY
in the
CONSUMER AGE

Emotions

Search for authenticity,
MEANING
& TRUTH

Be one with nature and the environment

1. Values

3. Exploits

Emotional Context:
- The emotional allure of the Great Outdoors stems from a sense of disillusionment with the competitive and meaningless values of the modern lifestyle. An inability to find purpose can cause people to opt out of contemporary society and turn instead to the purer values of simplicity and honesty, in a search for inner truths and a return to nature; the noble traveller.
- Hemingway-esque ideals pervade the concept of the Great Outdoors – the fight for what is right, the struggle for the right path, to protect the girl.

Social context:
- As nuclear annihilation receded as a global fear, concerns over the environment and global warming combined with increased competition at work and rises in employment hours, prompted a move away from the contemporary 'work till you die' western lifestyle. Answers were to be found in living in harmony with nature, a return to simplicity, the purity of eastern religions, and a return to primitive culture (Indians, Masai warriors etc – even though such ideas might border on ignorance and intolerance).

Personal Fears:
- Stress of work
- Loss of identity
- Becoming socially excluded
- Becoming subsumed within the system
- Modern life crushes the spirit
- Competitive social and work environment
- Exploitation by 'the system'
- Career failure

World Fears:
- We must put the brakes on
- If we carry on the way we are, depleting the world's resources and destroying nature, we are all doomed

Iconography:
- Mother Earth/Gaia
- Tents/teepees/wooden shacks, Indian rugs
- Farms and camp fires
- Unexplored hills, pine forests
- Long, windswept grass
- Horses, dogs, cattle
- Fluffy clouds & eagles
- Misty-eyed dishevelled girls, muscle-bound men
- Jeans, cowboy hats, suede
- Acoustic guitars/mouth organs
- Shelves of homemade jams and pickles
- Asian mysticism/Zen

Style/Aesthetic:
- Cities as polluted, overcrowded, corrupt, against the ideal of the country; a pastoral idyll, living in balance with nature
- Muted, sepia tones, hint of nostalgia
- Soulful youth
- Open expanses, distant, dreamy horizons

Visual spell

MISTY MOUNTAINS, CAMP FIRES, SANDALS, FORAGING FOR MUSHROOMS

4. Seduces with

5. Reward

Promise

Freedom, individuality,

the 'real' you

ECOTOPIA
OVER THE HILLS

Reality check
The imagery of the great outdoors promises remoteness, authenticity, a sense of adventure and discovery. Yet this is also the imagery of big business, as likely to promote a return to nature in some gas guzzling 4x4, the latest must-have trainers or high-tech clothing range. What remains of the real outdoors is under seige. And every year we scour the globe and use more air miles in the hope of unearthing some last outpost untouched by the modern world.

Is the Big Wilderness quest overrated? As Ranulph Fiennes once remarked, you can go to Everest and find yourself queuing, yet at the base of Ben Nevis there's no one to be seen.

Promise:
- Freedom from city strife
- Find fulfilment, creative expression, eternal optimism
- Experience 'real' life
- Self-sufficiency
- Manliness
- Commune with nature
- Mind/body holism
- Spiritual purity
- 'Head for the hills'

Future Vision:
- Ironically a mass migration to the outdoors would massively exacerbate our ills (country houses consume greater energy, more people would overstress the fragile environment). Making cities greener, less polluting and more energy efficient is the central challenge for our future.

LIFES

COMFORT
LIFESTYLE PERFECTION

MODERN LIVING
STYLE UTOPIA

SPE

STYLE

RETAIL THERAPY
SHE'S GOT TO HAVE IT!

ETHICAL CONSUMER
SAVE THE PLANET

LLS

Comfort

Lifestyle perfection

Will Hutton
The World We're In

The average new American house is now 2200 square feet, having expanded from 1,500 square feet in 1970 as the middle-class trades up to meet the new standards of opulence.

Ed Douglas
Writing in the New Scientist in an article, Better by design

The consequences of our fickle ways can be found in landfills everywhere. Americans use and throw away 2.5 million plastic bottles an hour. The British produce enough garbage to fill the Albert Hall every 2 hours. According to the authors of *Natural Capitalism*, Paul Hawken, Amory Lovins and Hunter Lovins, only 1 percent of all materials flowing through the US economy ends up in products still being used six months after manufacture. The waste entailed in our fleeting affairs with consumer durables is colossal.

The history of civilization can be charted as a steady inflation in our standards of comfort. Over the millenia mankind has moved from a hard rock in a damp cave to the designer 'must have', the Le Corbusier chaise longue. Since the Second World War Western countries have seen a sharp rise in living standards. Evidence of these new levels are everywhere: the temperature of our houses (constant heat in winter, chilled interiors in summer), ever-more luxurious materials on our floors and furniture, new fashions and shoes, the rich variety of food and drinks we consume, the cars we drive (now with climate-controlled interiors, heated seats, even heated steering wheels), and the comforts we demand when we travel (flat beds and masseurs on transatlantic flights).

Cosseted by our lifestyle, the real world doesn't really intrude. The comforts of the home become a retreat, an oasis, a safe haven from the harsh, dangerous and threatening world outside. But such luxuries also make us complacent, risk averse and toothless for adventure. Our dependence on material wealth together with our own very special modern problems of obesity, binge drinking, and drugs, further reinforces the perception in anti-Western eyes that the West has become gutless, gorged on luxury, insensitive to the problems of the poor and suffering in the Third World.

Personal Fears:
- Losing it all; financial misfortune, divorce, fire
- Household stains from children, animals and drunken dinner guests
- Paradise lost; a tear on the designer furniture
- The world beyond your door (anti-social behaviour, street violence and rising crime)

World Fears:
- Climate change, environmental and natural disasters (floods and earthquakes)
- World financial crash
- Global terrorism, anarchy
- (The 9/11 attack in the US and the 7/7 bombings in London have caused a retreat to the home, increasing needs for greater comfort and luxury)

Comfort

LIFESTYLE PERFECTION

1.Values

Cocoon living

2.Target

Aspiring middle class

Fears

Emotions

Feet up in front of the telly

The world outside the door

3.Exploits

Obedience to:
- Paradise at home
- Self-indulgence, luxury, the comforts of a modern, western lifestyle
- Interior perfection: the latest styles, Italian furniture, hi-tech kitchen gadgetry, walk-in fridge freezer, widescreen entertainment
- Wellness: stylists, spas, health weekends, exotic villa escapes
- Comfort food: luxury indulgences, Champagne, Belgian chocolates, foreign delicacies
- Cocoon culture: risk adverse, stay at home, lock the doors, curl up in front of the widescreen telly
- Booming house prices – potent symbol of pride and security

Rejection of:
- Back to basics – the simple things in life are best and sometimes free
- Make do with what you've got
- Post-war austerity (saving, recyling, patching up the old sofa)
- Delayed gratification
- Unnecessary consumption
- Modesty as a governing virtue
- Saving for a rainy day

Emotional Context:
- As individuals we have always sought happiness. Material possessions and the comforts they provide are often confused with this goal. Likewise to pursue comfort by avoiding discomfort is as pointless as seeking happiness by steering clear of unhappiness. One state is given meaning and resonance by its opposite. A hot bath has stronger appeal after a cold walk. A good meal after periods of abstinence.

Social context:
- From clothes to food, from furniture to home entertainment, the soft, the warm, the cuddly, the cute, combined with our obsessions over cleanliness, soothe our senses and make us feel good about ourselves. Never a static state, our ideas of comfort are always inflating. Greater luxuries are always, temptingly, just over the horizon. And the more comforts we enjoy, the more fearful we are of losing them.

Iconography:
- Designer living
- State-of-the-art kitchens, walk-in fridge-freezers, dustbusters and soft-wipes in the cupboard
- Widescreen TV, leather three-piece sofa set
- Soft Italian lighting
- Exotic sunken baths and power showers
- Luxury executive cars, leather interiors, heated seats, in-car entertainment systems
- Luxury spa travel, pampering, hedonism, body and soul wellness regimes

Style/Aesthetic:
- Soft, muted tones
- Perfect carefree existence
- Not a detail out of place
- Interiors populated with happy families
- Harmony, balance and symmetry

5.Reward

Paradise at home

Visual spell

Walk-in fridge-freezer,
42" tv
with surround sound, designer sofa

4.Seduces with

Reality check

Historically intellectuals have decried decadence. Social scientists, such as Werner Sombart, found the bourgeois obsession with comfort (shying away from the tragic in life) made man unheroic, gutless and mediocre. Religious narratives, whether of Babylon or the Great Flood, have equated the accumulation of wealth and comfort with greed and sin, inviting God's retribution. Today, environmentalists have framed the profligate consumer as the guilty party behind our climate concerns, as the price of what we regard to be acceptable standards of comfort and contentment continue to inflate.

Promise

Comfort,
cleanliness,
convenience

Promise:
- Safe haven from the dangerous world outside
- Paradise home: design and control your little perfect world
- Warmth, happiness, comfort and contentment
- A life of relaxation, indulgence and hedonism
- Soothe your problems away
- Put your feet up

Future Vision:
- The perfect world is always a purchase away; the softer sofa, the larger Jacuzzi, the brighter flat screen TV. Inflated norms of comfort, cleanliness and convenience, drive our spiralling consumer consumption and thus our needs for energy, directly contributing to the rise in CO_2 emissions, one of the the prime causes of global warming
- The cure; not simply cutting back, but a retreat from comfort, consumption and cleanliness

Modern Living

Style utopia

It's close to a hundred years since the invention of modernism as an architectural and design style by visionaries such as Walter Gropius and Le Corbusier at the beginning of the 20th century. Over that period the modern style has slowly evolved to become the central aspirational residential style. Its look encompasses both expensive and sophisticated Italian manufacturers, together with the mass-produced lines from popular retail stores such as Habitat and Ikea. What explains this success? Why have we globally turned against traditional indigenous styles and cultures in favour of a common international *Wallpaper** look?

Alain de Botton, writing in *The Architecture of Happiness*, explains this shift in aesthetic choice by reference to the writings of the German Art historian, Wilhelm Worringer, in an essay, *Abstraction and Empathy*. De Botton examines such changes from a psychological perspective; 'The determinant lay, he believed, in those values which the society in question was lacking, for it would love in art whatever it did not possess in sufficient supply within itself'. A rush for the modern aesthetic and style in contemporary times betrays similar anxieties and pressures. Unsettled by the world that is beyond our control – crime, civil disorder, poverty and terrorism – we retreat to a comfort zone we can organise and hone to perfection.

In Asian societies the rush for the International style reveals different concerns. Turning their back on traditional values is a rejection of a past. Ethnic masks and carvings might appear cute to western eyes, but to a younger demographic, who are but one generation away from the fields, such entities symbolise a past of struggle and hardship. And from Shanghai to Bangkok, that past is rapidly disappearing under tons of concrete.

Modern Living

Style utopia

Emotional Context:
- The modern look, written in our possessions, identifies and promotes who we are: young, forward thinking, successful, progressive, hip and stylish. But it is also a clear statement of who we are not: boring, staid, conservative, traditional, old, a failure.
- In its comforts and visual appeal, modern architecture and interiors can make us feel good about ourselves, fill us with pride and provide us with environments in which to be happy. But such happiness is tied to our need for perfection; how rapidly can the slightest blemish on the Italian furniture darken our mood and shatter our frail self-esteem?

Social context:
- Modernism was a movement defined by the inter-war years. It was fired by a utopian desire to create a better, more egalitarian world, through reinvention and simplicity in design.
- Across Europe, Tyler Brule, founder of *Wallpaper** magazine, reignited the Modern look. Unlike previous style publications, *Wallpaper** presented a truly global vision of lifestyle: architecture, dreamy interiors, design, but also fashion, beauty, cuisine, and travel. And its ideas became ubiquitous.

1.Values

THE
COMFORT ZONE

2.Target

YOUNG AFFLUENT,
INTERNATIONAL
AESTHETES

Emotions

IT'S WHO
YOU ARE

3.Exploits

Fears

BLEMISH
ON THE ITALIAN
FURNITURE

Obedience to:
- Lifestyle utopia in glass, steel and concrete
- The latest chic designer look
- Apartment / loft living
- World of cool, calm, ordered perfection, populated by dazed, young and beautiful people
- My home is my statement
- From the lemon squeezer to the toothbrush holder, no detail overlooked
- Under the influence; living by the dictates of coolhunters, design gurus and lifestyle bibles
- Cool destinations; hip, designer hotels and chic retreats

Rejection of:
- Middle-class values
- Fussy Victorian ornamentation
- Sentimental family heirlooms
- Cheap, mass-produced products
- Student hovels
- Dull conformity and tradition
- Disorder and chaos

Personal Fears:
- Messy kids, friends, lovers
- Animals in the house
- Wine stains on the Italian furniture
- The mother-in-law coming to stay
- Street violence and crime (fears over our safety are creating an architecture that is inward looking, defensive, obsessed more with security and seclusion than community)

World Fears:
- Curl up on the sofa, fire up the LCD screen, lock the doors, keep the chaos of the world outside (terrorism, conflict, poverty) at arm's length.

Iconography:
- Italian furniture: latest from Milan
- Glass and steel, wooden patios
- Infinity pools
- Latest tech gadgets: iPod, B&O
- Design hotels, chic spa retreats, bars and clubs
- Bikini-clad models (furry in winter)
- Child-free (mess free) lifestyle
- Super-star designers: Starck, Tom Dixon, Jaime Hayon

Style/Aesthetic:
- International modern: Paris, Milan, Shanghai
- Glossy Wallpaper look
- Simplicity and precision of materials
- Less is more
- World of perfection, comfort and beauty, unsullied by the 'real' world
- Cutting-edge cool
- Cloudless skies, golden light

Promise

HAPPINESS IN ORDERED PERFECTION

5.Reward

YOUR PLACE WITH THE BEAUTIFUL PEOPLE

Reality check

The modern style, in homes and architecture, is one of the West's most invasive and potent spells, effortlessly sweeping aside indigenous and traditional cultures to become the dominant, affluent, international style. The modern look becomes a reflection of what we want to be, that goes beyond style. In a world that is fraught with complex concerns (from terrorism to tax inspectors), we retreat to a cocoon that is calm, cosseting, ordered and thus anxiety free.

DESIGNER DREAMWORLD, POPULATED WITH ETHEREAL MODELS AND TASTEFUL (BUT MOSTLY USELESS) PRODUCTS

Visual spell

4.Seduces with

Promise:
- Happiness in lifestyle perfection
- Individualism; a life less ordinary
- What's hip, what's cool
- Move with the 'in' crowd
- You've arrived
- Surrender yourself to comfort, pleasure, hedonism
- Your inner sanctum

Future Vision:
- Modern living promises greater efficiencies, improved insulation, greener fridges and bio-tech washing machines. At the same time our houses get bigger, our fridges fatter, and our televisions double in size. How do we balance small, incremental savings on the green side, with our rapidly inflating modern needs and desires

Retail
Therapy

Instant gratification

With a generation sold on the 'feel-good factor', Retail Therapy offers itself as a 'cure all' for life's stresses; it promotes the idea that ailments such as feelings of being unloved, or bouts of loneliness and despair, can be alleviated by going shopping. It can also be true. Who hasn't felt transformed by a luxury purchase, or dispelled the blues with an afternoon of random shopping?

But behind the fun facade there's intent: contemporary fashion environments might look effortlessly 'cool' and stylish, but it's a seductive mix of colours, sounds and smells that's been finely tuned by an army of retail consultants and brand gurus. And 'the buzz' has a single purpose: lose yourself in the glamour of the moment and suspend rational 'can I afford it?' 'do I need it?', judgement. So powerful are these pleasure states, that people can attune themselves psychologically to derive feelings of genuine contentment, even happiness, by indulging in the process of accumulating material goods. But as cycles of fashion – from 'in' to 'out', 'hip' to 'unhip' – accelerate with ever-dizzying efficiency, this is 'therapy' that, measured financially across a lifetime, comes with a health risk: Retail therapy, far from being a cure for discontent, can often end up being its cause.

Obedience To...

- Neophilia: an obsession with novelty and things wrapped up in fancy packaging
- Instant 'I want it now' gratification
- Go for it: live for the moment
- New season's everything
- Slavish obedience to the dictates of the fashion gurus
- Latest styles of the stars and celebs
- Fashion as entertainment, one of life's pleasures, aimless fun
- What you wear is who you are
- Shameless attention seeking
- The ability to transform yourself through clothes, accessories and cosmetics
- Status rush: £24,000 handbags give you 'bragging rights' over your envious peer group
- Never, ever repeat a look

Rejection of...

- Old clothes, old image, old age
- Yesterday's fashion
- Restraint, delaying gratification (no one got anywhere by being shy and retiring)
- Dutifully paying credit cards on time
- Lifestyle detox: a voluntary month without shopping
- Finding pleasure in modest, more enlightening pursuits (life's dull enough without being censured by moral prudes)

Emotions

- It's common academic practice for intellectuals to mock the banality of materialism and our slavish pursuit of status. In reality this is a conflict of two mind-sets. They are men/women of letters, with a predisposition to finding reward in cerebral, often solitary pursuits, with an abhorrence of crowds and the frivolous delights of the high-street.
- Novelty seeking runs deep in our evolutionary past. The desire for 'all that glitters' is an emotion that strikes at base values. In denying the power of such stimuli, it would be disingenuous to suggest that acquisitions cannot ignite a sense of contentment – however temporary and expensive that 'fix' might be.

Social Context

- Barely fifty years ago, shopping was seen as a chore, a functional, domestic necessity, like taking out the rubbish. Since then our retail industries from manufacturing to design and marketing have become masters of the art of producing highly desirable product, rapidly, at low-cost.
- Today's retail interiors, cathedral-like in size, have made shopping centres the core of our communities, a sensory bombardment of lights, sound and vision. Like an extension of entertainment, 'retail therapy' is a pursuit shared by celebrities, pop-stars and fashion models. And in aping their looks, brands and styles, we hope that some of that magic might rub off on us.

3.Exploits

Fears

No style,
no presence,
no love

Emotions

Go for it girl

1.Values

Out with the old,
in with the
NEW

Global
Consumer

2.Target

Retail
Therapy
Instant gratification

Personal Fears
• Others stealing the limelight at parties
• Being overlooked, unnoticed (in style terms invisible)
• Having zero self-esteem
• 'Cool stress' at school: the constant pressure to always be 'hip and with it'
• Not fitting into size '0'
• Getting older
• Caught repeating a look
• Being a shopaholic (research has shown that as many as 17 million Americans fall into the category of being compulsive shoppers)
• Being last in line (as witnessed by the crazed storming of the Primark retail outlet in London's Oxford Street)

World Fears
• Early closing

Iconography
• New clothes, new fashion, new stuff
• Latest hot 'cool' style
• Beautiful happy people
• Celebs
• Sunshine
• Jet-set lifestyle
• Gold, glitter, jewellery
• Cute, shiny gizmos
• The catwalk
• Clubs & bars
• Beauty spas

Style/Aesthetic
• Seductive gloss 'Hip' photography
• Dreamworld
• Eternal youth & beauty
• Live for the moment 'Fun'
• Projection of a life of sex, success and happiness

5.Reward

Visual Spell

HIP, HOT, COOL;
THE NEWEST,
THE SEXIEST

She's got to
have it!

Promise

RE-INVENTION,
TRANSFORMATION,
THE 'NEW' YOU

Reality check
In America's darkest hour (9/11), President Bush made an appeal to the patriotic – go shopping to defeat terrorism. This might not seem as silly as it sounds. Yes, terrorist atrocities might steal headlines, but the future prosperity and prowess of nations will be marked less by conflict, than by the ability of its people to produce loads of stuff and (perhaps) more importantly, the ability of its people to consume loads of stuff. Concepts of retail therapy provide that powerful emotional accelerator.

4.Seduces

Promise
• Stand out amongst the plain
• Overshadow rivals, get your man/girl
• Dispel the blues – instant cure for unhappiness
• Transform your sad, unremarkable, little life
• Love yourself: you deserve it
• Buy perfection: style, beauty accessories, cosmetic surgery
• Excitement, novelty, pleasure
• Be sexy, desirable and adored
• Identify with the beautiful people
• Lose yourself in brand heaven

Future Vision
• With increased global competition and the growth of the internet, the retail experience must fight harder to reinvent itself and remain relevant to consumers. In the Far East, the future battle-ground for the brands, competition for grandiose architectural visions has dramatically escalated. By 2010, seven of the ten largest shopping malls in the world will be in China.

Oliver James,
Britain on the Couch,
(on the growth of discontent in Britain)

Dissatisfaction is caused partly by advanced capitalism which fosters discontent to sustain itself and partly by the human tendency towards upwards comparison which capitalism exploits. The disturbing consequence of this latter trait is that however such things improve materially, people 'adjust upwards'. They develop a new higher set of expectations the moment old ones are fulfilled.

Herbert Stein,
The Economist,
(on the growth of mobile phones)

It is the way of keeping contact with someone, anyone, who will reassure you that you're not alone. You may think you're checking on your portfolio but deep down you're checking on your existence. It is being alone that they cannot stand. And for many people, being alone really means being without mummy.

Daniel Pick,
Svengali's Web,
(on the Great Exhibition of 1851)

Artefacts and new social experiences were said to come at the citizen in a disorderly and impossible deluge: the brain was simply overwhelmed by the miscellany of items in the shop and the newspapers – an inane and motley output of titbits, from crockery to shares, solemn state occasions to the most tawdry gossip, vague metaphysical discussions and repots of the latest in science and history. This mad flow of news was said to make rationality difficult for any but the best attuned minds.

C.S.Lewis,
The Screwtape Letters,
(the demand for novelty)

In the first place it diminishes pleasure while increasing desire. This pleasure of novelty is by its very nature more subject than any other to the laws of diminishing returns. And continued novelty costs money, so that desire for it spells avarice or unhappiness, or both – inflaming the horror of the same old thing.

Tim Adams,
Observer Review on the BBC Series *'The Century of the Self'.*

In the wake of the Soviet atomic tests in 1958, Eisenhower for the first time made conspicuous consumption the first duty of the free: 'you auto buy', he sloganed. This was, of course, the very same exhortation made by politicians on both sides of the Atlantic after 11th September. Your democratic duty in the light of global terror was to indulge yourself: go shopping, save the world. The interests of the free market and the pursuit of personal freedom were indistinguishable.

Rick Poynor,
Obey the Giant.
Life in the Image World
(inside the Blue Whale – Bluewater shopping centre)

Of course, all this attention to sensory factors and quality of experience is not motivated by altruism. Bluewater is a machine for making money and these are the lubricants that increase its efficiency. The parkland outside is there to help visitors 'recharge their batteries', explains the celebratory Bluewater book, *Vision of Reality* (a sign in itself of the mall's ambition). The unstated hope is clearly that, rather than flopping into the car and driving home, the recharged shopper will return to the aisles with a spring in his or her stride, credit cards at the ready.

ETHICAL CONSUMER

Save the planet

There are many constructs that make an appeal to the rebel that resides in us all. Several are in this book. All work on the same basic precepts appealing to faux Marxist principles which purport to be anti-capitalist, anti-materialist, and anti-corporate. And we have proved more than willing to buy into such modes of behaviour, unaware that these style constructs, once co-opted by the media machine, are in effect highly efficient drivers of the global economy.

The ethical consumer and the eco-warrior have become the latest rebel prescriptions to make an impact on consumer lifestyle. With brands and products queuing up to imbue their products with 'green' virtues, will the eco-warrior become something we merely flaunt via our jeans and sneakers, rather than a genuine call to action? Hollywood superstars epitomise these confused double standards. Ever willing to turn up for the electric car photo shoot to enhance their hip credentials, celebs think nothing of flying to some distant location in a private jet for a weekend on their luxury yacht.

In the age of the armchair activist, soft sacrifices make us feel pleased about ourselves. We recycle, we don't use plastic bags and we buy long-life lightbulbs. These are relatively painless guilt-aversion strategies — but are merely tickling the body of the beast. Our larger transgressions have yet to be focused on. We live in ever larger houses, we drive heavier cars, fly more frequently, eat more than ever and rush to buy the latest fashions and tech appliances. Our consumer universes inflate.

If we are really serious about mitigating our carbon emissions, real sacrifices will need to be made. And that entails a painful retreat from comfort and consumerism. The truly ethical consumer is not a consumer.

Obedience to:
- Awakening the rebel that is in us all
- Opt out of the system – alternative lifestyle
- Green labels, energy ratings, eco-friendly products
- Energy saving and recyling
- Self-sufficiency and sustainability
- Alternative energy sources: wind, solar, biofuels
- Free trade, organic produce, low-meat diet
- Farmers' markets
- Eastern philosophy and meditation
- Fringe/world music
- Guerrilla activism, culture jamming, adbusting
- Demos and boycotts

Rejection of:
- Multinationals, commercialism and globalisation
- Dependence on oil and gas
- A return to nuclear power
- Factory farming
- Supermarket produce
- Sweatshops, cheap Asian labour
- The branding of everything
- GM (Frankenstein) science
- World Bank strategy
- SUVs: vehicle of Satan and all his siblings
- Flying, obsession with house makeovers, gold and diamonds
- Climate change deniers & sceptics: Bjorn Lomborg (author of *The Skeptical Environmentalist*)
- Superficial, materialist lifestyle
- The conservative 'business as usual' establishment

Personal Fears
- Loss of identity
- Voice of reason not heard
- Middle-class guilt
- Global warming will impact on my family and their future
- Energy will run out
- We're all utterly doomed – though secretly hopeful that we will all wake up in the morning and the problem will have gone away

World Fears
- Global warming leading to climate chaos
- India and China spoiling the consumer party
- Resources being depleted
- Rich/poor divide increasing
- Rampant capitalism destroying the planet
- Advertising is turning us into mindless materialists

1. Values

ALTERNATIVE LIFESTYLE

GLOBAL SHOPPER

2. Target

Emotions

IDENTIFY WITH A CAUSE

WORLD CATASTROPHE IN THE MAKING

Fears

3. Exploits

⊙ ETHICAL CONSUMER

SAVE THE WORLD THROUGH YOUR SHOPPING TROLLEY

Emotional Context
- The very real threat of global warming awakens fears for the future of the world, the stability of its environment and the survival of its wildlife. It also touches on other themes: disillusionment with the industrial world and our obsession with material comfort.
- Critics argue that a lot of these concerns are born of middle-class guilt. A new piety and Puritanism in a world of plenty in which we have nothing much to worry about. The ethical consumer becomes a badge with which to promote our virtues and altruism – and brands, by association with the cause, are falling over themselves to get our 'green' pounds, dollars and euros.

Social context
- The eco-warrior can be seen as coming from the same mould of the age-old class conflict: the bohemian against the bourgeois, the rebel against the establishment and the Marxist against global capitalism. But the central issue driving the debate, ditching oil for alternative energy, brings on an unlikely, and for some, unacceptable saviour: nuclear power.

Promise
- Join the fight
- The moral voice of reason
- People power will save the world
- Take action now before it's too late
- Carbon-neutral living and sustainability
- Low-energy lifestyle
- Natural 'highs'
- Commune with nature
- Future for our children

Future Vision
- Time is rapidly running out in the fight to prevent future global warming. Present levels of CO_2 have already created the conditions for climate change over the next 50 years. Vociferous voices claim that there is nothing we can do to prevent the inevitable. Despite this doom mongering, less energy use, turning our backs on oil, and forcing a search for cleaner, alternative energy are ideals well worth fighting for. But the disturbing fact that mankind has the ability to alter this planet's atmosphere fundamentally at all should be troubling enough to enforce change.

Promise

SUSTAINABLE, LOW ENERGY FUTURE

4.Seduces with

5.Reward

SAVE THE PLANET

Reality check

Lifestyle media and commercialism have created the image of the ethical consumer. And like any other fashionable style it comes with its own set of neatly packaged values: hate SUVs, drive hybrid cars, buy green T-shirts, recycle bottles, and holiday in distant eco-resorts. We can start to believe we are saving the planet. The harsh reality is these are but modest effects. If we are to be serious about making a sizable dent in our carbon emissions, we need to cut our consumption. But with the spectre of declining world growth hanging in the wings, this is an eventuality that few western governments are even willing to contemplate.

Ethical consumerism is an easy and painless style choice. An alternative economy is an entirely different challenge.

Visual spell

GAIA, MOTHER EARTH, WIND TURBINE ON THE ROOF

Iconography
- Gaia, Mother Earth
- Natural environments, forests, furry polar bears
- Natural fibres, knitted hats and scarves
- Ethnic diversity and cultures
- Low-tech living
- Solar, wind and biotech power
- Bohemian lifestyle, communes, tepees etc.
- Bicycles and electric cars

Style/Aesthetic
- Good v evil
- Fatcat v underdog
- Polluting industry v furry creatures
- Stinky cities v idealised natural environments
- Gas guzzling SUV v bicycle
- Grey-suited executive v jeans-wearing activist

BIG PHARMA
QUICK FIX CURE

MEGASTORE
*BIGGEST, THE BEST, THE CHEAPEST,
THE TASTIEST*

SUPERSTAR CHEF
THE NEW EPIC TASTE SENSATION

ALTERNATIVE MEDICINE
HARMONY WITH NATURE

FAT FUTURES
FAST FOOD LIFESTYLE

BINGE DRINKING
DAZED AND CONFUSED

Big Pharma

Aldous Huxley
Brave New World

(The controller) 'People are happy; they get what they want, and they never want what they can't get. They're well off; they're safe; they're never ill; they're not afraid of death; they're blissfully ignorant of passion and old age; they're plagued with no mothers or fathers; they're got no wives, or children, or lovers to feel strongly about; they're so conditioned that they practically can't help behaving as they ought to behave.'

Francis Fukuyama
Our Posthuman Future

The more typical threats raised by biotechnology, on the other hand, are those captured so well by Huxley, and are summed up in the title of an article by novelist Tom Wolfe, "Sorry, but Your Soul Just Died." Medical technology offers us in many cases a devil's bargain: longer life, but with reduced mental capacity; freedom from depression, together with freedom from creativity or spirit; therapies that blur the line between what we achieve on our own and what we achieve because of the levels of various chemicals in our brains.

No one can deny that modern medical science has made huge contributions to the health of the human race. The average life expectancy of men and women in the developed world has continued to advance. Living to be over one hundred will soon be commonplace. Running in parallel with the suppression of pain and suffering and the race to prolong life, the pharmaceutical companies are also tailoring drugs to alleviate sadness, depression, shyness, even aggression and the lack of intelligence. Of course some people might find all of the above part of the human condition. Who hasn't felt inadequate, shy, sad, depressed or angry at some point of their life? Soon we can choose. We can live with our anxieties and imperfections, or, in the not-too-distant future, we can reach for the medicine cabinet.

Many are sceptical of this brave, pain-free world of longer living. The best artists, writers and intellectuals across our history have often not been the most stable minds. Will freedom from suffering and concern take the edge off our internal struggles and conflicts, so often the humus for our so-allusive inspiration, itself the engine room of our creativity?

Obedience to:
- Instant relief cure for every ailment: tense nervous headache, lack of sleep, anxiety, depression, obesity, aggression, unhappiness
- Improved health and lifestyle; look better, feel better, live better
- Longer life
- Well-stocked medicine cabinet for every eventuality
- Get through life with as little discomfort as possible

Rejection of:
- Natural health cures (hoakum and baloney)
- Spiritual healing (mumbo jumbo)
- Treatment is unnecessary (who says?)
- Slob in a baseball cap (Michael Moore, after Fahrenheit 9/11, turned his critical focus onto the health care industry in his film *Sicko*)

Personal Fears:
- I look and I feel dreadful
- Nagging pain inside
- Throbbing headache
- Other people's illnesses
- I'm next in line for the dreaded lurgy
- Embarrassing problem, I can't discuss...
- Ever-present fear of debilitating illness and disease
- Old age and death on the horizon
- Safety and side effects of treatments

World Fears:
- World-wide pandemic
- Chicken flu, smallpox
- Bioterrorist attack

1. Values

HYPOCHONDRIACS

3. Exploits

REACH FOR THE **PILLS**

2. Target

Fears

TENSE NERVOUS HEADACHE, NIGGLING PAIN INSIDE

BIG PHARMA™

QUICK FIX CURE

Emotions

BE BETTER, BE MORE ACTIVE, BE MORE SUCCESSFUL

Emotional Context:
- The pharmaceutical industry is well attuned to contemporary mores. In our fast-track lives we have no time or determination to get well naturally. We need cures now, can't live with discomfort. Medicine answers all our anxieties. We want quick fixes, we want to do more, be better, be more active, be more successful. And for Big Pharma, such habits breed a lifetime of dependence.
- (It is now legal in the UK for Doctors to give Prozac to 8 year-olds – shouldn't we be addressing why they are sad in the first place?)

Social context:
- Ever since the invention of penicillin, medication has undoubtedly brought substantial improvements to people's lives. Today the pharmaceutical industry is a $550-billion business. It can cost upwards of $1 billion to bring a drug to market. The pressure to make profits creates its own momentum. Over 3,000 lobbyists are hired by drugs companies to buy favour on Capital Hill, Washington. Cheerleaders are employed as sales reps to promote new drugs to doctors. And across the world, advertising and marketing creates a culture of anxiety that breeds a lifelong dependence on expensive cures.

Promise:
- New lease of life
- Instant cure-all
- A better life
- Prolonged youth
- Feel great
- Rejuvenation and new vigour

Future Vision:
- Recent advances in drugs for disorders such as attention deficit disorder, depression, and sexual dysfunction, also have benefits for normal healthy people, allowing them to 'feel better than good', smarter and sexier, increasing their quality of life. Such benefits are likely to impact on all our future decisions. Who will deny intelligence drugs to their children when every other child in the class is taking them?
- Yes, new drugs and treatments can extend life – but it's the number of years of ill-health, living with disabilities or degenerative diseases that is increasing.

5. Reward

4. Seduces with

Younger, better, sexier, smarter

Reality check

Without a doubt our lives are better with modern drugs. But continued pressure to deliver new 'lifestyle' products can override a focus on health. Pharmaceutical companies have been accused of selling diseases and blurring the boundaries between what is considered a disorder and a normal condition. As a result we are taking more drugs when we are not even sick. Why run when you can buy pills to make you healthy? Why go on a diet when you can take anti-obesity pills and still stuff yourself stupid? Most of our health problems stem from bad diet, lack of exercise and stress. We should take more control of our lives before reaching for the medicine cabinet.

Promise

- NEW LIFE,
- NEW DAWN,
- NEW YOU

Visual spell

INSTANT,
BUG-BUSTING,
FEVER-FLUSHING,
MIRACLE CURE

Iconography:
- Say goodbye to nasty, ugly bugs and nagging pain
- Life-saving miracle return to health
- Soothing, instant cures; back at work, fit for play
- New dawn, new life, new youth
- The home-coming; tearful wife and kids
- Rejuvenation, a new beginning; running again on the beach with family and small dog
- Dancing, hip-hop grannies
- Future health; a sporty, long retirement; tennis, sailing, golf
- The seeding of a culture of anxiety, by juxtaposing the prospect of disability or some hideous ailment, with a life of carefree abandon

Megastore

① Values

**Biggest, the best,
the cheapest, the tastiest**

② Target — World consumers

Emotions
**Instant, clean,
hassle-free shopping**

③ Exploits

Fears
**GM food,
toxins, chemicals**

Obedience to:
- Customer satisfaction
- Masses of choice (15 varieties of sausages)
- Quality, matched to value for money
- Convenience, fun, open all hours, soft, calming music in the aisles
- Friendly, smiling service and staff
- Benefits the local community, employment
- Free trade, organic, 'green' produce

Rejection of:
- Anti-supermarket movement (supermarkets argue that they don't kill local economies, they provide much-needed employment)
- Buying locally (only if you can find a parking place and don't mind queuing in the rain…)
- Supermarkets are ungreen (have you seen the wind-turbine on the roof?)
- Supermarkets exploit the Third World (have you checked aisle 14 – look for the Fairtrade label)
- Battery farms, meat-retrieval machines (not us, only our cheaper rivals)

Emotional Context:
- The emotional and financial argument for the megastore is hard to resist: more, better-looking food, ok taste and quality, low cost, comfort, convenience, car parking, all in one easy to find location. Without subsidy or regulation it's hard to see how the local butcher, grocer or baker can survive. Even on the organic front they lose out to the buying power of the big brands.

Social context:
- With revenues higher than some major European countries, the largest megastore brands such as Wal-Mart and Tesco, have become a template for international business success. Economies in their own right, they have an impact that goes way beyond the humble supermarket trolley, controlling the employment of thousands, the movement of air and container ship traffic, the look of our cities and suburbs, our obsession with car culture, the size of our fridges and ultimately of ourselves.

Personal Fears:
- GM (Frankenstein) food
- Toxins in food
- Additives and high sugar content
- Salmonella (and now in chocolate)
- Unnatural, non-organic produce
- Being ripped off, high prices
- With the demise of the high-street and the corner-shop, we lose the small day-to-day exchanges and gossip that bind communities together

World Fears:
- Food health scare; bird flu, mad cow disease
- A world dominated by large international conglomerates (competition is so intense that by 2010 it is predicted that only 10 major brands will dominate)

Superstar Chef

① Values

**The new epic
taste sensation**

② Target — Global foodies

Emotions
**Better than sex;
like nothing I've ever tasted before…**

③ Exploits

Fears
Dinner party disasters

Obedience to:
- Perfection on a plate
- Food as an art form
- Cult of the TV chef
- The new restaurant sensation; signed book of new recipes in the reception
- Rare, exotic, obscure ingredients
- Cooking as the new porn
- Fusion food; Asian, Italian, French, Japanese, Spanish
- Chef as auteur: Wolfgang Puck, Mario Batali
- Macho bully boy chef: Gordon Ramsey
- Alchemist with a frying pan: Heston Blumenthal
- Chef as seductress: Rachel Ray, Nigella Lawson
- Kitchen stuffed full of high-tech equipment

Rejection of:
- Junk food (burgers, pizzas, chips)
- Processed oven-ready meals
- Motorway service stations
- Anything out of a can
- The ordinary and the mundane
- House wine
- Tasteless 'healthy', veggie food
- Obsessive diets (eat what you want)

Emotional Context:
- Just as we buy the clothes pop celebs wear to forge a personal link with our stars, the same is true with our obsession with celebrity chefs; book the restaurant, buy the book, watch the TV show, buy the branded kitchen knives, be reduced to tears when our attempt to create some culinary masterpiece fails in front of gloating dinner guests. Food has become yet another positional good; a mark of sophistication, a fetish, in the hierarchy of social competition.

Social context:
- The cult of the celebrity chef and our quest for even more 'intense taste experiences' has had a global impact. Restaurants, previously discreet and intimate, have become designer extravaganzas. Our supermarkets stock exotic all-year produce: mangoes from Thailand, tuna from Japan, beef from South America. Kitchens heave with the latest high-tech hobs, grills and walk-in fridge freezers. We demand new kitchen gizmos. Cook books dictate that every meal should be a work of art. Whatever happened to the humble beans on toast?

Personal Fears:
- Nothing in the fridge
- Dinner party disasters: over-cooked vegetables, burning the roast, failed soufflé
- Cheap local wine
- Service station food
- New restaurant opening unable to find your booking

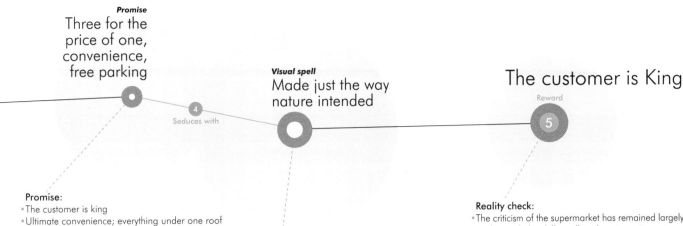

Three for the price of one, convenience, free parking

4
Seduces with

Made just the way nature intended

The customer is King

Reward
5

Promise:
- The customer is king
- Ultimate convenience; everything under one roof
- New cheap prices, three for the price of one
- Value from money, 20 percent less for more
- All-year supply of exotic fruit – even rare Himalayan Goji berries
- Fun for the family
- Easy parking
- Money-back guarantee

Future Vision:
- Ethical conflict is on the horizon. On the left, Fairtrade and lobby groups anxious to increase produce from the Third World. On the right, the organic food movement, issues of air miles, the distance food takes from field to plate, and the alliance for better food and farming, favouring local produce against the high-energy costs of global trade. Of course we could all eat less – though this is not an issue that the supermarkets are likely to endorse.

Iconography:
- A great day out for all the family
- Easy parking
- Palaces of choice, colour and variety
- Fresh, ripe produce from sunny, healthy orchards and fields, populated by happy, colourful, foreign growers contentedly harvesting plump fruit especially for you – made the traditional way, just like their grandparents did

Style/Aesthetic:
- Colour and cleanliness
- Safety and quality
- Warm smile, friendly service
- Perfect, natural products – fresh from the earth

Reality check:
- The criticism of the supermarket has remained largely unchanged; they kill small traders, turn city centres into ghost towns and have dubious ethical and environmental policies. Although several companies have countered these negative images (Wal-Mart famously turning green), the superstores key defence is that they offer value for money and that shoppers vote with their feet. But feet are unthinking. Consumers are not made aware of the link between their purchases and the social consequences of their actions. And more often than not you get what you pay for – cheap, tasteless food, made without care or attention.

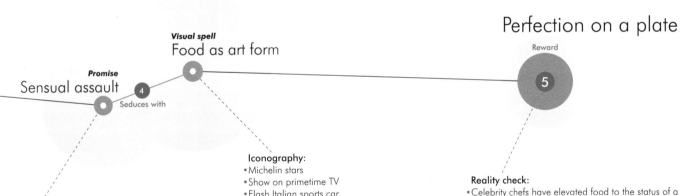

Perfection on a plate

Reward
5

Food as art form

Sensual assault

4
Seduces with

Promise:
- New taste sensation – better than anything you, your neighbours, your rivals have ever tasted before
- Worth catching the flight for
- A night to remember
- Appeal to the senses: cool interiors, sexy waitresses, gourmet cuisine

Future Vision:
- Celebrity chefs have created a global food industry that shows no signs of abating. But with good food (ever reliant on butter, cream, often wine and salt), the crucial issue remains: flavour equals fat. As obesity, health issues and the environment (issues over food miles), become global concerns, where next for the globe-trotting, superstar chef?

Iconography:
- Michelin stars
- Show on primetime TV
- Flash Italian sports car
- Straight from the farm local produce
- Here's one I prepared earlier
- Best-selling book series
- State-of-the-art kitchen
- Latest kitchen gizmo
- Dining with the stars; Madonna, Robert de Niro

Style/Aesthetic:
- Glossy, seductive photography
- Food as porn
- Food perfection; fresh, deep colours, succulent, steaming

Reality check:
- Celebrity chefs have elevated food to the status of a religion. Our food obsessions have inflated hand in hand with the spread of global affluence. Though such indulgences can veer close to gluttony, super star chefs can also bring about positive social change: Rick Stein encouraging the move to local farm produce, Carlo Petrini creating the slow food movement, and Jamie Oliver using unemployed kids in his kitchens and instigating the 'feed me better' campaign that shamed the government into changing food standards in British schools.

Obedience to:
- Nature versus nasty toxic chemicals
- Power of the spirit against cold rational science
- Aromatheraphy, reflexology, acupuncture, osteopathy, homeopathy, herbalism, natural food supplements
- Spiritual healing
- Mind over body
- Power of positive thinking
- Tibetan, Ayurvedic, Chinese cures
- Faith healers
- Holistic approach to health; living in harmony with your surroundings
- In many ways, an obsessive belief in alternative medicine is an addiction to hope, that despite all the odds, some mystical force will shine down and cure us

Rejection of:
- Big bad Pharma
- Global corporations
- Modern science
- Obsessive reliance on facts and empirical evidence
- Controlled trials (no room for spiritual magic)
- Mass-market cures
- Unnatural chemical ingredients

Personal Fears:
- Stress of modern life
- Pollution of cities
- Unhealthy office environments
- GM food
- Debilitating illness
- Toxins and chemical additives in food and cosmetics (Paradoxically, alternative beauty therapies that claim to be natural often contain more toxins and chemicals than mainstream products)

World Fears:
- World-wide pandemic caused by unnatural practices in science and agriculture

Fears

The technological age
is corrupting our souls

Emotions

Belief, faith,
positive thinking

2.Target

Those distrustful
of modern science

Power
of the spirit

1.Values

3.Exploits

Emotional Context:
- Sceptics argue that in trials alternative medicines have fared no better than placebos. But the placebo effect may also have a chemical basis. The emotional expectation of a benefit can lead to the release of dopamine in the brain causing pain regions to be less active. Highly skilled Tibetan doctors, just by their presence, can have profound effects, even before they have laid hands on the patient.

Social context:
- The conflict between alternative medicine and science touches on several themes — (mostly nothing to do with medicine) — the 'touchy feely' vs the need for hard empirical fact, faith vs science, ancient Asian wisdom as opposed to mindless pop culture, the friendly practitioner vs the faceless global multinational. Distrust of science (GM food, mad cow disease) has led to over $65 billion been spent on 'natural' cures, alternative and complimentary medicines. All dispensed by practitioners that need no qualifications to operate and an industry that is unregulated.

Promise:
- A miracle cure
- A natural remedy
- Have faith and your illness will disappear
- Live life in balance with the environment
- Spiritual well-being

Future Vision:
- The power of positive thinking as a mantra could equally well be applied to the millions been made by the complementary and alternative health business.
- The internet provides a global conduit for the distribution of a vast array of products, services and cures, where the only proof offered for their fantastic effectiveness is the amount of passion they inspire.

Iconography:
- Chinese medicine cabinet
- Natural, herbal cures
- Asian, Indian, Chinese images and carvings
- Power of the sun, the earth, water
- Soothing oils and candle light
- Weird names; Ginkgo Biloba, Weleda Aconite
- Massage, meditation and acupuncture
- Tibetan healing paintings
- Chakras, Yin & Yang symbols
- Crystal healing
- Repetitive chanting

Style/Aesthetic:
- The natural world
- The old, traditional world; wisdom of the past
- Power of the spirit and the soul

5. Reward

Rejuvenation, recovery

Reality check

We need to remove labels, alternative or modern from all cures. Medicine either works or it doesn't. Either it can be tested to bring benefits or not. Just as people shouldn't confuse natural with safer, they should also not be lulled into a lifestyle that makes us dependent on a supermarket trolley full of pain-relieving drugs.

Most of our most common ailments derive from the stresses and strains of modern life: excessive work, lack of exercise and bad diets. And if alternative practices such as meditation, acupuncture and yoga alleviate that stress, so much the better.

4. Seduces with

Miracle, natural, **herbal cure**

Promise

Mystic Asian symbols, candle light, burning incense, healing oils

Visual spell

Alternative Medicine
Harmony with nature

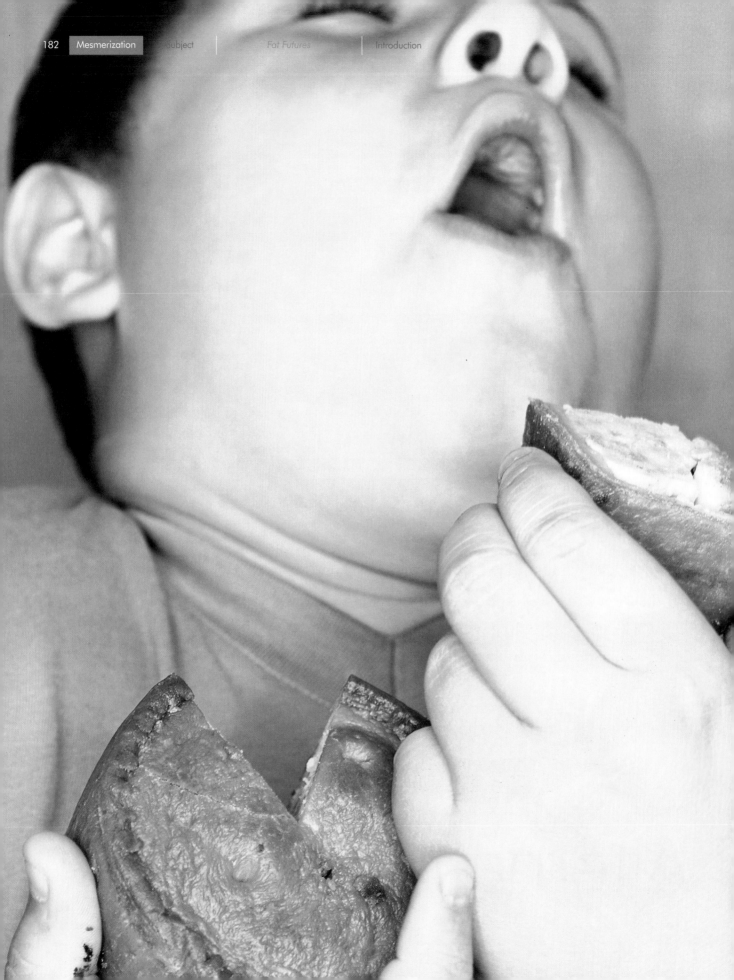

Fat Futures

Alison Motluk
New Scientist (Supersize surprise)

Ask anyone why there is an obesity epidemic and they will tell you that it's all down to eating too much and burning too few calories. That is undoubtedly true – you cannot get round the first law of thermodynamics. It's also true that we live in an 'obesogenic environment': Calorific food is plentiful and cheap and our lifestyles are increasingly sedentary. Most of us have to make an effort not to get fat.

It used to be simple; eating loads and being lazy made you fat. Fast food, combined with TV culture, has always been an obvious factor. But a third culprit, particular to our times, has crept into the equation; the conveniences and comforts of modern lifestyle are making the developed nations of the world obese.

In the US, two-thirds of the population is classified as being overweight. In the UK the proportion is close to 50%. China blames westernization and urbanisation for an alarming rise in its own obesity rates. Part of the cause is an increase in world wide affluence. Supermarkets offer more for cheaper prices; we buy more, we eat more. In restaurants, food portions and plate sizes are getting larger.

Our aversion to any form of exercise is another contributing factor. City transport systems, elevators in buildings, escalators at department stores, discourage us from walking. The modern age sells us every comfort and convenience: from larger cars, to ever-more efficient vacuum cleaners and washing machines. All have replaced human exertion. Office work is a major cause of obesity. For the majority of the world-wide working population, 'the job' is a lifetime starring at a screen.

Personal Fears:
- Low self-esteem
- Being stigmatised for being overweight
- Heart disease
- Type 2 diabetes
- I hate myself – food is my only friend, my only refuge, my single, dependable comfort
- Checking the scales

Fat Futures

Fast food lifestyle

3.Exploits

2.Target

Hungry youth

Fears

1.Values

Feet up in front of the telly

The world hates me; food is my only friend

Emotions

Feed me!

Obedience to:
- Fast food, convenience food, soft drinks
- Snack culture
- Freedom of choice
- Super-sized meals
- Instant gratification
- Comfort eating
- All-you-can-eat
- Cure for the blues
- Diet pills
- TV dinners; feet up in front of the DVD player
- Why walk when you can take the car

Rejection of:
- Judgement day on the scales
- Latest diet fad
- Weight watchers
- Low carbohydrate diet
- Exercise: walking, running, cycling
- Doing the housework
- Active team sports
- Gym membership
- Food police
- Slow food movement
- Flagrantly skinny, self-righteous people

Emotional Context:
- Fast food and convenience food punch all the emotional buttons: desire, hunger, taste and enjoyment. Greed has always been our most compulsive addiction.

Social context:
- Obesity is the result of several powerful factors; general world-wide affluence, supermarkets offering more and cheaper food, high levels of caloric sweeteners seeping into products to enhance their appeal and plate and bottle sizes that are always inflating. And then there are social causes; working parents too tired to cook real meals and unable to stand up to the demands of their kids for 'instant' (often junk) food; our modern-day aversion to exertion – doing the house work, driving when we should walk, playing computer games as opposed to active team sports. Lastly there's comfort: our stay-at-home culture, a night in front of the telly.
- A recent BBC report suggested that obesity is contagious – having a friend who is overweight raises your own risk of being obese.

Iconography:
- Super-sized meal
- Two for the price of one
- Eat-all-you-like buffets
- Cool crowd; pop and celeb endorsements of soft-drinks
- Snappy, jolly cartoon characters
- The happy family meal
- Free toys and gifts (usually linked to a high profile film release)

Style/Aesthetic:
- Fast food with a friendly face
- Ease, convenience, cleanliness
- Cool animation and hip graphics

5.Reward

Visual spell

HAPPY HOUR
with a cheesey face
and a snappy tune

SUPERSIZED
snack culture

Reality check

Temptation is everywhere in the contemporary urban environment: advertising promotions on TV, marketing campaigns on large billboard sites, superstar chef recipes in magazines, soft drink dispensers in schools and hospitals and ranks of fast food outlets on every high street. Its message is hard to resist; food is fun, food is hip, food is cool and sings a catchy tune. It's a persuasive message that adds up to one of the most compulsive desire states on the planet; hard to resist, even harder to stay thin.

NEW
TASTE SENSATION,
LIVE FOR THE MOMENT,
INDULGE YOURSELF

Promise

4.Seduces with

Promise:
- Instant taste sensation
- Super value for money
- Enjoy the moment – indulge yourself
- Fun for all the family

Future Vision:
- Being fat is more than mere food – it's more driving, more food transportation, more waste, more energy and emissions, and more medical bills.
- With obesity shaping up to become one of the most pressing global health concerns, it's no surprise that the pharmaceutical industry has such issues firmly in their sights. On the horizon the Barbie pill; not only do you lose weight, you feel sexy to boot.

Personal Fears:
•I can't remember
•Socially inept without a drink
•Group exclusion
•Head-splitting hangover
•Loss of libido and potency
•Cirrhosis of the liver
•Alcoholic dementia
•Facing up to 'cold' reality without a drink
•Link with alcohol and cancer

World Fears:
•Last orders

Fears

BINGE DRINKING
DAZED&CONFUSED

1.Values

Emotions

LIVE LIFE TO THE MAX,
GO ON THE PISS,
GET HAMMERED

2.Target
NIGHT OWLS

GO

I CAN'T
REMEMBER...

FOR IT!

3.Exploits

Obedience to:
•Hard-partying and hedonism
•Live life to the Max
•Let yourself go
•Having a laugh
•Booze bonding
•Super-sized wine glasses
•Happy hour – 2 for the price of 1
•It's good for you (red wine, even beer in moderation has proven to be beneficial to health)
•One for the road
•Getting an ASBO (Badge of honour)
•Stylish self-destruction

Rejection of:
•No fun brigade
•Moral prudes; drinking is a vice
•Conservative parents
•Government health campaigns
•Doctor's orders
•Low-alcohol beers
•Abstention (how dull is that?)
•Alcohol fuels violence

Emotional Context:
•For kids, stressed from all angles – social competition, pushy parents, getting a job – relief comes in the form of easily available medication: drink. And alcohol works; it relaxes you, makes you feel happier, chattier, sexier and dispels the blues. You say more or less what you normally say, but louder, faster, with more expletives – and in the morning you feel miserable and look shit.

Social context:
•The social effects of alcohol make grim reading: child abuse, domestic violence, rape, anti-social behaviour, and low work productivity. In the UK one in four adults are binge drinkers. And of these drinkers an increasing number are teenage girls, a large percentage from middle-class affluent families. 60 percent of young girls admitted to losing their virginity under the influence of alcohol.
•Binge drinking isn't confined to the streets – a lot of hard drinking takes place behind the closed curtains of 'prim' suburbia.

Iconography:
- Music, lights, beautiful people
- Drop-dead gorgeous salsa dancing bar girls/boys
- Sussed, lager-drinking dork, attracts the babe
- Sussed, vodka-drinking babe, gets the hunk
- Blokey camaraderie and lad culture; two pints and a packet of crisps, pool, darts, poker
- Cuban bands, rock music, jazz, blues
- Beach parties populated with the young and beautiful
- Celebs stumbling out of rehab, new mark of cool

Style/Aesthetic:
- The authentic you
- Afterdark club world
- Edgy, underground, sexy
- Youthful, exciting, fun

Visual spell

EDGY, UNDERGROUND CLUBS, SEXY, SASSY DANCERS

5. Reward

CAR CRASH CHIC

Reality check

Fifty years of glamorising drinking in the media has ingrained perceptions of alcohol consumption as being sexy, socially acceptable and cool; nights of abandon, cavorting with sassy dancers in some edgy South American bar.

Yet the uncomfortable reality remains largely untold; teenage girls tottering into the gutter, vomit on the floor of A&E, battered and abused housewives, a diseased liver under the surgeons' knife.

A sure sign that the drinks companies are getting nervous of being lumped together with 'big bad tobacco' as public health threat number one, has been the recent implementation of their responsible 'Drinkaware' campaign.

Promise

LEAVE
IT ALL BEHIND,
LET YOURSELF GO

4. Seduces with

Promise:
- An escape from dull office and family life
- Night of frivolous, sexy, fun
- Feelgood – leave your troubles behind
- Credibility; part of the cool crowd
- Still standing – mark of a man
- Still dancing – 'go for it' girl chic

Future Vision:
Alcohol's effect is pretty basic and has remained virtually unchanged since the Stone Age. It has always fuelled aggression, men have always pissed in doorways and woken with mind numbing headaches with their boots on. Now change is on the horizon. Drugs have been developed that can sober up a drunken rat in less than five minutes. New forms of drink are being developed that give all the fun parts of drinking without the bad – such as aggression and liver damage.

FEA

SPE

MEGA CATASTROPHE
FEAR INC

FRANKENSTEIN SCIENCE
DON'T MESS WITH THE CREATION

CLIMATE CHAOS
THE HEAT IS ON

AR
LLS

CONSPIRACY THEORIES
THE BIG COVER UP

XENOPHOBIA
US VS THEM

MEGA CATASTROPHE

Fear Inc

In the modern world, fear is ever present: from petty fashion and style concerns, insecurities over our weight, looks, food and health, to the bigger crisis beyond our control: nuclear disaster, terrorist attack and climate change, and the irrational: ghouls and psychotic monks, fears govern who we are and condition how we behave and react to the world.

It is also big business. We take pills to tame phobias, alleviate stress and calm tensions. Every facet of our lives we insure: from expensive possessions, to homes, cars and holidays.

Anxieties over future illness and injury see a sizable proportion of our income invested in expensive health plans for ourselves and our family. Scared of the world beyond the door, we transform our homes and offices into small fortresses. In the street, CCTV cameras and identity cards monitor our every move. Technical advances, such as the mobile phone, though selling themselves on the promise of freedom, only add to the anxiety state: the nagging fear that we can never be out of touch with loved ones and small children.

Are those brief moments when we are momentarily distracted by feelings of great beauty, happiness or excitement simply an alleviation of the ever-present fear state?

1.Values

STAY AT HOME, LOCK UP, STOCK UP

2.Target

WORRIED WORLD

Emotional context
• As our lives grow richer in comfort and luxury, the fear that it will all be suddenly taken away, or will end in disaster, becomes proportionately greater.
• The prospect of a mind-numbingly appalling catastrophe influences a large part of our internal governance: don't talk to strangers, they'll rob you, don't travel to distant places, you'll be kidnapped, don't have sex, you'll get HIV.

Social context
• Obsessions with self-preservation magnify our fear of the unknown. Constant states of paranoia increase suspicion: we distrust foreigners, science, the police, government.
• Our climate of fear tells us that we live in times of great turbulence and uncertainty. In historical terms our lives have never been safer or more comfortable.
• With the everyday saturated with concerns, we begin to fear modern life.

3.Exploits

Fears

A WORLD RUNNING OUT OF CONTROL

Emotions

ANXIETY
FIRING ON ALL CYLINDERS

Obedience to...
• Don't do that, don't go there, don't eat this
• Protect, secure, insure
• Risk avoidance: go for the safe option
• Stay at home: cocoon lifestyle
• Obsession with home security: bigger locks, alarms, video surveillance
• Neighbourhood watch, emergency numbers, larder crammed with essentials to sit out a coming disaster
• Don't stay out late, don't talk to strangers, don't let your children play in the streets
• Don't travel to iffy foreign destinations
• Dependence on the nanny state and health and safety inspectors: regulate, legislate, isolate
• Well-stocked medicine cabinet for all eventualities
• Flashlight, baseball bat by the bedside

Rejection of...
• Spirit of carefree adventure
• Risk taking and dangerous sports
• Adrenalin junkies who live for the moment
• Science and technological progress (can't trust it – tech-melt-down in the making)
• The Future is bright (wishful thinking: disaster is always on the horizon)
• Faith in innate human goodness and world harmony (naïvety – take a look back through world history)

Imagery/Style:

- Run for the hills
- Mass hysteria in the street: women and children first.
- Violent, unexpected death and injury
- Terror on our doorstep: national monuments, transport systems, airports attacked
- Epic environmental collapse: burning of the rainforest, melting ice-caps, rising sea levels, dying polar bears
- Pollution and toxic pollution killing our habitat and its wildlife
- Shock news headlines: massacres of innocents, refugee camps, homeless children
- The uncontrollable earth: volcanic eruptions, tsunamis, hurricanes, floods
- Stock market meltdown: rapidly declining indices, suicidal traders
- Super surveillance society: CCTV everywhere, identity cards, global tracking

Promise

- Peace of mind
- Better safe than sorry
- Prevention better than cure
- Take a pill and alleviate your stress
- Ring of confidence: better locks, better security systems
- Sleep soundly at night (insure against everything)
- Guardian angel (video surveillance)
- Lifetime protection for you and your family

Future View

- From anxieties such as climate change, to concerns over international terrorism, our fears are getting bigger and more global. They highlight an even greater concern: our world problems are of a magnitude that are so epic, that they are beyond the ability of our nation states and their leaders to control.

4.Seduces with

Promise

FEAR IS EVERYWHERE:
IN THE SKY,
IN THE STREET,
IN YOUR FOOD,
UNDER YOUR BED...

5.Reward

Visual spell

GUARDIAN
ANGEL

SELF
PRESERVATION

Reality check

Fear is natural for self-preservation. As the old adage goes, it is better to mistake a stick for snake, than a snake for a stick. But a media environment over-saturated with images of fear has distorted our ability to assess danger. Unable to deal with big numbers and percentages, we are left with an unbalanced picture of risk. The end result: fear fosters passivity and restraint, undermines boldness and adventurism and increases our dependence on the 'nanny' state. We fall prey to professions that peddle fear: insurance salesmen, financial advisors, lawyers, cosmetic surgeons and health and safety inspectors.

Personal Fears

- Fear is everywhere:
- We look in the mirror we see old age
- We look at the news we see disasters
- On every street corner wait muggers, rapists and murderers
- Every plane, car, train is a potential disaster waiting to happen
- In the supermarket we fear mad cow disease and toxins in food
- In the hospital hide superbugs and avian flu
- In the City we see financial collapse and fraud

Joseph LeDoux
The Emotional Brain (an example of fear stimulus – walking through the woods)

From the point of view of survival, it is better to respond to potentially dangerous events as if they were in fact the real thing than to fail to respond. The cost of treating a stick as a snake is less, in the long run, than the cost of treating a snake as a stick.

Theodore Zeldin
Conversation

Technology has not totally eliminated the tone of humility set by religion, which reigned unchallenged in the past, and which partly survives in the dread of terrible, apocalyptic catastropies.

Guillermo Lemarchand
Scientific American

Michael Archer, a biologist in Wales, thinks the gold-coated copper phonograph records affixed to each Voyager spacecraft – which contains, among other indications of intelligent life, 118 photographs of our planet, ourselves and our civilisations – are giant dinner invitations to the cosmos.

Simon Conway Morris
New Scientist
(on the search for intelligent life in the cosmos)

The fact that aggression has arisen independently in so many species on earth suggests that the trait will be found wherever life is... Conflict is inherent to most successful species. I'd suggest that if the telephone rings, put it down straight away.

Jamil Tanvir
Sunday Times

If worry wasn't essentially part of us, and you took away every conceivable worry that a human could have, you would think that all you'd be left with is happiness... but in reality people just fill the vacuum by inventing a million new worries overnight. Worry is just a part of the human condition, so there's really no point in worrying about it.

Desmond Morris
The Naked Ape

Animals are free of worry... because, in order to have worry you need to be able to have an internal voice that can put fears into words and develop a narrative of 'maybes' and 'what ifs'. You also need to have a concept of the future. Language has blessed us with the ability to plan for the future, but also to worry about bad things and ultimately death.

Frankenstein
DON'T MESS WITH THE CREATION
Science

Personal Fears:
- Lack of identity
- Voice of reason smothered by the modern world
- Toxins and additives in food, chemicals in water
- Pollution in cities
- Dangerous microwaves from radio masts, mobile phones
- Cancer from solvents, foods, materials, buildings, modern lifestyle
- No future for our children

World Fears:
- The modern world is in danger of destroying our fragile ecosystems
- Global warming brought about by unchecked economic expansion
- Frankenstein food (science in the pay of the mega corp)
- Toxic clouds
- Nuclear accident

2. Target

1. Values

3. Exploits

Fears

Sciencephobics

Simple ways were better

Uncontrolled experiment
running out of control

Emotions

The natural world is being destroyed

Obedience to:
- Don't mess with nature
- The weird and the wonderful can't all be explained by science
- Don't trust the boffin in his lab – he's in the pay of the great corporate machine
- Yes science has brought advances – but it has also invented the means by which we can destroy ourselves
- A return to traditional knowledge, new-age science, and spiritual purity
- Common sense – the simple ways were better
- People power; community action, activism and protest groups

Rejection of:
- Future faith in technological progress
- Globalization
- Agribusiness corporations
- Corporate greed (not creating benefits, just profit)
- The pharmaceutical industry and modern medicine
- Nuclear and oil industry
- The idea that science can improve on nature
- Genetic engineering
- Rationalism; over-reliance on fact and empirical evidence
- Theories of reductionism; everything can be reduced and explained by simple formula

Emotional Context:
- Post the nuclear age, after accidents like Chernobyl, science was seen as dehumanising and not to be trusted. Large advances were viewed with suspicion together with the fear that such 'benefits' would have unseen consequences and destroy the natural world. Combined with our inability to make science understandable (quantum physics and string theory was baffling even to practitioners), anti-science phobias have led a retreat back to folk science, natural and alternative thinking, superstition and even magic.

Social context:
- In the C17th, Francis Bacon warned of the illusions posed by 'the cave, herd, theatre and marketplace'. Science, like everything else in the world, has to be heard through the mouthpiece of popular media. Academics, partly by their refusal to debase complex ideas to sound bites, make notoriously bad entertainers. Only the most sensational topics get aired. With not enough time to explain data properly, results become over-sexed, over-interpreted and over-sold. The most sensational headlines provoke disproportionate intention, contributing to an inflation of global fear, and by association, further distrust in science.

Premise:
- Stable and sustainable future (solar, wind power)
- A return to natural alternative cures, science and thought
- Mystery and fantasy (why does everything have to be explained?)
- The human perspective
- Slow, low-tech lifestyle
- Clean air, clean water, clean future

Future Vision:
- Recent progress in science promises huge advances in modifying nature: plants, animals and man. All will have subtle and sometimes unpredictable consequences. Francis Fukuyama writes in his work *Our Posthuman Future*, that genetic modification is similar to giving a child a tattoo that she or he can never remove. At the international scale the issues are even more daunting. If as a country we choose to ban certain avenues of future science, what's to stop less scrupulous nations from developing modifications that will give their people intellectual superiority over the rest of us?

5. Reward

Nature's
way is better

Reality check

In the really big issues – GM food, stem cell science and global warming, pressure from both corporate, government and green interest groups have made it increasingly difficult to ascertain who has paid for what in research. As a result trust in science has been eroded. In the mainstream media, pseudo science, bad science, and folk science all share space with established science. In electronic media, such neat distinctions are nonexistent. Who mediates or decides the conditions for truth? Is it any wonder that in US schools evolution is losing the battle in the conflict with Intelligent Design?

4. Seduces with

PREMISE

Don't trust technological progress

Visual spell

Clones, blood sucking zombies, Frankenstein food, nanoclouds, grey goo

Iconography:
- Frankenstein, GM food
- Dolly the sheep
- Horrors of global warming; melting icesheet, dying polar bears
- Boys from Brazil: human clones, zombies running amok
- Nanotechnology and grey goo
- Artificial intelligence: robots taking over
- The tipping point; global environmental disaster in the balance
- Nuclear meltdown, Chernobyl, mushroom cloud

Style/Aesthetic:
- Dr Jekyll; mad scientist in his lab
- 'Controlled' experiment running out of control
- Corporate stooges hired to cover up a disaster
- Chain reaction
- Total global chaos

CLIMATE
CHAOS

The Heat is On

Malcolm Gladwell
The Tipping Point
What must underlie successful epidemics, in the end, is a bedrock belief that change is possible, that people can radically transform their behaviour or beliefs in the face of the right kind of the impetus.

James Lovelock
The Revenge of Gaia
Humanity, wholly unprepared by its humanist traditions, faces its greatest trial. The acceleration of the climate change now underway will sweep away the comfortable environment to which we are adapted. Change is a normal part of geological history; the most recent was the Earth's move from the long period of glaciation to the present warmish interglacial. What is unusual about the coming crisis is that we are the cause of it, and nothing so severe has happened since the long hot period at the start of the Eocene, fifty-five million years ago, when the change was larger than that between the ice age and the 19th century and lasted for 200,000 years.

One of the most acrimonious debates in recent times has been bitterly contested between the growing environmental movement and the climate change deniers. With a clear majority of the world's scientists now united in their belief that human activity has contributed to global warming, the mud slinging has moved onto a different stage; who are the culprits in big business? From the automotive industry to air travel and food production, a blame culture has developed in which polluters point the finger at others they perceive to be more guilty. The less comforting reality is that public consumption across the board sits at the heart of the problem. Comfort, convenience, cleanliness and choice, are the marketing mantras that increase energy use.

No less disconcerting is the realisation that our very ability to indulge in these luxuries and comforts in the first place, is dependent on the security of our jobs, in turn bonded to the productivity of industry, such success reliant on continued worldwide growth, itself geared to our own greater consumption. Our livelihoods today are in conflict with our future survival.

Yes, our scientists, engineers and designers will develop more efficient machines, cars and homes. But on the political and economic front, the big social vision is disconcertingly missing. No one has yet come up with a blueprint for a future in which global economic prosperity can be made compatible with the need to use less energy.

CLIMATE
THE HEAT IS ON
CHAOS

Emotional Context:
- Human existence has always been framed and given meaning by fear. Fear of religious persecution, fear of Nazism, the red menace, nuclear annihilation and today climate chaos. Our sense of wellbeing is often overshadowed by guilt; that enjoyment of life and affluence is in some way sinful and that retribution has long been overdue. Some argue that climate chaos provides that highly comforting sense of doom. A necessary corrective to an age of profligacy and extravagance.

Social context:
- Climate hysteria has become big business, feeding Hollywood movies, documentaries, books, magazine and newspaper headlines. It has also created streams of funding for scientists, lobbyists and environmental advisers, all banking their future on climate chaos, or on the obverse, the myth of climate chaos. Political rhetoric and vested interests create their own momentum, clouding and confusing the issues.
- What facts and figures that have been gleaned from what remains a bafflingly complex science, have been used to support arguments both for and against action. Uncertainty encourages prevarication. Doubt makes it ok to do nothing. All the more reason not only to get the facts straight but to make it understandable to the public.

1. Values

RISING TEMPERATURES WORLDWIDE

2. Target

YOU!

Emotions

SAVE, TURN OFF, RECYCLE, REUSE

3. Exploits

Fears

TOTAL ENVIRONMENTAL CHAOS

Obedience to:
- Urgent wake up call – act now, or face future disaster
- The heat is on; rising temperatures world-wide
- Greenhouse effect (CO_2 trapping heat in the atmosphere)
- Total weather chaos: hurricanes, heat waves, floods
- Melting ice sheet (less ice means less reflectivity, thus more heat)
- The tipping point (past the point of no return)
- The hockey stick effect (sharp increases on the horizon)
- Positive feedback (leading to faster warming)
- Al Gore's 'An Inconvenient Truth'
- We only have a decade to save the planet

Rejection of:
- America (lack of leadership, failure on Kyoto)
- Big oil
- Gas guzzling SUVs
- Global corporations and international trade
- International flights
- Mass consumption
- China and India (though the average US citizen is responsible for over 20 times more emissions)
- Climate deniers (who claim that climate change is a con created by left-leaning extremists out to destroy capitalism)
- Nuclear power (though some, like scientist James Lovelock sees this as the lesser of two evils)
- Carbon trading as an easy 'get out of guilt' card
- Eating meat (1 kilogram of beef creates more damaging emissions and pollution than driving a car for three hours)
- Green Fatigue – 'Global Boring'
- Greenwashing – companies claiming to be green when they're not

Personal Fears:
- Powerlessness – nothing I can do will help
- Voice of reason smothered by the modern world
- Future of our children

World Fears:
- Melting ice caps
- Hurricanes, heat waves and flooding
- Gulf stream shutting down
- Melting of Greenland's ice sheet causing rising sea levels
- Mass extinctions; polar bears, rare frogs
- Positive feedback (Albedo effect, ocean and cloud reflectivity) contributing to faster warming
- Worldwide famines, civil unrest, economic meltdown, total chaos (Ironically, those who have done nothing to cause global warming – the poor of the Third World and Africa stand to lose the most from climate change through sudden drought, violent and extreme weather)

Iconography:
- Alarmingly coloured NASA images of the disappearing ice caps
- Street protests (Kyoto, Seattle)
- Pop stars rocking for trees
- Film stars in hybrid cars
- Renewable energy: wind, solar
- Back to nature; sandals, bicycles
- Melting glaciers and marooned polar bears
- Receding snows of Kilimanjaro
- Heat waves in Europe
- Drought in Ethiopia
- Floods in Bangladesh
- Dirty power stations in China

Style/Aesthetic:
- Total global chaos
- Us and them (Greenies v big bad corp)
- Hysteria; run for the hills

4. Seduces with

5. Reward

PREMISE

PEOPLE POWER CAN CHANGE THE WORLD

Visual spell

MAROONED POLAR BEAR ON MELTING ICEBERG, NEW YORK, LONDON FLOODED

SAVE THE FUTURE
BEFORE IT'S TOO LATE

Reality check

Sceptics tell us that climate change is the norm and that humans have been altering the landscape and thus the climate for hundreds of thousands of years. Arguing that climate change is the result of thousands of factors, they believe that just concentrating on cutting CO_2 emissions is both wrong and naïve. Even the most dramatic reductions might achieve nothing. Yet several hard facts remain irrefutable. The Greenland ice sheet is melting. The earth is getting warmer (albeit by 0.8 degrees over the last century). Man-made emissions have increased. The alarming fact that mankind can have such a dramatic impact on the earth's atmosphere should be justification alone for change.

Promise:
- Save the world; recycle and drive hybrid cars
- You can change the future
- Green, sustainable, alternative energy for all

Future Vision:
- Those hoping for a single, simple, easy to sell solution will be disappointed. It will be painful. But it needn't all been negative. To back off from oil (an ideal in its own right) would be both a seismic shock and a catalyst for radical innovation. Setting vigorous restrictions on emissions will drive technological progress towards creating a more efficient lifestyle. A spur for the world's innovators, thinkers, designers and visionaries to build new economies and businesses that are compatible with a low-energy future. Growth, but not as we know it.

Conspiracy Theories

The Big Cover-Up

b7c

1. Values

You're dumb if you believe what you're told

2. Target

Anxiety junkies

3. Exploits

Fears

We're being lied to

Emotions

Be suspicious, be alert

Obedience to:
- Don't believe a word of what you're told
- Warning: duplicitous forces at work
- Events outside our control
- From Roswell to the *Da Vinci Code*, a big secret that due to the nature of its revelations must be kept from the public at all cost
- Secret codes, enigmas, religious sects and mad monks
- Historic and religious events, covered up by covert government or mainstream religion
- Revelatory messages encrypted in obscure texts
- The occult, ancient societies
- New world order orchestrated behind the scenes
- Whistle blowers

Rejection of:
- Traditional institutions
- Dictates of church and state
- Government and authority
- Mainstream explanations in the media
- The need to classify information in the interests of national security
- The men in black

Emotional Context:
- For those who believe that everything the establishment says is a total fabrication, such paranoia is a short step to submitting to beliefs that are a total fabrication; the aliens of Roswell, the moon landing was filmed in a studio, 9/11 was a CIA plot, that Princess Diana was assassinated by MI6. Psychologists have discovered that those with high levels of dopamine in the brain are more susceptible to finding significance in coincidence and creating meaning from small events where there is none.

Social context:
- Cynicism and disillusionment with the murky operations of contemporary government has added credence to the belief that most world events are manipulated by interests behind the scenes. It isn't new. Nazism and Communism drew on imaginary plots to instill hatred. Theories of a nuclear Iraq prompted the invasion of 2001. Hizbollah blamed 9/11 on Jewish involvement. Many see the shady Bilderberg group (a collection of power brokers and intellectuals) as behind-the-scenes manipulators of world events.

Promise:
•The truth is out there...but only for the initiated...

Future Vision:
•Christopher Hitchens, correspondent on the *Wall Street Journal*, sees conspiracy theories as being 'the exhaust fumes of democracy', the by-product of a vast amount of unmediated information circulated among a vast number of people. An explosion of misinformation is the result. As the internet grows in power this will only inflate.

Personal Fears:
•We're being constantly lied to
•We are in the dark
•Events are being manipulated behind the scenes
•'They' are not working in our interests, but for the powers that be

World Fears:
•Forces of evil on the march. Judgement Day is coming
•World instability

5.Reward

The truth is out there

FBI

Reality check
•When popular media, TV, films and culture mix reality with the bizarre, the absurd and the plain wacky, it should be no surprise that conspiracy theories abound and proliferate. Our daily news supplies us with a fair quota of the unexpected and the surreal. After all, what could be more improbable than the sight of the President of the United States calmly reading a story about a pet goat, as two commercial airliners crashed into the twin towers of the World Trade Centre?

4.Seduces with

Promise

Join the inner circle
(those in the know)

Visual spell

Secret worlds, secret societies

Iconography:
•Flying saucers and alien abduction
•Mystic symbols and glowing secret codes
•Freemasons, church vaults
•Messages hidden in paintings. Paranoid monks and secret societies
•Being followed by 'agents'

Style/Aesthetic:
•Dark powers behind the scenes
•Someone is watching you

Personal Fears:
- Insecurity at home, travelling, and at work
- Fear of foreigners
- The crazy world beyond my gate
- Violence in the street
- Coming face to face with terrorism
- Criminal aliens, foreign gangs, drug traffickers and vice rings
- Job insecurity

World Fears:
- World instability
- Spread of global terror
- Unstoppable tides of immigration
- The end of our civilisation as we know it

Fears

1. Values

DEFENSE OF THE REALM
(I.E. YOUR BACKGARDEN)

2. Target

MR & MRS WORRIED

Emotions

TAKING OUR JOBS, OUR HOMES & OUR WOMEN

KEEP *THEM* OUT

3. Exploits

Obedience to:
- Fortress mentality – keep them out
- Defence of the realm, the homeland
- Patriotism
- Preservation of 'our' way of life (security & wealth)
- Not in my back yard
- Suspicion of foreigners
- Hard line on border control
- 'Us' and 'Them'
- Hatred as old as the hills – identify your foe – make him a scapegoat for all your ills
- Distrust of any man with a 'funny' name, wearing 'funny' clothes

Rejection of:
- One big equal world – all the people as brothers
- Opening the flood gates on immigration
- Bogus asylum seekers and political refuges
- Racial equality and multiculturalism
- Promotion of ethnic identities
- Ethnic education (only fronts for terror schools)

Emotional Context:
- From Asia, to Europe and the US, xenophobia is universal. It has innocent beginnings – a pub joke, a football chant, a flippant remark on a TV chat show. But enflamed by politicians and religious leaders, xenophobia can easily morph into nationalism, racism, and at worst case, genocide. Post 9/11, fear of foreigners has veered into hysteria. Passengers have refused to board flights with people wearing 'heavy clothes, speaking Arabic'. Such tensions can create genuine phobias; 'I'd rather be paranoid than dead'.

Social context:
- Since the collapse of the World Trade Centre, the world has undergone, in the words of Martin Amis, 'a moral crash', 'the spiritual equivalent, in its global depth and reach, of the Great depression of the 30's'. Across the world personal freedoms have come under siege as the police expand their powers to identify and detain foreign suspects. The media, fuelling insecurity and paranoia, increases this polarization. Crude stereotypes of immigrants as being terrorists and economic migrants adds to the paranoia. The majority are skilled professionals – doctors, nurses, technicians – beneficial to national prosperity.

XENO**PHOBIA**
US vs THEM

5.Reward

4.Seduces with

Promise

SECURITY FOR **YOU** AND YOUR FAMILY

Visual spell

HOARDS AT THE GATE

SLEEP SOUNDLY AT NIGHT

Reality check:
In the context of the Third World, the media paints a picture of the West as the promised land. It's difficult to understand the potency of this message. 'Maddened by the media', its soap operas, game shows, music videos and commercials, Africans and Asians will risk starvation and drowning at sea for the desire state: wide screen TVs, luxury cars and the comforts of the modern home. When this quest is rejected, the ensuing resentment and hatred will find an easy welcome in the arms of the extremist.

Promise:
- A safe future for you and your family
- Sleep peacefully at night
- Keep the hoards at bay

Future Vision:
- As the threat of immigration becomes a central issue across Europe, right-wing political parties are gaining ground. As the barriers go up on fortress Europe, are we in danger of writing the narrative for a future clash of cultures? Passions stoked by TV and the Internet are already increasing divisions at a time when the best hope for our future lies in the plurality of our identities and ideas.

Iconography:
- 9/11
- Global acts of terror
- Suicide bombers
- Daily atrocities on the news
- Radical Islam
- Russian, Albanian, middle European mafia
- Increased gun violence
- Prostitutes on the street
- 25 grams of enriched uranium – making its way to a city near you at this very moment
- African boat people

Style/Aesthetic:
- Hoards of migrants at the gate

POLIT

& RELI

SPE

**MASTERS OF
THE UNIVERSE**
WAR ON TERROR

THE GREAT SATAN
RESIST WESTERN IMPERIALSIM

HEAVEN
REWARD IN THE AFTERLIFE

TICAL

CAL

GIOUS

LLS

ANTI-GLOBALISATION
PEOPLE POWER

OIL
FILL HER UP

SUPERCITY
ENVY OF THE WORLD

THE POOR MOUTH
BADGE OF VIRTUE

CHINA SYNDROME
ASIAN HORDES ON THE HORIZON

MASTERS OF THE UNIVERSE

Niall Ferguson
Colossus: The Rise and Fall of the American Empire

In military confrontations, the United States has the capability to inflict amazing and appalling destruction, while sustaining only minimal damage to itself. There is no regime it could not terminate if it wanted to – including North Korea's. Such a war might leave South Korea in ruins, of course, but the American Terminator would emerge from the rubble more or less unscathed. What the Terminator is _not_ programmed to do, however, is to rebuild. In his wake, he leaves only destruction.

Nick Cohen
What's Left?: How Liberals Lost Their Way

What fuelled the anti-globalization movement was a passionate and often well merited hatred of the rich world in which its supporters lived. Like the theorists, the protesters believed their rich countries in general and America in particular constituted a global hegemon which oppressed suffering humanity. The psychological pressures behind the error were easy to explain. Contrary to the fashionable post-modern theory of the time, people don't always hate the 'alien other'; more often they hate what they know. British left-wingers were likely to have a deeper loathing of British Tories than for Saddam Hussein or Kim Jong-il because they had seen them up close all their lives and learned to find the thought of a victorious smirk on their enemies' faces intolerable.

US power features prominently in the pages of the world's press and news channels. Black Hawk helicopters, Humvee military vehicles and over–teched GI's are the symbols of its unrivalled military dominance which currently absorbs more than $500 billion a year. But just as a single image eroded the will to fight in Vietnam (the My Lai massacre), the weird, surreal, perverted images of the torture at Abu Ghraib prison, totally destroyed the moral cause in Iraq. US intervention, anywhere, has never been more unpopular.

Many in the civilised world, the Europeans being the most vocal, are even questioning the need to have a global policeman. Would there even have been conflict with the Muslim world if the war mongers hadn't been so inept? Have they inadvertently created the enemy by giving it unity and a cause?

Just as the West and the Middle East slide inexorably towards a deepening quagmire, China, after two centuries of relative decline, has been quietly recovering its stride. Single minded in its vision of expansion, foreign policy is an instrument used only to procure vital resources, especially oil, to feed its voracious industry. With a reluctance to interfere with the internal affairs of other nations, or use its power for humanitarian ends or to influence change, its international style, in contrast to the US, couldn't be more different. Its war is different. It's purely commercial. And the US is firmly in its sights.

Emotional Context:
- At the heart of the American Way is self-righteousness. Four thousand years of other nations' often brutal and failed social experiments from sun-god worship to more recently fascism and communism has culminated in the ideal social state: democracy and market capitalism. Within such a system everyone, irrespective of colour, creed or status, has the potential to be successful. The American Way is the freedom to be unequal.

Social context:
- US policy acts with two faces: the hard-line hawks project fear of impending terrorist activity (which no doubt Al Qaeda will inevitably oblige), justifying the need to expand US power abroad to maintain US security at home. At the same time the Doves peddle soft-line idealism – the promotion of justice, freedom and democracy, which in turn bring stability for US markets and commercial interests.

Fears:
- Axis of evil: North Korea, Iran, Iraq
- Dominant radical Islam
- Collapse of US power
- International terrorism
- Mounting casualties abroad (though the 'enemy' may be closer to home. Since the 1960's more Americans have died from national gun crime than have been killed on the battlefields of the world)
- More screw-ups in the Middle East (i.e. Islamists taking over in Saudi Arabia)
- Rising power of China (how to get tough with rogue states when China is all too willing to step into the breach?)
- Weak Europe (more work for the US)
- Looming healthcare crisis, ageing population, mounting national debt

Obedience to:
- Protection of US interests (i.e.oil security)
- War on terror, tyrants, oppressors and aggressors
- Moral superiority tempered by total military dominance on land, sea and air
- Peace through strength; pre-emptive action and interventionism
- Preventing the descent into chaos in the Middle East
- US as a force for good, crucial to the promotion of liberty and free markets everywhere
- Empire consolidation; maintaining competitive advantage
- See the enemy, know the enemy (listening and video surveillance of suspicious activity worldwide)
- CIA expression – 'Limited hangout' – own up to as little as possible, bury the rest

Rejection of:
- Woolly liberal, soft–talk peaceniks (thinly disguised Bolsheviks, subversives and anti–capitalists)
- UN indecisiveness
- Weak, old–school European diplomacy
- Committee consensus multi–lateral agreement
- Left–leaning media; terror thrives given the right conditions, chaotic government unable to confront radicalism and an ever–compliant Media ready to give it air time
- Imperial overstretch

1.Values
FREEDOM, DEMOCRACY, MILITARY SUPERIORITY

2.Target
PATRIOT AMERICA

3.Exploits
Fears
WATCH THE SKIES

Emotions
WE'RE THE GOOD GUYS ★★★

MASTERS OF THE UNIVERSE
WAR ON TERROR

Promise:
- US power is crucial to the promotion of liberty and justice for all
- 'We're the good guys'
- Freedom & democracy
- Stability & security
- Free markets & world prosperity

Future Vision:
- The conflicts in Iraq, Afghanistan, Israel and now with Iran over its nuclear ambitions only further exacerbates the quagmire which is the Middle East. The neocons, largely responsible for the chaos of Iraq, have struggled to understand the nature of the enemy they are up against, blithely unaware that it is their own incompetence and lack of foresight that have both created the enemy and fuelled the rise of radical Islam.

Promise

FREEDOM TO BE UNEQUAL

Visual spell

SUBURBAN HOME & GARDEN, WALK IN FRIDGE FREEZERS, SUVS, WALL TO WALL TVS

4. Seduces with

5. Reward

THE US CENTURY

Reality check:

For the powerful military contractors contemplating budget cuts as a result of the end of the cold war the rise of international terrorism saw a welcome return to the good old days. Conflict was opportunity; the spread of democracy a Trojan horse for new markets for US companies. But behind all the gesturing and tough talk of liberty and justice, the more unnerving implication is clear: the stability and future security of the world is irrevocably tied to oil. It begs the question – if all the military expenditure poured into fighting for oil (author Joseph Stiglitz puts the cost of the Iraq war at $3 trillion), had been intelligently invested in energy research would we have found an alternative? And could we all sleep better at night?

Iconography:
- Military might and technical superiority
- Precision bombing & surgical strikes
- Stealth warfare, war by wire, 'smart' bombs
- Drones and robot warriors
- Humvees, Blackhawks, GIs
- Ballot boxes, self determination, Coke and hamburgers
- Satellite TV and mobile phones
- CNN, MTV, Disney, Hollywood
- Benefits of a free market economy; suburban homes, walk in fridge freezers, sleek SUVs, 42" TVs

Style/Aesthetic:
- Patriotism and pride in one's country
- Truth, justice, the American way
- Faith in the future
- Protector of world security

The Great ☆ Satan

The U.S. is responsible for all the injustices of the world

Mary Midgley
The Myths We Live By

Fanatics are not just stern moralists, they are obsessive ones who forget all but one part of the moral scene. They see no need to respect ideals that seem to conflict with their chosen ones, or to work out a reconciliation between them. This frame of mind is not, of course, peculiar to full-time fanatics. It is easy to fall into it whenever one is, for the moment, completely absorbed in some good cause, and good causes often do seem to demand that kind of absorption.

Charles Allen
God's Terrorists – The Wahhabi Cult and the Hidden Roots of Modern Jihad.

Said's *Orientalism*, with its central charge that Western scholarship was a weapon of imperialism, became *the* text in Arab and Middle Eastern studies in the 1980s and 1990s, and has itself contributed mightily to the revisionism and myth-making which have given many Muslims a highly distorted understanding of their own history; in particular, giving further credence to the widespread Muslim self-image of the Umma as innocent victim of Western oppression.

Anti-Americanism, rather than being a recent concept, had its origins in the universities and institutions of the Western world in the 20th century. It reflected more the insecurities of academics, who feeling displaced in a world of obsessive consumerism, blamed American culture and its mindless materialism for corrupting the social values of the world. This lifestyle dominance, in its brands, cars, language and now its technology, has made it the world scapegoat for a myriad of ills, from environmental degradation, to the soullessness of high rise cities, and the erosion of the rural idyll.

Ian Buruma and Avishai Margalit write about the origins of such animosity in *Occidentalism: A Short History of Anti–Westernism*. Since ancient times, humans have lived in terror of being punished for their effrontery in challenging the gods, by stealing fire, or gaining too much knowledge, or creating too much wealth, or building towers that reach for the skies. The problem is not with the city per se, but with cities given to commerce and pleasure instead of religious worship. In the case of Osama bin Laden and Mohammed Atta this religious impulse curdled into a dangerous madness.

Writer of *Identity and Violence*, Nobel Laureate Amartya Sen, in looking for the seeds of such madness, argues that conflict violence and hatred is sustained by the illusion of unique identities, divided along religious lines, that ignore a person's common humanity and the plurality of our afflictions.

Resignation of one's autonomy to the group also devolves one of responsibility. Scientific research has shown that we have a natural propensity to form groups for our own protection. Part of that defence includes a prejudice to those outside our circle. Such discrimination can easily be inflamed to create violence.

The Great Satan

The **US** is responsible for all the injustices of the world

1. Values

Resist westen aggression and imperialism

2. Target

Disenchanted, angry, young Muslims

Emotions

Fight injustice

Fears

Being subsumed by U.S. power

3. Exploits

Fears:
- The Middle East and its people being subsumed and enslaved by US power
- I'm a nobody, unrecognised and unloved
- Loneliness and a sense of dislocation
- Exclusion from a world of plenty
- Lack of direction and opportunity
- Personal, social and sexual failings (the constant humiliation of being spurned by the opposite sex can transmogrify into resentment and hatred and a desire to 'purify' the world of the promiscuous (as occurred in the Bali Nightclub bombing in 2002).

Obedience to:
- Total obedience to the Word, rule of Shariah
- Return to the purity of an idealised past
- Total devotion to a cause
- Purity of the soul uncorrupted by Western ideas
- Do not accept the rule of the Kaffir (non muslim)
- Counterbalance the injustices suffered at the hands of the West
- US and its allies are the devil incarnate
- Rebirth through destruction
- Fight to prevent Islam being subsumed by Western liberal democracy
- Demonise your enemy; Westerners are weak, effete, cowardly, superficial, spiritually and morally bankrupt, obsessed by material comfort and sex

Rejection of:
- Bullish, arrogant US Power
- The endless killing of innocent Muslims
- The duplicity of US diplomacy (front for expansionism and the preservation of Israel)
- Freedom and democracy (a deceit cloaking commercial ambitions)
- Global dominance of US corporate power and brands
- Pornography of western pop culture and fashion
- Banality of lifestyle and materialism
- Cities as dens of vice and prostitution
- Cosmopolitanism (abhorrence of intercultural marriage)
- Cold, soulless, scientific rationalism
- Idolatry

Emotional Context:
- For young Muslims, a sense of fury over their impotence to be heard together with an ever-expanding sense of injustice, is further enflamed by propaganda and the rhetoric of radical and religious extremists; as a bystander you have no power or voice. But cross the line and become a martyr, you are all powerful and your voice is amplified across the media channels of the world.

Social context:
- Originating in the Crusades, the concept of Jihad was given added momentum with the collapse of the Ottoman Empire after World War 1.
- Many intellectuals in the Middle East view religion as a retrogressive force, holding back modernisation and with it the benefits of education and scientific advance that can do so much to alleviate poverty – so often the breeding ground for resentment.
- The great satan is also a reading of world affairs in which every ill, of every oppressed individual and people, has its origins in western imperialism. In historic terms, many of these grievances have some truth: Vietnam, Korea, South America, Iraq.
- Global envy of US power plays a large part in this animosity. The destruction of the Twin Towers symbolised the destruction of an imperial icon. From the Middle East to Asia many shared in this schadenfreude over the misfortune of the over-bearing, arrogant US Empire.

Promise:
- Nobility of self-sacrifice/dying for a cause
- Death is Victory
- Paradise in the afterlife
- Salvation & deliverance
- Destruction of US power
- You shall be heroes (your actions will be celebrated in songs, on websites and posters)
- Group solidarity (shared pact/sense of duty)
- Individual autonomy surrendered for the cause
- Family will be proud

Future Vision:
- A more serious ramification of the war on terror will be a tendency to associate every Muslim with violence. An erosion of trust will lead to less social interaction, business and trade, increasing inequality and further fomenting future anger and discord.
- Though the Great Satan is a term applied to hatred between West and East, recent massacres between Sunni and Shia Muslims have shown that radicals and militants are more than willing to carve each other up in the name of religion.

4. Seduces with

Promise

Nobility of self-sacrifice, **dying for a cause**

Visual spell

Destruction of the cities of the infidel

5. Reward

Paradise
in the afterlife

Reality check

The dehumanizing image of the West — a racist bigoted view of all Westerners as being godless materialists, unfeeling, guided by greed and sexual obsessions — goes some way to explaining how brutal acts of atrocity perpetuated by those fired by radicalism against total innocents, can be justified under the banner of 'religion'. Terrorism wraps itself in the world's grievances and the problems of the world's oppressed, to conceal its real intentions. Likewise, an appeal to heroism, for recognition, is attractive to those who feel diminished by Western successes, the benefits of which they are excluded from and a material lifestyle they cannot share in. Instead they reject it, finding glory in a cause that destroys it.

Iconography:
- Destruction of symbols of US power (cities)
- Atrocities committed by the West and its allies
- Suicide bombers (from kids to grandmas)
- Heroic nature of cause
- Purity of the past against corruption of modernism
- Courageous lone warrior against the masses of fearful, effete westerners
- David v Goliath
- Babylon / Sodom & Gomorrah (God destroys the cities of the infidels and the sinful)

Style/Aesthetic:
- Individual against global power
- Faithful against infidel
- Pure against impure
- Spiritual superiority v cold, soulless rationalism
- Divine light of righteousness v dark evils of imperialism and global dominance
- Apocalypse Now

HEAVEN

Since the dawn of civilisation from early sun worship to the Pharaohs and the Crusaders, religion has been a highly compelling belief system, an essential component of any society, bringing order, obedience, moral instruction, community and brotherhood. Ideas of a God found welcomed acceptance within minds plagued by insecurity and misfortune and for those struggling to find understanding, meaning and peace of mind. Early myth makers and gurus latched onto this psychology of uncertainty – the sense of unknowing, of curiosity and superstition – to tailor narratives that promised salvation and an alleviation from suffering, with a place in an afterlife paradise in exchange for obedience and subservience in the present.

Heaven is central to almost all faiths. Millions are prepared to devote, or even sacrifice, their lives, to a contract that is beyond earth-bound rationalisation. Without conviction as to this central tenet – the promise of paradise – religions would not have had such a compelling hold over us.
Some might interpret this as gullibility. But maybe people are content to live with their illusions. In social terms belief has advantages: certainty is better than uncertainty, feelings of spiritual unity are mentally healthier (in terms of happiness and lack of stress) than a sense that life has no purpose.

Though it is tempting in our modern technological age to write off religion as simple moral tales and fables, belief is on the ascendancy, gathering acceptance with a new generation of fundamentalists, creationists and dubious cults. Countering such popular movements, recent publications such as Richard Dawkin's *The God Delusion* and Christopher Hitchens' *God Is Not Great: How Religion Poisons Everything*, have shown few qualms in vigourously questioning the validity of faiths. Paradoxically, such critiques of religion, rather than encouraging a meeting of minds, are more likely to have the opposite effect – making faiths more defensive and polarised in their views. The continued strength of religious conviction in America, despite clear advances in education, information and scientific innovation, is one such anomaly.

Personal Fears
- Being unloved and alone
- Being invisible, unrecognised, lost in the modern, uncaring world
- Feeling soulless, 'empty inside', spiritually bankrupt
- Being excluded from the community
- Fear of past sins catching up with you
- Fear of death (in the light of those past sins)…

World Fears
- Intolerance, persecution and hate
- The dominance of imperial powers and global corporations
- The threat of nuclear catastrophe
- Natural disasters
- Ever-present anxiety of impending doom
- The inescapable judgement day
- The discomforting prospect of an afterlife in eternal damnation

HEAVEN
Reward in the afterlife

1. Subject

YOU ARE THE CHOSEN ONES

Emotions

3. Exploits

SALVATION, SPIRITUAL ENLIGHTENMENT, AN END TO SUFFERING

2. Target

WORLD POPULATION

Fears

ETERNAL DAMNATION: ROASTING IN THE FIRES OF HELL

Obedience to:
- Future reward for a life of obedience to the word of the scriptures, its commandments and moral codes
- Inner spiritual transformation
- The promotion and defense of the faith
- Adherence to the discipline of prayer, ritual and religious instruction
- Belief in forgiveness, redemption and the remission of sins
- Charity towards the less well-off (donations are an investment in paradise)
- Peace, love and harmony, instead of war (though religious tension over the next century looks set to increase conflict)
- Megachurches – 'Big Brother' in Guatemala seats 12,000 of the faithful and even comes with a heliport
- Rise of the Pastorpreneur – mass-market religion with export potential
- The coming Apocalypse – only by the destruction of our present sinful world can a more perfect 'kingdom of the chosen' come into being

Rejection of:
- Erring from the path of righteousness and falling victim to temptation and deviant acts of depravity and indulgence (sex, drink, drugs and rock & roll)
- Unbelievers and heretics
- Doubters and sceptics (the impudent who dare mock the veracity of the Testament)
- Pagans who worship false gods
- Blasphemy
- Devoting one's life to material comforts and pleasures
- Faith in the ability of modern, empirical science to explain the mysteries of creation (religion is not a thing that can be subjected to test-tube analysis)

Emotional context
- In the Middle Ages, belonging to the right faith was simple survival. In a period of history where sudden, unexpected death literally lurked around every corner, the promise of faith was succinct: safety and protection for the group – and if you devoted yourself to the cause, a place in heaven awaited you. The way of darkness was equally as focused: if you sinned you were cast out, eternal damnation yours in the fires of hell. Paintings, portraying horrific visions of heretics being brutally tortured and disembowelled by devils, the equivalent of today's snuff movies, made such transgressions abundantly clear.
- The neurology of the mind is so malleable that through indoctrination, repetition and the power of prayer, we are able not only to create a 'reality' and 'truth' of god within us, but also its sense of ecstasy, even its miracles – Heaven of sorts.

Social Context
- It's easy to ridicule the legitimacy of the Biblical account, handed down as it was, by disciples and wandering ascetics, in different languages over hundreds of years. But beyond the myths and fantasies, the place of religion in people's lives was much more fundamental than prayer and ritual. It was community and social fabric: a network of trust and reciprocity, a guide for how to conduct yourself within family, society and in business.
- The Pilgrim Fathers, in claiming the New World, toiled to create a Garden of Eden on earth untainted by sin. More ominously, contemporary fundamentalists interpret paradise as the need to purge the world of unbelievers.

5.Reward

4.Seduces with

Promise

GUIDING LIGHT
IN THE DARKNESS

Visual spell

PARADISE:
THE ANGELIC HOST,
NYMPHS IN WATERFALLS,
SOFT CHORAL MUSIC

YOUR SPECIAL
PLACE AWAITS YOU

Reality check:
Religions that have survived for more than two thousand years are not going to give up that tenure lightly. In order to get this far religions have needed armour-plated defense strategies to overcome the test of time. Doubt was tantamount to heresy, temptation the voice of the Devil, lack of faith weakness, and criticism a test of faith. In the modern age, empirical science and neurology are interpreted as an attack on the soul (a conflict of cold mechanical rationalism against the spiritual and the emotional) and the revolutionary insights of Darwinism explained away as 'intelligent design'.

Promise
- You are the fortunate ones: God's chosen children
- When the rest are damned you will be saved
- Share in the protection and goodwill of the all-seeing one
- Find strength and security in community
- Shut out suffering, anxiety and despair
- Follow the guiding light in the darkness
- Gain superiority and strength over unbelievers
- Those who wrong you today will find hellish retribution on judgement day
- There is purpose to life: in heaven you will be recompensed for your good deeds

World View
- The big problem for faith in the future is to remain relevant to young people in the age of multi-media everything: the internet and mobile communications. In the US, Christian fundamentalists and evangelical movements, have seen a rapid rise in popularity with congregations of all ages. And with cable channels, internet sites and ever-slicker architecture, they have also embraced the modern age.
- In contrast Islamist groups have derived their power by blaming the modern age for our lack of faith: we have become corrupt and sinful by indulging in the entertainments and pleasures of popular culture and lifestyle.

Imagery/Style
- In the age of blockbuster movies and cities overcrowded with towering monuments to household brands, it's hard to appreciate the impact temples and cathedrals had on ordinary people a thousand years ago. Religious buildings, overshadowing all else in the landscape, were mesmerizing in scale, colour, imagery and sound. Central to the whole religious experience, was heaven: a fantasy of serenity and beauty, decorated in gold and soft pastel hues. Like the original Eden, wild animals shared this paradise with enchanting angels and nymphs. Candle light, choral music and the chanting of monks, provided a sensory lyricism that was hard to resist. Such intense emotional stimulus locked religion in 'hearts and minds'.

Matt Ridley,
The Origins of Virtue

A parochial perspective characterises most religions – because most religions were developed by groups whose survival depended upon competition with other groups – fostering an 'in group' mentality. Even genocide was a central part of God's instruction as morality. When Joshua killed 12,000 heathen in a day and gave thanks to the Lord afterwards by carving the ten commandments in stone, including the phrase 'Thou shalt not kill', he was not being hypocritical. Like all good group selectionists, the Jewish God was as severe towards the out group as he was moral to the in group.

Felipe Fernandez Armesto,
Truth

We are followers of ill glimpsed guides. Most of the early thinkers whose influence has helped to form the world left scarce and sketchy indications of their teachings. This is part of their remarkably enduring attraction: unrecorded or poorly recorded thoughts can be reinterpreted to the taste of every generation, without the disciplines of fidelity to an unquestionable text.

Richard Dawkins
The God Delusion
(Quoting from an article by Richard Dawkins and Jerry Coyne, in The Guardian)

Why is God considered an explanation for anything? It's not – it's a failure to explain, a shrug of the shoulders, an 'I dunno' dressed up in spirituality and ritual. If someone credits something to God, generally what it means is that they haven't a clue, so they're attributing it to an unreachable, unknowable sky-fairy. Ask for an explanation of where that bloke came from, and odds are you'll get a vague, pseudo-philosophical reply about having always existed, or being outside nature. Which, of course, explains nothing.

Susan Blackmore,
The Meme Machine

Beauty inspires the faithful and brings them closer to God. Some of the most beautiful buildings in the world have been constructed in the name of Buddha, Jesus Christ or Mohammed. Then there are the beautiful statues and alluring stories about Hinduism; stained glass, inspiring paintings, and illustrated manuscripts, uplifting music sung by tremulous choir boys and vast choirs, or played on great organs. Deep emotions are inspired to the point of religious ecstasy or rapture which then cries out for and receives an explanation. The ecstasy is real enough, but from the memes' point of view, beauty is another trick to help them reproduce.

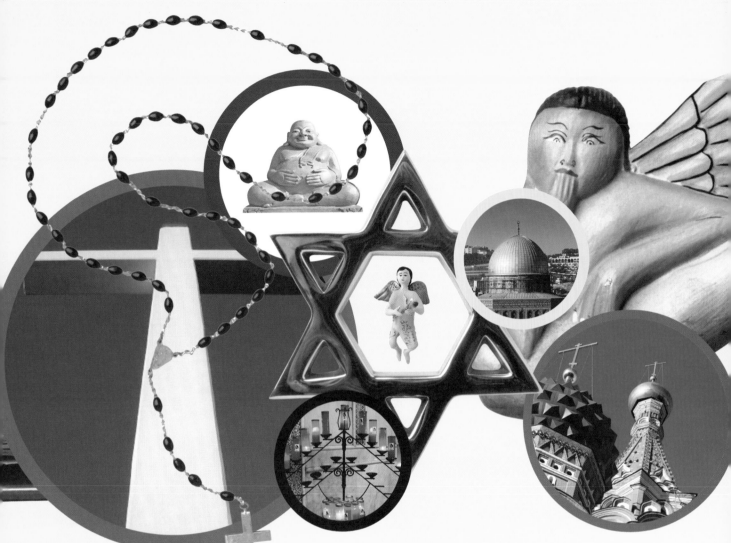

John Keay,
India – A History

Buddhism was not a belief system, nor a rival faith to the post Vedic cults and practices which prevailed under Brahmanical direction, but more a complementary discipline. About gods, worship, offerings, prayers, priests and ritual, the Buddha claimed no special knowledge. He offered merely heightened insight, not divine revelation. It was his followers in the generations to come who would elevate the Buddha and other semi-enlightened ones (Bodhisattvas) into deities, thus claiming for Buddhism the authority and the supernatural paraphernalia of a religion.

Abraham Eraly,
The Mughal Throne (Mughal Emperor, Akbar)

'The vulgar believe in miracles,' he said, 'but the wise man accepts nothing without adequate proof' – not that he doubted the possibility of miracles, but he knew that the potency of miracles was not in the shrine or in the saint, but in the faith of the supplicant himself.

Jacques Barzun,
From Dawn to Decadence

Rousseau reminds the reader that two-thirds of mankind are neither Christians nor Jews, nor Muhammadans, from which it follows that God cannot be the exclusive possession of any sector or people; all their ideas as to his demands and his judgments are imaginings. He asked only that we love him and pursue the good. All else we know nothing about. That there should be quarrels and bloodshed about what we can never know is the grossest impiety.

Anti-globalisation

Protect traditional interests and cultures
① Values

Third-world countries
② Target

Emotions
Individual rights

③ Exploits

Fears
Relentless march of global brands and corporations

Obedience to:
- Globalisation devastates the developing world and only lines the pockets of the multi–nationals
- Markets have no conscience
- The need to protect traditional cultures and identities
- Support social issues, workers' rights and fair trade
- Transparency of government
- The eradication of third world debt
- Fight against inequality, unemployment and corruption
- Reduce the wealth gap between rich and poor nations
- Street action and global protests at G8 and World Bank conferences and meetings

Rejection of:
- Under-aged workers and sweat-shop labour
- Globalisation as a simple 'cure all' for poverty
- Washington-centric world view (IMF, World Bank, WTO)
- Over reliance on standard economic models for all
- Faceless bureaucrats and suits
- Large infrastructure projects (power stations & dams)
- Bio–piracy (multinationals patenting traditional foods and medicines)

Emotional Context:
- Globalisation is a conflict of two mindsets: bankers who see the answer to all poverty in the implementation of 'one size fits all' economic prescriptions and the myriad lobbyist groups and NGO's that fight for a complex array of narrow interests (often in conflict with each other). This highly emotional debate is confused by researchers who often warp evidence to suit the demands of their pay-masters. Just as the heavy handedness of bankers finds few friends, fear of NGO assault can often hamstring development projects that depend on speed to prevent impending famine.

Social context:
- The most vociferous voices of protest have often drowned out the success stories of globalisation in Eastern Europe, China and much of Asia. Africa remains a quagmire. Wars, conflict and corruption have made parts of the continent hostile to growth and investment. Much of the problem with globalisation is management. Countries need stability and basic institutions – efficient banks, and robust legal systems – to enforce contracts and inspire trust, to encourage commerce and entrepreneurship.

Personal Fears:
- Becoming disenfranchised by the great global machine
- Having no voice
- Grey corporate bureaucracy
- Lack of recognition
- Corruption

World Fears:
- Dominance by multi-national power
- Environmental degradation and pollution
- Global warming

The Poor Mouth

① Values

The comfortably well off
② Target

Emotions
Compassion, Empathy, Charity

Fears
Compassion fatigue
③ Exploits

Front page shock image

Obedience to:
- Alleviation of inequality and world poverty
- Saving millions from famine and starvation
- Debt relief
- Poverty everywhere is of our making
- Victorian, Dickensian, Enlightenment values of compassion and benevolence
- Parable of the good Samaritan – feel good about giving
- One world community; share wealth and resources
- Reach for the purse; we spend more on our pets than the world's poor
- A world dichotomy – one billion people starving, one billion people obese

Rejection of:
- Compassion fatigue
- Uncaring western governments
- Global corporations
- Sweatshop labour
- War and conflict
- Complacency and inaction
- Charity should start at home

Emotional Context:
- With western audiences cocooned in the comforts of a modern lifestyle, ever more provocative images are needed to stir people out of inaction. Compassion is the emotion these images hope to induce. But there is also an appeal to vanity; the self promotion of their altruism in very visible badges and bracelets. Critics have long questioned whether benevolent acts to alleviate one's own guilt were selfish and therefore not real benevolence. For those at the receiving end, such pedantic debates are irrelevant. The end result is what matters; a good deed remains a good deed despite being done out of vanity.

Social context:
- For charities, ever reliant on the media to provide the 'advertising' for a cause, a logo on CNN translates into big donations. The need to conform to the demands of 24-hr news creates a pressure on photojournalists that can often result in issues being oversimplified in the rush to deliver the stock, shock image, to raise the millions that are needed. Likewise, using a celeb to ensure good coverage, again an essential part of the charity mix, can sometimes detract from the purpose of institutions such as Unicef and Oxfam by focusing more on glamour than the complexity of the task in hand.

Personal Fears:
- Puritanical guilt – help your neighbour
- Misfortune happens to us all – one day I might need to be on the receiving end
- Retribution follows a selfish act
- Innocent lives are being lost every day (millions every year)

World Fears:
- Africa, the failed continent, is at Europe's back door – the threat of uncontrolled immigration
- Poverty is a breeding ground for fanaticism and future terrorism
- The widening poverty gap between the wealthy north and impoverished south will lead to future friction
- The sophistication of markets worldwide, in technology and marketing, will only increase this gap

Sustainable future, fair trade

Street protests; walrus masks & turtle costumes

People power over faceless corporate power

4 Seduces with

5 Reward

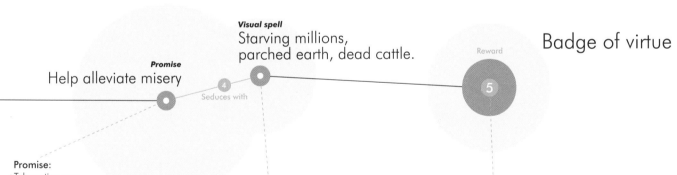

Promise:
- The voice of the people
- Self-determination
- Sustainable future
- Micro-economics – small is beautiful
- Respect for the environment
- Big business kept at bay
- Preservation of traditional ways and culture

Future Vision:
- International protest groups and the anti-globalisation movement is growing in worldwide prominence. As e-protest becomes even more mobile and connected (via the internet and the mobile phone), the ability of guerrilla activists to stage mass protests without warning anywhere in the world, becomes a real force to be reckoned with. Used responsibly, e-protest has the potential to be a highly effective counterbalance to the relentless expansion of global corporate power.

Iconography:
- World Bank protests and street battles
- Smashing shop-fronts of global brands: McDonalds, Starbucks
- Dressing up as goats, turtles and penguins
- A world of contrasts; comfy suburbia v the reality of life in Africa, Sudan, Ethiopia

Style/Aesthetic:
- Us and them
- Rich v poor
- Fat cats v starving children
- Third world v global business
- Green jungle v concrete jungle

Reality check:
- Naomi Klein's influential *No Logo*, described globalisation as being predominantly an 'American capitalist prescription'. The global spread of Starbucks, Nike and McDonalds are obvious symbols of a one-way process that only enriches the coffers of the multinationals.
- The rhetoric of global trade has been used to push Third world countries into eliminating trade barriers on their own goods, whilst developed nations continued to protect their own. Considering the ever increasing divide between rich and poor nations it would be a sad indictment of 'civilisation', if national interests can't be made to give ground to 'universal' interests.

Starving millions, parched earth, dead cattle.

Badge of virtue

Help alleviate misery

4 Seduces with

5 Reward

Promise:
- Take action now
- Save a life today
- Help alleviate disaster
- A better, fairer future
- Your conscience can sleep soundly at night

Future Vision:
- As news becomes more commoditised, media stations are increasingly being perceived and used as 'consumers of disaster imagery', forcing charities to resort to brand strategies to ensure their cause secures the front page against the competition. The expansion of the internet has added to the range of causes on offer from thousands of small NGO's and single issue advocacy groups. But with so many discordant demands, there are fears that conflicts over narrow interests will over burden the fight on poverty; farmers rights, environmental rights, animal rights, indigenous tribal rights, democratic rights, all crowd into the problem of whose 'freedoms' take preference over others.

Iconography:
- Hopeless, innocent, starving women and children
- Babies with bloated bellies and flies on their faces
- Dead cattle and parched earth
- Food queues at tented refugee camps
- Benevolent white politicians positioning for photo opportunities
- Saviours: the celeb, rock star entourage (Africa's image problem: How can the continent modernise and encourage investment when images printed in the western press repetitively endorse negative ideas of endemic poverty, disease, inept and corrupt government)

Style/Aesthetic:
- The hard, emotional reality
- Shock imagery: displaced and starving poor
- Death and disaster on an epic scale

Reality check:
- The inequities of global trade and the subsidies and trade barriers used to protect western nations and their farmers, have always beset the stability of African economies. The continent's core predicament is not a lack of money but the problem of failed states, corruption, incompetence and mismanagement. Further compounding the issues, large donations, badly directed, can sometimes exacerbate the situation; a dependency on foreign aid often undermines local markets and investment initiatives, leading to more corruption.
- Beacon of Hope – health programmes, against diseases such as AIDS, tuberculosis and malaria (financed by charities such as the GAVI Alliance and the Gates Foundation), have been some of the great success stories of the past decade.

Oil

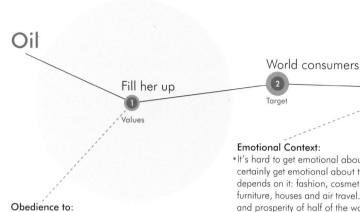

Fill her up
1 Values

World consumers
2 Target

Emotions
Freedom & prosperity
○ **3** Exploits

Fears
Maybe it really is running out…
◎

Obedience to:
- Fill her up
- Powering the nation
- Step on the gas
- Business as usual

Rejection of:
- It's running out
- The environmental movement: oil is dirty, polluting and endangering wildlife
- Liberal lefties: oil is responsible for the spread of global terror
- The Green lobby: oil is global warming culprit number one
- Alarmist photojournalists – images of dying polar bears and melting icebergs

Emotional Context:
- It's hard to get emotional about oil. But we can certainly get emotional about the lifestyle which depends on it: fashion, cosmetics, cars, electronics, furniture, houses and air travel. The wealth, comfort and prosperity of half of the world is locked into a hydrocarbon economy.

Social context:
- The future for oil isn't optimistic. Increased competition for dwindling reserves is forcing the West to deal with the increasingly belligerent Middle East. Such rising animosity is partly responsible for the spread of global terrorism and a prime reason behind the recent US-led invasion of Iraq in the interests of maintaining 'oil' stability. With the average US citizen consuming twice as much energy as his European equivalent and ten to twenty times more than a Chinese or Indian citizen, maybe it's time for the US to lead a search for alternatives.

Personal Fears:
- Maybe it really is running out?
- City pollution
- $200 a barrel

World Fears:
- It is running out
- Islamists taking over Saudi Arabia, the largest world exporter of oil, and turning off the taps, leading to economic chaos
- China and India competing for energy, and in the struggle to secure oil, the threat of future conflict

China Syndrome

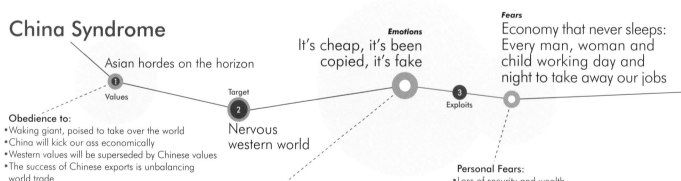

Asian hordes on the horizon
1 Values

Target
2

Emotions
It's cheap, it's been copied, it's fake
◎

Fears
Economy that never sleeps: Every man, woman and child working day and night to take away our jobs
○ **3** Exploits

Nervous western world

Obedience to:
- Waking giant, poised to take over the world
- China will kick our ass economically
- Western values will be superseded by Chinese values
- The success of Chinese exports is unbalancing world trade
- China will be the cause of global instability (Taiwan, South China Sea)
- Chinese expansion is causing environmental damage: desert encroachment, air pollution, dams
- The Chinese turn a blind eye to child labour, prison labour and human rights abuses
- Chinese tourists are taking over our beaches, our hotels and our cultural destinations
- China's advantage is built on cheap labour: for the West to compete effectively, its hard-won social systems and welfare benefits will need to be sacrificed

Rejection of:
- The Chinese miracle will run out of steam
- China lacks innovation
- With all economic activity controlled by the Party, the system is massively corrupt and inefficient
- China, victim of its own success, is losing its competitive edge; higher costs and labour
- Chinese hegemony over the world is an illusion

Emotional Context:
- Made complacent by wealth and comfort, Empires have always felt threatened from outside. For the US the Russian menace provided this fear for almost half a century. This time being overshadowed economically by China is becoming the big fear of contemporary times.

Social context:
- The Chinese have always seen themselves as being first as a civilisation. Many advances, such as paper, printing and gunpowder, originated in the East and gradually filtered out to the West. The Chinese saw their world as being the celestial kingdom; heavenly harmony on earth. The Great Wall kept the barbarians and foreigners out. Though communism might have reversed their dominance, many now feel that the superiority of old will see a resurgence.
- Historic humiliations (the Opium Wars and the Boxer Rebellion), provide further impetus

Personal Fears:
- Loss of security and wealth
- Prospect of greater competition from the East
- Rise of one (China), eclipses the success of the other, Europe and the US will slide into recession

World Fears:
- Europe overrun with Chinese coach tours and tourists
- Massive rise in global warming caused by dirty Chinese power plants (though about 25% of CO_2 emissions in China come from products made for Western markets).
- China is 2nd in military power: conflict is inevitable
- China is also the 2nd largest consumer of oil – and is becoming increasingly predatory to secure it
- Chinese industry has a brash disregard for western copyright (20% of brands in China are fake)
- China has no political will to meddle in international affairs, or use its power to rein in rogue states
- Twenty years ago Red China pledged to fight western capitalism to the death. Now that battle will continue commercially

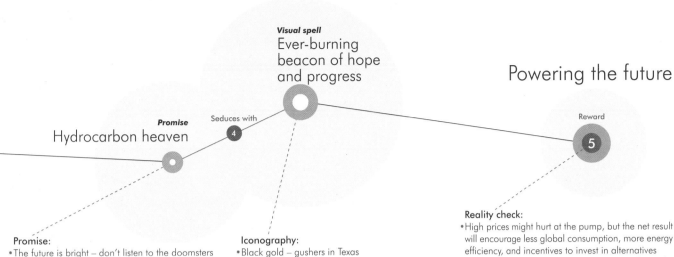

Visual spell

Ever-burning beacon of hope and progress

Promise

Hydrocarbon heaven

Powering the future

Seduces with **4**

Reward **5**

Promise:
- The future is bright – don't listen to the doomsters
- Business as usual
- Newer, cleaner fuels
- Hydrogen power on the future horizon
- No need to panic (yet)

Future Vision:
- The easy oil has gone. Some are predicting that production is close to peaking. What remains is becoming ever more difficult and expensive to extract. Making future predictions is compounded by the problem of assessing how much oil remains. Countries like Saudi Arabia refuse to allow outsiders to audit its reserves. Adding to the murky picture of how much is left, the big global oil companies habitually raise estimates to enhance their short term share prices.

Iconography:
- Black gold – gushers in Texas
- Quarter-mile-long oil tankers
- Pipelines across snowy or windswept landscapes
- Oil waving the flag for freedom; go anywhere, anytime
- The automobile at the centre of the American way of life (which is rapidly becoming the global way of life)
- Glowing logo of an international oil brand as a beacon of security and progress

Style/Aesthetic:
- The future's bright, optimistic. A new dawn, promising clean, new energy is virtually on the horizon. Don't panic.

Reality check:
- High prices might hurt at the pump, but the net result will encourage less global consumption, more energy efficiency, and incentives to invest in alternatives (biofuels, solar, wind, hydrogen), delaying the peak in oil reserves by at least 100 years. Conversely, low oil prices, and a return to profligacy, will mean less incentives to save and explore alternatives, bringing the peak in production forward to 25 years from now.

Promise

Western power has reached its zenith; the only way is down

Visual spell

New high-tech, state of the art, star architect, building on the skyline

Rising Sun

4 Seduces with

Reward **5**

Premise:
- Western economic power has reached its zenith
- Prepare for relegation to the second league
- To compete effectively those in the West will need to work harder, for longer, for the rest of their days

Future Vision:
- Chinese growth worldwide remains undiminished. The country retains almost $1 trillion in foreign exchange reserves. It is also the second largest consumer of oil. Big on production and even bigger on consuming, few in Asia doubt that the next century will be theirs. Despite this optimism, China has massive structural and political problems to surmount, before it can cruise to full capitalism.
- Is China lining up to be the new Big Bad Red Menace, or is a more positive force in the making?

Iconography:
- 'To get rich is glorious'
- Every month a new building on the skyline
- Star architects lining up with bold new visions
- Beijing Olympics: bigger, more efficient, than anything the West has fielded
- Regimented production lines, dutiful workers, at it day and night
- Everyday a bright new high-tech factory
- New motorways, slick transport systems, airports
- Bigger department stores, billboards, markets
- Sun setting on western and US hegemony

Negative imagery:
- Tiananmen Square – a single student standing in the way of a tank
- Slave labour camps
- Political prisoners
- Beating up Tibetan monks

Reality check:
- Fear of China's remarkable growth is rapidly turning the country into big bad ogre: taking away our jobs, our wealth, economic wellbeing and spoiling our beaches and the global environment. But is the fear that the West will be rapidly eclipsed by China overdone? Poor labour conditions, income disparity, pay, restrictive and corrupt government, are already hampering greater productivity and efficiency. Unless the country can make the jump to more sophisticated technologies, become innovative and create value through branding and marketing, China will remain the effective sub-contractor of the West.

SUPERCITY

Envy of the world

Deyan Sudjic
The Edifice Complex

Everyone wants an icon now. They want
an architect to do for them what Gehry's
Guggenheim did for Bilbao and Jorn
Utzon's Opera House did for Sydney.
When the Walt Disney Hall finally
opened in Los Angeles, most of the
speeches at the opening ceremony
talked more about what the new concert
hall was going to do for the city's image
than about the acoustics.

The well known picture postcard silhouette of Manhattan, with skyscrapers
crowned with the logos of household products and brands, from Woolworth
to Chrysler, Trump Tower and Citigroup, was without doubt the most potent
symbol of the power, prestige and dominance of American culture and commerce.
In bricks, glass and steel, here was material evidence of the success of market
capitalism. Such grandeur epitomized the values of the American dream;
ordinary men and women could make a mark on the world's stage. And it was
a vision that went global. For cities in Asia, South America and the Middle East,
the high-rise skyline become the aspirational look. Now, over 120 years after
the first tall building was completed in Chicago, North America is finally
surrendering its high rise supremacy to Asia and China.

Since the mid-seventies and the construction of the Sears Tower and the World
Trade Centre, the race to build the world's tallest building has speeded up. In
1998 the Petronas Towers in Kuala Lumpur brought Malaysia fleeting prominence.
Taiwan ploughed more than $1.8 billion into lifting Taipei 101 into first place,
at 448 metres. A brief supremacy that is likely to last no more than 2 years.
In Dubai, anxious to break every building and architectural record on record,
(biggest man-made island, longest indoor ski-slope, largest department store),
ambitious investors are bravely pushing its Burj Dubai towards the 800 metre
mark. But with Shanghai and Moscow waiting in the wings, how long it keeps
its crown remains to be seen.

SUPERCITY
ENVY OF THE WORLD

Personal Fears:
- Not going high enough
- Being upstaged by rival cities or architects
- Running out of funds
- Recession on the horizon (most of the world's tallest buildings are completed at the cusp of a recession)
- Being sued by clients for malpractice

World Fears:
- Global financial collapse
- World terror attack 9/11 style (towering skyscrapers glorify commerce and power. Reinterpreted in the eyes of the terrorist such edifices read as symbols of all that is rotten in the West, the personification of greed and materialism – thus ripe for destruction)

2.Target

MEGALOMANIACS

3.Exploits

Fears

BEING UPSTAGED BY RIVALS

1.Values

FUTURE UTOPIA

Emotions

BIGGER THAN YOURS

Obedience to:
- New city on the world map
- My glass tower's bigger than yours
- Prestige architect to provide the vision
- Architecture as a reflection of national power in steel and concrete
- Symbol of progress (as opposed to traditional cultural symbols of a redundant past)
- Gigantism; stamp my mark on the world
- Aspirational totem in the sky; if one man can achieve this, so can I
- The architect as sculptor, artist, icon builder
- Go East (high rise buildings in Asia now exceed those in the North America)
- The next hot international business destination
- Inflating real estate values, rental, land yields

Rejection of:
- Preserving the past
- Conservative city planners
- Red tape and health and safety prerogatives
- Narrow interest protest groups obstructing planning – 'preserve the spotted newt'
- Concrete production accounts for 5% of world CO_2 emissions

Emotional Context:
- To build big, to build high, to build with style, is the ego magnified in glass, titanium and concrete; immortality for dictators, businesses or tech billionaires.
- Like playing with lego, even the most sophisticated cities in the world engage in a childish drive to build higher than their neighbours – a temporary superiority that might last no more than a couple of years before the attention of the world's media deserts you.

Social context:
- Celeb architects are increasingly drawn to the parts of the world undergoing the fastest economic transformation: Beijing, Shanghai, Singapore. Nothing expresses the wealth and economic progress of a city more than a skyline dominated by a showcase of the world's elite architects. It's a formula that's contagious; around half of the world's tallest buildings have been built since the year 2,000 – the majority in Asia.

Iconography:
- New dominant silhouette on the skyline
- Cool new civic plaza as the social heart of the city (small children, mime artists and roller skaters)
- Dramatic view from the top floor; men as ants
- Future plans: beaming financiers and architects posing in front of perspex scale models
- Super slick computer 'walk-throughs'
- The new 'blob' organic style – anything goes
- Centre spread of style bible, *Wallpaper**
- Backdrop for cool fashion and car commercials

Style/Aesthetic:
- Power in glass and steel
- Call up the usual suspects: Foster & Partners, Frank Gehry, Renzo Piano, Rem Koolhaas, Zaha Hadid, Santiago Calatrava, Herzog & de Meuron

Visual spell

POWER IN GLASS AND STEEL

4. Seduces with

Promise

SYMBOL OF TECHNOLOGICAL, CREATIVE AND SOCIAL PROGRESS

5. Reward

OVERSHADOW YOUR RIVALS

Reality check

Since the pyramid of Cheops, the purpose of grand monumental architecture hasn't changed. It's about glory, economic power, superiority and immortality. In the US, household products, Woolworths and Wrigleys, became towering high-rise icons. The purpose of the Petronas Towers in Asia was to place the Malaysian PM at the centre stage of Asia politics. Frank Gehry's titanium-clad Guggenheim made a cultural destination out of previous back water, Bilbao. Since then competing cities across Europe have raced to build on this successful formula, with more dramatic architectural visions hoping to pull in the world's tourists (though the art to fill them is a diminishing commodity).

Promise:
- Your city the envy of the world
- Future utopia
- Centre of the universe
- Symbol of technological, creative and social progress
- Supercity superiority
- 'Castles in the clouds'

Future Vision:
- With more people now settling in cities than in the country, it is to urban living that we should turn to for efficiencies in lifestyle and energy conservation. Hi-tech advances in design, materials and building techniques can create buildings that consume 35% less energy. Contrary to its image as being dirty and polluting, cities are the future of green.

BIBLIOG
& IN

GRAPHY

DEX

Allen, Charles. *God's Terrorists – The Wahhabi Cult and the Hidden Roots of Modern Jihad,* Da Capo Press, 2006.

Anderson, Chris. *The Long Tail: How Endless Choice Is Creating Unlimited Demand,* Random House Business Books, 2007.

Armesto, Felipe Fernandez. *Truth: A History and a Guide for the Perplexed,* St Martin's Press, 2001.

Armstrong, Karen. *The Great Transformation: The World in the Time of Buddha, Socrates, Confucius and Jeremiah,* Atlantic Books 2006.

Austerlitz, Saul. *Money for Nothing: A History of the Music Video from the "Beatles" to the "White Stripes",* Continuum International Publishing Group Ltd, 2006.

Barzun, Jacques. *From Dawn to Decadence: 500 years of Western Cultural Life,* Harper Collins Ltd, 2001.

Berlin, Isaiah. *The Sense of Reality: Studies in Ideas and Their History,* Farrar Straus & Giroux, 1997.

Berlin, Isaiah. *The Roots of Romanticism,* Princeton University Press, 2001.

Blackmore, Susan. *The Meme Machine,* Oxford Paperbacks, 2000.

Botton, Alain de. *The Consolations of Philosophy,* Penguin Books Ltd, 2001.

Botton, Alain de. *The Art of Travel,* Penguin Books Ltd, 2003.

Brooks, David. *Bobos in Paradise: The New Upper Class and How They Got There,* Simon & Schuster Ltd, 2000.

Buruma, Ian. *The Missionary and the Libertine. Love and War in East and West,* Vintage Books USA, 2001.

Buruma, Ian & Margalit, Avishai. *Occidentalism: A Short History of Anti-Westernism,* Atlantic Books, 2005.

Calvino, Italo. *Why Read the Classics?,* Vintage, 2000.

Carey, John. *Faber Book of Science,* Faber & Faber, 2005.

Cashmore, Ellis. *Celebrity Culture,* Routledge, an imprint of Taylor & Francis Books, 2006.

Chadha, Radha & Husband, Paul. *The Cult of the Luxury Brand: Inside Asia's Love Affair with Luxury,* Nicholas Brealey International, 2006.

Clarkson, Jeremy. *Born to be Riled,* Penguin Books Ltd, 2007.

Cohen, Nick. *What's Left?: How Liberals Lost Their Way,* Fourth Estate, 2007.

Crick, Francis. *The Astonishing Hypothesis: The Scientific Search for the Soul,* Simon & Schuster Inc, 1994.

Damasio, Antonio. *The Feeling of What Happens: Body and Emotion in the Making of Consciousness,* Harcourt Publishers Ltd College Publishers, 1999.

Dawkins, Richard. *The God Delusion,* Bantam Press, 2006.

Dennett, Daniel. *Darwin's Dangerous Idea: Evolution and the Meanings of Life,* Penguin Books Ltd, 1996.

Dylan, Bob. *Chronicles: Volume One,* Pocket Books, 2005.

Edelman, Gerald & Tononi, Guilio. *Consciousness: How Matter Becomes Imagination,* Penguin Books Ltd, 2001.

Edelman, Gerald. *Second Nature: Brain Science and Human Knowledge,* Yale University Press, 2007.

Emsley, John. *Vanity, Vitality, and Virility: The Science Behind the Products You Love to Buy,* Oxford University Press, 2004.

Ferguson, Niall. *Colossus: The Rise and Fall of the American Empire,* Penguin Books Ltd, 2005.

Figes, Orlando. *Natasha's Dance: A Cultural History of Russia,* Penguin Books Ltd, 2003.

Frank, Robert. *Richistan: A Journey through the 21st Century Wealth Boom and the Lives of the New Rich,* Piatkus, 2007.

French, Patrick. *Younghusband: The Last Great Imperial Adventurer,* Flamingo, 2004.

Fukuyama, Francis. *The Great Disruption: Human Nature and the Reconstitution of Social Order,* Free Press, 1999.

Fukuyama, Francis. *Our Posthuman Future: Consequences of the Biotechnology Revolution,* Picador USA, 2002.

Gladwell, Malcolm. *The Tipping Point: How Little Things Can Make a Big Difference,* Abacus, 2002.

Gleick, James. *Faster: The Acceleration of Just About Everything,* Random House USA, 2005.

Graaf, John de, Wann, David and Naylor, Thomas H. *Affluenza: The All-Consuming Epidemic,* Berett-Koehler, 2005.

Gray, John. *Heresies: Against Progress and Other Illusions,* Granta Books, 2004.

Gray, John. *Black Mass, Apocalyptic Religion and the Death of Utopia,* Penguin Allen Lane, 2007.

Greenfield, Susan. *The Private Life of the Brain,* Penguin Books Ltd, 2002.

Hattersley, Roy. *In Search of the Third Way,* Granta 71, Granta Press.

Heath, Joseph & Potter, Andrew. *The Rebel Sell: How the Counterculture became Consumer Culture,* Capstone Publishing, 2006.

Hutton, Will. *The World We're In,* Abacus, 2003.

Huxley, Aldous. *Brave New World,* Vintage.

James, Oliver. *Britain on the Couch: A Treatment for the Low-serotonin Society,* Arrow, 1998.

Johnson, Steven. *Everything Bad is Good for You: How Popular Culture Is Making Us Smarter,* Penguin Books Ltd, 2006.

Jones, Steve. *Coral: A Pessimist in Paradise,* Little, Brown, 2007.

Kapuscinski, Rzszard. *The Shadow of the Sun: My African Life,* Penguin Books Ltd, 2002.

Keay, John. *India: A History,* HarperCollins Publishers Ltd, 2001.

Ledoux, Joseph. *The Emotional Brain: The Mysterious Underpinnings of Emotional Life,* Phoenix Press, 2004.

Lomborg, Bjorn. *The Skeptical Environmentalist,* Cambridge University Press, 2001.

Lorimer, Kerry. *Code Green: Experiences of a Lifetime,* Lonely Planet Publications, 2006.

Lovelock, James. *The Revenge of Gaia: Why the Earth is Fighting Back and How We Can Still Save Humanity,* Allen Lane, 2006.

Maalouf, Amin. *Leo the African,* Abacus, 1994.

Mallaby, Sebastian. *The World's Banker: A Story of Failed States, Financial Crises and the Wealth and Poverty of Nations,* Yale University Press, 2006.

McCloud, Kevin. *"Grand Designs": The Blueprint for Building Your Dream Home,* HarperCollins Publishers Ltd, 2006.

McEwan, Ian. *Enduring Love,* Vintage, 1997.

Midgley, Mary. *The Myths We Live By,* Routledge, an imprint of Taylor & Francis Books Ltd, 2003.

Miller, Geoffrey. *The Mating Mind: How Sexual Choice Shaped Human Nature,* Vintage, 2000.

Monbiot, George. *Heat: How to Stop the Planet Burning,* Allen Lane, 2006.

Obama, Barack. *The Audacity of Hope,* Crown Publishers, 2006.

Packard, Vance. *The Hidden Persuaders,* Cardinal, 1958.

Pamuk, Orhan. *Istanbul: Memories of the City,* Faber and Faber, 2006.

Pick, Daniel. *Svengali's Web: The Alien Enchanter in Modern Culture,* Yale University Press, 2000.

Poole, Steven. *Unspeak,* Little, Brown, 2006.

Porter, Roy. *Enlightenment: Britain and the Creation of the Modern World,* Penguin Books Ltd, 2001.

Pountain, Dick and Robins, David. *Cool Rules: Anatomy of an Attitude,* Reaktion Books, 2000

Poynor, Rick. *Obey the Giant: Life in the Image World,* Birkhauser, 2001.

Rees, Martin. *Just Six Numbers: The Deep Forces That Shape the Universe,* Basic Books, 1999.

Ridley, Matt. *The Origins of Virtue,* Penguin Press Ltd, 1997.

Ridley, Matt. *Mendel's Demon: Gene Justice and the Complexity of Life,* Weidenfeld & Nicolson, 2000.

Ridley, Matt. *The Red Queen: Sex and the Evolution of Human Nature,* Harper Perennial, 2003.

Seabrook, John & Foster, Hal. *Nobrow: The Culture of Marketing – The Marketing of Culture,* Vintage Books USA, 2001.

Sen, Amartya. *Identity and Violence: The Illusion of Destiny,* Allen Lane, 2006.

Shell, Ellen Ruppel. *Fat Wars: The Inside Story of the Obesity Industry,* Atlantic Books, 2004.

Soros, George. *The Bubble of American Supremacy: Correcting the Misuse of American Power,* Phoenix Press, 2004.

Stebbins, Michael. *Sex Drugs and DNA: Science's Taboos Confronted,* Palgrave Macmillan, 2006.

Sudjic, Deyan. *The Edifice Complex: How the Rich and Powerful Shape the World,* Penguin Books Ltd, 2006.

Thomson, Garry. *The Sceptical Buddhist,* River Books, 1993.

Trefil, James. *Are We Unique?: A Scientist Explores the Unparalleled Intelligence of the Human Mind,* John Wiley & Sons Inc, 1997.

Walden, George. *New Elites: A Career in the Masses,* Penguin Books, 2001.

Wheen, Francis. *How Mumbo-jumbo Conquered the World: A Short History of Modern Delusions,* Harper Perennial, 2004.

Whybrow, Peter. *American Mania: When Too Much Is Not Enough,* W W Norton & Co Ltd, 2005.

Wilson, A.N. *The Victorians,* Arrow, 2003.

Wilson, Edward O. *Consilience: The Unity of Knowledge,* Abacus, 1998.

Zeldin, Theodore. *An Intimate History of Humanity,* Vintage, 1995.

Acknowledgements

Ideas for anything, when they are young, rough and unformulated, are at their most vulnerable. So the first acknowledgement must go to those who showed support for the project in its earliest days.

It was my wife, Narisa, who, even when the first concept sketches were made for mapping popular culture, voiced unreserved enthusiasm. Then there are those whose wisdom and critical judgement along the way, were essential in maintaining momentum. Foremost of these, I am grateful to Hansjörg Mayer, himself a publisher, whose interest and knowledge on the subject, provided an important impetus. Input from the academic side came from the husband and wife team, Professor Philip Stott and the historian and writer, Anne Stott, together with valuable insights from the former Director of the Royal Anthropological Society, Jonathan Benthall, and a former school friend, now an executive at Leo Burnett, Harry MacAuslan.

Design is half of this book. I especially thank all of Why Not, the graphics company. From its bosses, Dave Ellis and Andy Altman, (who has skilfully guided most of the projects we have done in the past), to the designers of the book itself, the ever creative and meticulous, Chris Curran, together with Geoff Williamson, also part of the design team.

On the publishing side, and instrumental in the completion of this project, is the editor at Thames & Hudson, Lucas Dietrich, who together with my wife, Narisa Chakrabongse and Paisarn Piammattawat of River Books, expertly coordinated the publishing of the final books. Tim Evans, again of Thames & Hudson, also provided valuable support and assistance throughout.

Stock Library Images courtesy of Shutterstock, Corbis Images and GettyImages
Other photography by Christian Hogue, Gee Thomson, Manit Sriwanichpoom and Paisarn Piammattawat.

Designed by Why Not Associates
Designers, Chris Curran and Geoff Williamson